Why are you here?

Searching for the meaning of life

John Blanchard

EP BOOKS
Faverdale North
Darlington
DL3 0PH, England

web: http://www.epbooks.org

e-mail: sales@epbooks.org

EP Books are distributed in the USA by:
JPL Distribution
3741 Linden Avenue Southeast
Grand Rapids, MI 49548
E-mail: orders@jpldistribution.com
Tel: 877.683.6935

First published 2014

British Library Cataloguing in Publication Data available

ISBN 978–1–78397–068–1

Printed in the UK by Bell & Bain Ltd, Glasgow

Thanks

As the manuscript for this book was being prepared I shared it chapter by chapter with a number of friends. I am grateful to Rob Barlow, Andrew Blanchard, Stephen Blanchard, Tim Bongers, Paul Hill, Simon Gay, Tony Pietersen and Martin Thomson for their valuable input. I am especially grateful to Marlene Williams, who in repeatedly reviewing the text left no stone unturned—and found several stones I did not know existed! I am also indebted to Trudy Kinloch for her superb editorial work. Without their help this book would not be as it is; I accept personal responsibility for any remaining weaknesses.

My special thanks to Professor Sinclair Ferguson, who in spite of massive demands on his valuable time, has written such a generous Foreword.

JOHN BLANCHARD
Banstead, Surrey
November 2014

Contents

Why are you here?

Foreword

Professor Sinclair B. Ferguson, M.A., B.D., Ph.D.

To be invited to write a foreword to any book is a privilege. But it is a particular honour when the author is a friend and thus signals that he is willing to entrust his reputation to you! In the case of John Blanchard his good name is safe with me. But if you are new to his books, let me give you a few hints of what you can expect to find in these pages as you read on.

There are three hallmarks of JB's writing, and they are all present in *Why Are You Here?*

Christianity. Just in case you are wondering exactly what kind of book this is, you should expect to find that its every page is an exposition, exploration, and explanation of the Christian faith. But in case you are tempted now to return it to the shelf, please read to the end of this sentence: this is real Christianity, not the flimsy version of the TV soaps, or the crooked versions that seem to inhabit the world of TV satellite programmes. So if you are not a Christian, and in your more honest moments are prepared to admit that you are not actually clear what it is that you are rejecting or simply ignoring, please give John Blanchard the time it takes to read a few chapters to find out what the Christian faith really is. You may discover that it isn't what you thought it was. More than that, I suspect you may discover that Christian faith not only makes sense in and of itself, but it makes sense of everything else.

In addition, in *Why Are You Here?* you will find—

Integrity. You can trust John Blanchard. He does not write books in order to become a best-selling author (although he is; some of his works have had massive distribution in many languages). He writes because he has a genuine interest in and concern for other people. JB is now at an age when he could sit back and take things easy—along with many in his peer group. But instead he continues to accept invitations from all over the world to speak and lecture. It isn't that he hates gardening and despises golf (the very reverse in the case of golf!). It is because he has far more important things to do, and he values enormously every opportunity he is given to explain the Christian faith to others.

Integrity also permeates his writing. He is honest and he is gracious. He doesn't—as unfortunately some well-known opponents of Christianity do (and, sadly, some of those they criticise) rubbish people who disagree with him. And something else—he doesn't pick the weakest, wackiest, most way-out versions of unbelief and treat them as though they were the best possible representation of atheism or agnosticism. He is able to do this, incidentally, because he believes we are all made in the image of God. And so he is able to treat people with respect, and to honour their gifts and their intellects. Speaking for myself, I like that very much. It gives me confidence that this is someone I can speak to, discuss with, reason with, listen to, and trust.

Clarity. There's a great story told about two scholars who were walking out of a lecture given by an enormously distinguished fellow academic. One said to the other, 'What did you make of that?' His companion replied, 'To be honest, I believe there were only two people in that room who could possibly have followed his reasoning, it was so unclear and opaque. He was one, and I am the other. And I can assure you, he was quite wrong!'

There is no fear of that with John Blanchard. At no point will you find yourself asking, 'What is he trying to say?' But in addition to the sheer clarity of what he writes, nothing here is dull, merely ordinary, or uninteresting. Indeed, no matter who you are, or how well-educated, I think I can safely predict that in these pages you will learn something you did not know.

All of us have brains and memories. John Blanchard's appear to be composed of some form of biological velcro strips. As Oliver Goldsmith so wonderfully describes the village schoolmaster in his poem, *The Deserted Village*: 'And still they gazed, and still the wonder grew, That one small head could carry all he knew' He reads widely. But more than that he has that special gift of being insatiably curious about things, and—this is his genius—he always seems to be asking *if* and *how* and *why* things make sense.

Even if it is simply to improve your general knowledge, *Why Are You Here?* is worth reading! But its value is much greater. It will help you to connect the dots, so that the big picture, although composed of seemingly endless millions of facts and details, really does begin to make sense.

This quest to make sense of things has perennially occupied the minds of philosophers and scientists. It underlies the passion of so many great intellectuals to 'get to the root of things'. Historically this was often thought of as 'the problem of the one and the many'—given the almost limitless multitude of facts and things, is there something that unifies reality, and that makes it intelligent to speak about living in a 'universe'? Or as the eighteenth-century philosopher Gottfried Wilhelm Leibniz put it, 'Why does something exist rather than nothing?'

Unless we can answer that question, at the end of the day nothing really makes sense much beyond itself. And unless you share the perspective of Richard Dawkins (a biologist, not a philosopher), that the question is itself meaningless (along with all other fundamental 'why' questions), you will, I suspect, be glad that you happened upon *Why Are You Here?* and were willing to read it to the end.

I hope you will. I certainly do not mean to delay you any longer from making a beginning!

Sinclair B. Ferguson
Professor of Systematic Theology
Redeemer Seminary
Dallas
Texas.

Introduction

Why are we here? What's life all about?
Is God really real, or is there some doubt?
Well, tonight, we're going to sort it all out,
For, tonight, it's 'The Meaning of Life'.[1]

These are the opening lines of the first song in *The Meaning of Life*, a film made by the British comedy group Monty Python and released in 1983. The group's first televised comedy sketch show, *Monty Python's Flying Circus*, was broadcast on 5 October 1969 and ran for forty-five episodes that aired over four series. It turned the six men into a phenomenon and led to touring stage shows, films, albums, books and a hit stage musical. The group's influence on comedy, pushing the boundaries of what was considered acceptable at the time, has been compared to the Beatles' influence on music. They made such a mark that the word 'Pythonesque' now appears in the *Oxford Dictionary of English* to describe the kind of absurd or surreal humour the group presented. When they set up a reunion show at London's O2 Arena in 2014 (their first in over thirty years) all the thousands of available tickets were sold in 43.5 seconds, and extra shows had to be staged.

The Meaning of Life looks at the various ages of man, with sketches on Birth, Growth and Learning, Fighting Each Other, Middle Age, The Autumn Years and Death, and has the group's typical blend of violence, absurdity and vulgarity (one reviewer called it 'constant crudeness') all designed, as the group put it, to offend 'absolutely everybody'.

The opening song asks questions that have fascinated people for thousands of years, and today millions are still looking for the answers. A presenter closes the show by reciting Monty Python's rather tame response: 'Well, that's the end of the film. Now, here's the meaning of life … well, it's nothing very special. Uh, try and be nice to people, avoid eating fat, read a good book every now and then, get some walking in, and try and live together in peace and harmony with people of all creeds and nations.'[2] She then adds some pointless crudity before claiming that what the 'jaded, video-sated public' want is 'filth', such as 'people doing things to each other with chainsaws during Tupperware parties, babysitters being stabbed with knitting needles by gay presidential candidates, vigilante groups strangling chickens, armed bands of theatre critics exterminating mutant goats.'[3]

The Meaning of Life was never meant to be taken as a serious answer to the question our title asks, and the sketches rarely do more than take bizarre, off-the-wall swipes at some of modern society's behaviour. Although the film's final scene would have been carefully crafted, it merely lumps together the bland and the brutal and leaves the question hanging in the air, giving us not the slightest clue as to where the answer might lie. The furthest it goes is to suggest a few things we should try to do, but it gives no reason for doing them. The show begins with questions that should interest everybody—but ends by answering none of them.

Questions about the meaning of life have fascinated men for as far back as we can trace. *The Epic of Gilgamesh*, an ancient Mesopotamian poem that is among the earliest surviving works of literature, dating from about 2,000 BC, has Gilgamesh, the semi-mythic King of Uruk (now Iraq) scouring the earth in a search for the meaning of the universe, life, death and immortality. The famous Greek poet Homer (c. 8th Century BC), author of the *Iliad* and the *Odyssey* and rated as the greatest among his peers, spent years wrestling with the question and decided that man was meaningless, doomed at the end of a miserable life to complete annihilation. The Greek philosopher Epicurus (341–270 BC) wrote that man's only meaning lay in his physical parts and that 'when death is present we no longer exist'.[4]

As the centuries rolled on, many other heavy hitters were just as depressing. The English political philosopher Thomas Hobbes (1588–1679) said that man was nothing more than a physical object moving through space. The Scottish philosopher David Hume (1711–1776) taught that all we could say about our experiences was that we were having experiences. The Russian writer and philosopher Leo Tolstoy (1828–1910) looked back to a time when he asked, 'What is life for? To die? To kill myself at once? No, I am afraid. To wait for death till it comes? I fear that even more. Then I must live. But what for? And I could not escape from that circle'.[5] The teaching of the German philosopher Martin Heidegger (1889–1976) has been summed up as saying, 'Life is cast up between nothing and nothing'.[6] The bottom line of French philosopher Jean-Paul Sartre (1905–1980) was, 'Man is a useless passion'.[7] The Czech novelist Franz Kafka (1883–1924) said, 'The conveyor belt of life carries one somewhere—but one doesn't know where. One is a thing—an object, rather than a living creature.'[8]

The Algerian-born French philosopher and novelist Albert Camus (1913–1960), who won the Nobel Prize for Literature in 1957, came to the conclusion that 'life is like a bad joke'.[9] The English philosopher Bertrand Russell (1872–1970) wrote, '(Man's) origin, his growth, his hopes and fears, his loves and his beliefs, are but the outcome of accidental collocations of atoms.'[10] The modern American theoretical physicist Steven Weinberg calls human life 'a more-or-less farcical outcome of a chain of accidents',[11] while one modern thinker says, 'Man is a grown-up germ, sitting on one cog of one wheel of a vast cosmic machine that is slowly but inexorably running down to nothingness.'[12]

Others have taken a more optimistic view, but the fact remains that everybody is faced with the question this book is asking. The Welsh scholar Rheinallt Williams (1911–1993) claimed, 'There is nothing which arises more spontaneously from man's nature than the question about life's meaning.'[13] The English journalist, author and broadcaster Bernard Levin (1928–2004), described by *The Times* as 'the most famous journalist of his day', suggested, 'There are probably more people today seeking some larger meaning or purpose in their lives and in life in general than there have been, certainly in the West, since the day of unquestioned faith.'[14] It is impossible for anyone who thinks seriously about life to avoid the issue, yet raise the question with a group of ten people and there would be a range of different opinions. Some of these would amount to nothing more than sound bites. Some people try to shut the question down by saying that it is pointless to ask it, but this approach gets us nowhere. The Indian-born Canadian-American apologist Ravi Zacharias tells of an incident on the campus of the University of the Philippines in Manila. When a student in the audience shouted out, 'Everything in life is meaningless,' Zacharias replied by saying, 'You don't believe that.' When the student came back with, 'Yes, I do,' Zacharias responded, 'No, you don't.' By now the student was getting exasperated, and shouted, 'I most certainly do; who are you to tell me I don't?' When Zacharias politely replied, 'Then please repeat your statement to me,' the student did so: 'Everything in life is meaningless.' Zacharias then told him, 'Please remain standing; this will only take a moment. I assume that you assume that your statement is meaningful. If your statement is meaningful, then everything is not meaningless. On the other hand, if everything is meaningless, then what you have just said is meaningless too. So, in effect, you have said nothing.' The student quietly sat down, but as the meeting broke up he was seen pacing around the back of the auditorium muttering, 'If everything is meaningless, then ...'[15]

Today, what is known as postmodernism claims there are no absolute rights or wrongs, looking for absolute truth is pointless, moral questions are relative, and personal interpretation of whatever we read is all that matters. The English author Dave Tomlinson describes postmodernism's stance: 'Truth is what you find for yourself, not what someone imposes on you ... It no longer says, "Here is the truth—believe it!" It says, "Try this for size."'[16] In *The Closing of the American Mind*, the American philosopher and academic Allan Bloom (1930–1992) claimed, 'There is one thing a professor can be absolutely certain of: almost every student entering the university believes, or says he believes, that truth is relative.'[17] In a poll taken in the United States, sixty-four per cent of those taking part agreed that the statement, 'There is no such thing as absolute truth' was true![18] Even solid history is sometimes brushed aside: according to another American survey over thirty per cent of those polled said they did not believe that the Holocaust, the appalling massacre by the Nazis of six million Jews and others in

the Second World War, ever happened.[19] We will drill into this idea
later on, but the point can be made here that if there is no absolute
truth, how can we know that postmodernism itself is true? The
whole idea trips over its own feet. For example, how can we have
absolute belief in relative morality? As the English author John
Benton puts it, 'If you say that there is no such thing as the truth,
that is to make an absolute statement of truth. It is to say, "It is
absolutely true that there is no such thing as absolute truth," which
is self-contradictory.'[20] On the other hand, throwing in the towel
and saying that we can never be sure that there is absolute truth
makes no sense, as it would mean that we can never be sure that
we can never be sure! In the musical show *Wicked*, the wizard says,
'The truth isn't a thing, or fact, or reason. It's simply what everyone
agrees on', but this is nonsensical as it reduces truth to personal
opinions, which by definition have no agreed basis.

In the American science fiction television series *The X-Files*, in
which FBI special agents Fox Mulder and Dana Scully investigate
unsolved cases involving paranormal phenomena, the recurring
tagline is 'The Truth Is Out There.' Moving from science fiction to
fact, the book you are now reading is written on the assumption
that in facing up to the question of whether life has any meaning,
the truth *is* 'out there'—and can be found. Discussing this with
a friend recently, he had only one comment: 'Well, the answer is
either "Yes" or "No".' It is difficult to argue with that! It makes no
sense to go through life without thinking that there must be some
meaning to it, and without making any attempt to find out what
that meaning might be. This book is a straightforward search for
the answer. We will begin by concentrating on a man whose life and
work have captured the imagination of millions, and whose ideas
lead us on to the question our title asks.

The genius

At the time of writing, the most easily recognizable scientist in the world is the English theoretical physicist Stephen Hawking. As he once admitted, 'The downside of my celebrity is that I can't go anywhere without being recognized. It is not enough for me to wear sunglasses and a wig. The wheelchair gives me away.' His is a remarkable story and it is worth taking this short chapter to follow it through. This is not a book about Stephen Hawking, but what he has to say on the biggest issues we face in life, and the reasons he gives for answering our title's question as he does, will prepare the way for us to take a much closer look at it.

Stephen William Hawking was born in Oxford, England on 8 January 1942. By a fascinating coincidence this was 300 years to the day after the death of the Italian physicist, mathematician,

astronomer and philosopher Galileo Galilei, who played a major
role in the revolution that marked the beginning of modern
science. Stephen's parents, Frank and Isobel, had both studied at the
University of Oxford, and he followed them there in 1959. Before
that he had been for eight months at St Albans High School for Girls,
then at Radlett School and St Albans School. His father wanted him
to enrol at London's prestigious Westminster School, but he fell
ill on the day of the scholarship examination (necessary because
his parents could not afford Westminster's fees) so he remained at
St Albans. He was not brilliant academically, with the exception
of scientific subjects. He had what he later called 'a passion to
understand how things work' and at one stage, with the help of a
mathematics teacher, he built a computer from recycled components
that included clock parts and an old telephone switchboard.

Fascinated by mathematics, he decided to study the subject at
university. This disappointed his father, who wanted him to study
medicine at his own *alma mater*, Oxford's University College.
Stephen met him half-way. Awarded a scholarship there as a
seventeen-year-old in October 1959, he enrolled to read natural
sciences, specializing in physics, as it was not possible to read
mathematics there at the time. For some eighteen months he was
bored and lonely, and even though he was one of the youngest
students he found the academic studies 'ridiculously easy'.[21] He
calculated that he worked 'about 1000 hours in my three years,
an average of an hour a day'.[22] His aim was to undertake graduate
studies in cosmology at the University of Cambridge, but he would
need a first-class honours degree before Cambridge would accept
him. When the oral examiners at his Oxford Finals asked him
about his plans, he got their attention by saying, 'If you award me
a First I will go to Cambridge. If I receive a Second I will stay at
Oxford—so I expect you will give me a First'.[23] They did; he was

awarded a first-class BA (Hons.) degree and in 1962 he enrolled at Trinity Hall, Cambridge.

His main interest was in theories about the origin of the universe, and in 1965 he wrote a thesis on the subject. He gained a Ph.D. in 1966, then became a Research Fellow at the university's Gonville and Caius College.[24] Several years later the university appointed him Lucasian Professor of Mathematics, a post he held from 1979–2009. He then became Director of Research at the university's Centre for Theoretical Cosmology. His work on the basic laws that govern the universe has since earned him such global recognition that following a theoretical argument he advanced in 1974, 'Hawking radiation' has become a term used to define radiation emitted by black holes, regions of space-time from which gravity prevents anything, including light, escaping.

His achievements have led to him being showered with honours. He has twelve honorary degrees, was awarded a CBE in 1982 and was made a Companion of Honour in 1989. He became a Fellow of the Royal Society (at thirty-two years of age one of the youngest scientists ever to be honoured in this way), an Honorary Fellow of the Royal Society of Arts, a lifetime member of the Pontifical Academy of Sciences and a Member of the US National Academy of Sciences. He received the Albert Einstein Award in 1978, the Wolf Prize in 1988, the Prince of Asturias Award in 1989, the Royal Society's Copley Medal in 2006 and Russia's Fundamental Physics Prize in 2012. In 2009 he received the Presidential Medal of Freedom, the highest civilian award in the United States. In a poll conducted by the BBC in 2002 he was named in a list of '100 Greatest Britons'.

ALS

During his final year at Oxford he began to have increasingly serious health problems and shortly after his twenty-first birthday he was diagnosed with amyotrophic lateral sclerosis (ALS), the most common of the five motor neurone diseases, known in the United States as Lou Gehrig's Disease. The doctors gave him two and a half years to live, but although his condition steadily deteriorated—after a fall there were times when he could not remember who or where he was—he refused to let his disease detract from his output. He has described himself as 'a scientist first, a popular writer second and, in all the ways that matter, a normal human being with the same desires, drives, dreams and ambitions as the next person.'[25] At about the same time as ALS was diagnosed he met Jane Wilde, a friend of his sister, and they soon planned to marry—but there was a problem. To get married he would need a job, but to get a job he would need to get his Ph.D. With this in mind, he 'started working hard for the first time in my life.'[26] He and Jane were married in July 1965 (he was walking with a stick by then, and beginning to lose strength in his arms) and they spent their honeymoon at a physics conference at Cornell University in upstate New York. Eight months later he gained his Ph.D.

Regarded as one of the most brilliant scientists since the German genius Albert Einstein (1879–1955), Hawking's ground-breaking work in physics and cosmology has included several books that have introduced his ideas to countless people outside of academic and scientific circles. One of the most popular of these is *A Brief History of Time*, first published in 1988 and subtitled 'From the Big Bang to Black Holes'. While it was being written he got a chest infection on holiday in Switzerland. He became so ill that at one point doctors offered to turn off his life support machine, but Jane refused to give permission and they returned to Cambridge. The weeks he spent in intensive care were 'the darkest of my life'.[27] He felt trapped in his own body, but pressed on to complete the book, which remained a world best-seller for four years, earning a place in *the Guinness Book of Records*, and was translated into over forty languages.

He was swept along on a tidal wave of fame, but his family life was deeply affected. His marriage broke up and he and Jane were divorced in 1995. In the same year he married Elaine Mason, who had been one of his nurses from the start of his need for 'wraparound care'. Their marriage was 'passionate and tempestuous'[28] but it ended in divorce in 2006.

Despite losing his voice permanently following a tracheotomy, his brilliant adaptations to cope with his growing disability led the Canadian physicist Werner Israel to compare what he was doing to Mozart composing an entire symphony in his head.[29] Today, with virtually all control of his body gone, he is wheelchair bound, and for vocal communication directs a computerized voice system through a cheek muscle attached to a sensor. Some people are merely famous for being famous; Stephen Hawking has earned his fame.

The God question

In *A Brief History of Time* Hawking tackles questions such as, 'How did the universe begin—and what made its start possible?' 'Does time always flow forward?' 'Is the universe unending—or are there boundaries?' 'Are there other dimensions in space?' 'What will happen when it all ends?' It is easy to see how all of these relate to the question of whether life on our particular planet has any meaning. He flirts with the idea of 'A Theory of Everything' (TOE), one that would fully explain and link together all known physical phenomena, but asks this fundamental and inescapable question:

'Even if there is one possible unified theory, it is just a set of rules and equations. What is it that breathes fire into the equations and makes a universe for them to describe?'[30] At one point he muses, 'So long as the universe had a beginning, we could suppose it had a creator,'[31] and in the second edition of the book adds 'It would be very difficult to explain why the universe should have begun in just this way, except as an act of a God who intended to create beings just like us.'[32] He begins the final chapter by asking the very questions that lie behind the one we are asking: 'We find ourselves in a bewildering world. We want to make sense of what we see around us and to ask: what is the nature of the universe? *What is our place in it, and where did it and we come from?*' (Emphasis added).[33] In what may be the best-known sentence in the entire book, he ends the chapter by saying that if we found out why we and the universe exist, 'it would be the ultimate triumph of reason—for then we would know the mind of God.'[34] This left open for him the possibility that the meaning of life is to be found not in ourselves or in the natural world, but in a Creator who brought it and us into existence. The importance of this will become clearer in the following pages—and buttoned down in our final chapter.

For some time now it has been popular to say that believing in God as the Creator of the universe is a religious hangover from earlier centuries, and that leading thinkers have long since abandoned the idea. Some of those who take this line are determined to defend it, regardless of where the evidence might point. In 1997 the Harvard geneticist Richard Lewontin wrote this: 'Our willingness to accept scientific claims that are against common sense is the key to an understanding of the real struggle between science and the supernatural. We take the side of science in spite of the patent absurdity of some of its constructs, in spite of its failure to fulfil many of its extravagant promises of health and life, in spite of the tolerance of the scientific community for unsubstantiated just-so stories, because we have a prior commitment, a commitment to materialism ... Moreover, that materialism is an absolute, *for we cannot allow a Divine Foot in the door*' (emphasis added).[35] He was saying that in looking for possible explanations as to why the universe seems to be so amazingly designed and precisely fine-tuned to sustain human life, we should begin by ruling God out.

As we have already seen, Stephen Hawking left Lewontin's door open (though his suggestion that we could 'know the mind of God' was over the top). However, twenty-two years later he took a very different line. When he co-authored *The Grand Design* with the American physicist and screenwriter Leonard Mlodinow (who also worked on the science fiction television series *Star Trek: The Next Generation)* he began by asking questions such as, 'How can we understand the world in which we find ourselves?', 'How does the universe behave?', 'What is the nature of reality?', 'Where did all this come from?' and 'Did the universe need a Creator?' The book goes on to conclude that the Big Bang was the inevitable consequence of the laws of physics and nothing more, and adds, 'Because there is a law such as gravity, the universe can and will create itself from nothing.'[36] Of course this is no more than an assumption, and we will look at this issue later. The book's real punchline is this: 'Spontaneous creation is the reason there is something rather than nothing, why the universe exists, why we exist. It is not necessary to invoke God to light the blue touch-paper and set the universe going.'[37]

The programme

On 29 September 2012 the Discovery HD television channel screened *The Meaning of Life*, a sixty-five-minute programme by Stephen Hawking, and one of a series under the overall title *The Grand Design*. The trailer asked the questions, 'Is there a meaning to life?' and 'Is there a purpose to our existence?' before adding, 'Hawking investigates what physics can reveal.'

After introducing himself as 'a physicist, a cosmologist and something of a dreamer' he told viewers, 'We humans are a curious species. We wonder. We seek answers. So can we answer the greatest question of all: *is there a meaning to life?* You may think that that is a philosophical question, *but I think that philosophy is dead* and I believe science holds the key. Science has changed everything; not just the world around us, but as we see ourselves.' We will come back to the philosophy issue in Chapter 3, but this statement set the stage for the rest of the programme, which featured brilliant space photography, dazzling computer-generated graphics and time-lapse sequences, as well as a kaleidoscope of scenes ranging from brain surgery to a couple enjoying a tranquil boating trip on the River Cam. It was a riveting production, bursting with colour and wrapped in richly textured music, but the most important feature was the verbal message, largely spoken by an actor but written, we can be sure, by Stephen Hawking. Here are some of the main points he made:

'We all have hopes and dreams, but the first thing we must accept as we search for the meaning of life is that this is *nothing more than physics.*'

'The entire universe works according to the laws of nature, such as the law of gravity. These laws control everything. I see no reason why we humans should be an exception to the rule. After all, we are made of exactly the same materials, operating to the very same principles.'

'If we are just biological clockwork, perhaps there is no meaning to life—perhaps no meaning at all.'

'We know that all life on earth evolved from complex molecules called amino-acids. These molecules collided randomly to create the first simple living things. Over billions of years these life forms became ever more sophisticated and eventually complex, multi-cellular creatures, animals with brains, arrived.'

It was not difficult to see where all of this was leading, and as the programme came to an end Hawking was front and centre:

'The entire 13.7 billion-year history of the universe exists as a model inside our minds. *So where does this leave us with finding a meaning to life?* The answer I think is pretty clear. Meaning itself is simply another piece of the model of reality that we build inside our own brain. Love and honour, right and wrong are all part of the universe we create in our minds … *The meaning of life is what you choose it to be.'*

That last sentence triggered the writing of the book you are now reading.

Why are you here?

The brilliant failure

In *The Grand Design*, Stephen Hawking takes two giant steps in trying to answer questions about the universe and the meaning of human life. The first of these is to say, 'Traditionally these questions are questions for philosophy, but *philosophy is dead*. It has not kept up with developments in science, particularly in physics.'[38] (emphasis added). This is a strange statement, for two reasons. The first is that the word 'philosophy' can be traced back to the ancient Greek word *philosophia*, which is built up from *philia* (love) and *sophia* (wisdom). The use of the word 'philosophy' has broadened out over the centuries, but its roots are important. Philosophy is technically described as 'the study of the fundamental nature of knowledge, reality and existence, especially when considered as an academic discipline.'[39] If there is no such thing as truth about anything—let alone the meaning of life—there is no point in looking anywhere for it. As we can take it that Stephen Hawking is genuinely searching for truth, it seems odd of him to ditch philosophy along the way; and without a passionate longing to discover what truth is, any search is likely to be half-hearted at best and futile at worst.

Hawking also contradicts himself, as the statement 'philosophy is dead' *is itself a philosophical statement.* It is not based on the physical examination of anything, nor is it the result of tests or experiments. It is simply a claim he makes, rather than a fact for which he can produce evidence of any kind. The American philosopher of science Tim Maudlin, who has extensively studied the fundamentals of physics, metaphysics and logic, is well qualified to assess Hawking's claim that philosophy is dead, and he does so with a flourish:

> 'Hawking is a brilliant man, but he's not an expert in what's going on in philosophy, evidently. Over the past thirty years the philosophy of physics has become seamlessly integrated with the foundations of physics work done by actual physicists, so the situation is actually the exact opposite of what he describes. I think he just doesn't know what he's talking about. I mean there's no reason why he should. Why should he spend a lot of time reading the philosophy of physics? I'm sure it's very difficult for him to do. But I think he's just … uninformed.'[40]

The American analytical philosopher William Lane Craig is equally clear that Hawking and Mlodinow are wide of the mark when they say that philosophy has breathed its last:

> 'The professional philosopher will regard their verdict as not merely amazingly condescending but also as outrageously naïve. The man who claims to have no need of philosophy

is the one most apt to be fooled by it. One might therefore anticipate that Mlodinow and Hawking's subsequent exposition of their favoured theories will be underpinned by a host of unexamined philosophical presuppositions. That expectation is, in fact, borne out. They assert their claims about laws of nature, the possibility of miracles, scientific determinism, and the illusion of free will with only the thinnest of justification. Clearly Mlodinow and Hawking are up to their necks in philosophical questions.'[41]

The simple fact is that *The Grand Design* is packed with philosophy from beginning to end—the philosophy of science—which makes it strange to put philosophy's obituary on one of its opening pages.

Science and scientism

The second giant leap in *The Grand Design* takes us to the subject of the present chapter. Stephen Hawking says that while philosophy has not kept up with modern developments in science, particularly in the realm of physics, 'scientists have become the bearers of the torch of discovery in our quest for knowledge.'[42]

At the beginning of his book *The Search for God: Can Science Help?*[43] the Welsh scientist, Sir John Houghton, a winner of the Albert Einstein World Award for Science, lists four views relating to science that have been adopted in man's search for truth. The first says that the scientific method is the only valid way, the second that faith is the only way, the third that faith and science overlap, and the fourth that faith and the scientific method are mutually exclusive.[44] Stephen Hawking votes firmly for the first of these and claims that science is the only way to truth. This is the line taken by what is currently known as 'New Atheism', an aggressive version of the old model. New Atheism claims that even allowing for adjustments that need to be made in the light of modern discoveries, science has replaced God as the source of reliable information about ourselves and the universe in which we live. As the English evolutionary biologist and passionate atheist Richard Dawkins puts it, 'Religion is no longer a serious candidate in the field of explanation. It is completely superseded by science.'[45]

In a debate at the University of Oxford in 1998 the English chemist Peter Atkins, a one-time lecturer in physical chemistry at Lincoln College, Oxford, an Honorary Associate of the National Secular Society and a well-known atheist, took the same line: 'I am on the brink of discovering everything, and I commend you to use your brains, because your brains are the most wonderful instruments in the universe—and through your brains you will see that you can do without God. There is no necessity for God, because science can explain everything.' This is pretty radical stuff, but he was not saying anything new; many years ago Bertrand Russell claimed, 'What science cannot tell us, mankind cannot know.'[46] Yet these are not scientific statements, but merely personal opinions. To make matters worse, Hawking, Dawkins, Atkins and Russell are all shuffling the cards under the table, then producing not science, but scientism. This is technically defined as 'the view that the characteristic inductive methods of the natural sciences are the only source of genuine factual knowledge and, in particular, that they alone can yield true knowledge about man and society'.[47] Simply put, scientism is a worldview claiming that everything can be reduced to a scientific explanation of its parts. Scientism sometimes trades under names such as materialism or naturalism, terms that point to its ancient roots. Materialism can be traced as far back as Greek philosophers such as Thales of Miletus (c. 624–546 BC) and Democritus (c. 460–370 BC). Democritus, for example, sometimes called 'the father of materialism', taught that all reality consisted of nothing but a vast number of atoms whirling around in space.

This explains why scientism is sometimes called reductionism, though I prefer the term coined by the Scottish physicist and brain scientist Donald MacKay (1922–1987) who founded the Department of Communication and Neuroscience at the University of Keele. In *The Clockwork Image*[48] he calls scientism 'nothing-buttery', a neat way of telling us that scientism claims there is nothing but matter and the things caused by matter. According to scientism, even human beings, the most complex and amazing creatures we know, are just collections of biological bits and pieces, and when we have come up with an explanation of these we have discovered all that can be said about us. If this is the case, and we are just collections of chemicals that determine what we think and do, how can we know that there is any meaning to life, let alone know that scientism itself is true? If the random shuffling of mental molecules is the only reason we come to conclusions about anything, what is the value of those conclusions? The claim that science is the only way to discover truth is itself a distortion of the truth. Materialism is no more than a particular philosophy *about* science and, as we will see later, it leads to a dead end in trying to find an answer to the question this book is asking.

Before going any further, let me make it clear that nothing I have said in this section should be taken as a criticism of science. Nobody can deny the phenomenal contributions that science and technology make to our lives. What is more, the pace of change is amazing, and at times has taken experts by surprise. In 1878, Sir William Preece (1834–1913), then the Chief Engineer of the British Post Office, said of the telephone (which had been successfully demonstrated two years earlier) 'The Americans have need of the telephone, but we do not, we have plenty of messenger boys.' At about the time the patent for the new invention was granted, an internal memo at the Western Union telegram company read, 'This "telephone" has too many shortcomings to be seriously considered as a means of communication. The device is inherently of no value to us.' In 1899 a Commissioner of the US Office of Patents declared, 'Everything that can be invented has been invented.' In 1943 the then Chairman of IBM said, 'I think there is a world market for maybe five computers.' In 1949 an article in *Popular Scientist* suggested that computers might eventually weigh as little as 1.5 tons. After Apple announced the release of the iPad, the research firm Simpson Carpenter concluded that 'there isn't a compelling incentive to get mainstream consumers to buy it'. Less than eighteen months later some eighteen million iPads were in use. If I had played golf in the seventeenth century I would have used a ball made of a hatful of boiled feathers stuffed into a leather pouch. The ball I use today has ultra-low compression, an ionomer cover, and a seamless dimple pattern. There is now more computing power in an average digital wristwatch than there was on the first lunar landing craft in 1969.

Science and technology are combining to revolutionize our lives and are making vast contributions to human well-being, but the claim that science is the only way to discover truth about the universe in which we live and the meaning of our place in it is simply wrong. What has become known as the scientific method (defined in *The Oxford Dictionary of English* as 'systematic observation, measurement, and experiment, and the formulation, testing, and modification of hypotheses'[49]) continues to produce staggering results. Scientism goes much further and says there are no limits to what science can achieve. One does not have to be a scientist to see that this is enthusiastic nonsense. Even when it keeps to its proper field, science is not infallible. The Nobel Prize-winning American theoretical physicist Richard

Feynman (1918–1988) maintained, 'Scientific knowledge is a body of statements of varying degrees of uncertainty—some unsure, some nearly sure, but none absolutely certain.'[50] In 2009, Lord Rees of Ludlow, an English astronomer who became President of the Royal Society, went so far as to say, 'Ultimately, the history of science is a history of best guesses'[51] while in the same year Richard Dawkins told BBC radio listeners, 'Science often makes progress by correcting its mistakes.'[52]

This confirms that science is an ongoing process of learning in which things once said to be true are later found to be false. As the American astronomer, astrophysicist and cosmologist Carl Sagan (1934–1996) put it, 'The most fundamental axioms and conclusions may be challenged. The history of science is full of cases where previously accepted theories and hypotheses have been entirely overthrown, to be replaced by new ideas that more adequately explain the data.'[53] The British-Austrian academic Sir Karl Popper (1902–1994), generally regarded as one of the twentieth century's greatest philosophers of science, went even further: 'The demand for scientific objectivity makes it inevitable that every scientific statement must remain tentative for ever. It may indeed be corroborated, but every corroboration is relative to other statements which, again, are tentative.'[54] This means that many announcements of scientific 'facts' are corrections of statements previously announced as scientific 'facts'; in true science, the latest word is not necessarily the last word. A *New Scientist* cartoon had a student asking her teacher a question, then pointing out that his answer contradicted one he had given the day before. The teacher then replied, 'Jennifer, that was yesterday—we must remember that science is making tremendous strides.' For nearly 1,500 years science maintained that our planet stood motionless at the geographical centre of the universe; modern science proves that this is nonsense. Science once claimed that atmospheric space was filled with a substance called ether, which held the planets in place; this is now laughed out of court. Reporting on an outstanding new finding by the Hubble Space Telescope a few years ago, a leading scientist said, 'We will have to rewrite the laws of physics.'

More importantly, while true science relies on observation and experiment, there are things that cannot be explored or explained by the scientific method.

Limits

We begin with the fact that a scientific description of something is not the only valid one. If you ask a visitor to your home whether they would like an infusion of *Camellia sinensis* leaves in a liquid compound of oxygen and hydrogen, they would wonder what in the world you were talking about. If you offered them a cup of tea they might be delighted to accept—but you would be asking exactly the same thing, using non-scientific words. A scientist's description of a sunset, giving accurate explanations of how the time of day and the angle of the earth's orbit in relation to the sun come into play, then describing the effect of dust particles in refracting the sun's rays to produce different colours, is no more valid than that of an awestruck onlooker revelling in the beauty of what he is seeing. If a husband tells his wife, 'I want to juxtapose my oral orbicular muscle in a state of contraction with yours, so that we can have a reciprocal transmission of carbon dioxide and microbes', she might think he was overworked or the worse for drink—but that is the scientific way of saying, 'I want to kiss you.' The scientifically worded proposition is no more valid than the romantic one— and might well be less productive! If you invited me to listen to somebody rubbing the entrails of a dead sheep with the hairs of a dead horse I would quickly find an excuse to decline, but if you used non-scientific language and invited me to a concert given by a world-class violinist I might want to look at my diary. Scientific descriptions are valid, but they have not cornered the market. Nor will they ever do so.

Just as clearly, there are many important things that are beyond the reach of science and the scientific method. Sir Peter Medawar (1915–1987) the Brazilian-born British biologist who won the 1960 Nobel Prize in Physiology or Medicine, wrote, 'There is no quicker way for a scientist to bring discredit upon himself and upon his profession than roundly to declare—particularly when no declaration of any kind is called for—that science knows, or will soon know, the answers to all questions worth asking.'[55] The American physician-geneticist Francis Collins, best known for his leadership of the Human Genome Project, put the same truth in a nutshell: 'Science is not the only way of knowing.'[56] I have written about this elsewhere[57] and can give only a brief summary of some of science's shortfalls here.

- *Science is unable to tell us why the universe came into being.* Scientists have come up with some fascinating theories about what the universe was like immediately after the so-called Big Bang, but they are unable to tell us why it should have happened in the first place. They speak about a point of infinite density, but have no way of explaining exactly what this was or why it was there. The English scientist Michael Poole, a Visiting Research Fellow at King's College, London, writes, 'As soon as scientists begin to ask why there is a Universe to study, or why nature operates in a regular, uniform way, or whether there is a mind beyond the laws they observe, they are looking for different types of explanations from a scientific one.'[58] In *Black Holes and Baby Universes* Stephen Hawking admits, 'Although science may solve the problem of how the universe began, it cannot answer the question: why does the universe bother to exist? *I don't know the answer to that*' (emphasis added).[59]

- *Science is unable to explain why the laws of nature exist, or why they operate as they do.* The English scientist Edgar Andrews, Emeritus Professor of Materials at the University of London, writes, 'If we ask science why the laws are such as they are, and not otherwise ... science can do nothing but shrug its mathematical shoulders and reply, "That question lies outside my terms of reference".'[60]

- *Science is unable to explain the amazing fine-tuning in the universe that enables life to exist on our planet.* We will look at this in the next chapter, but can give one illustration here. Paul Davies, an English physicist who at one time promoted atheism and whose research interests are in the fields of cosmology, quantum field theory and astrobiology (he even has an asteroid named after him) claims that for all the related elements to be so precisely integrated by chance is the equivalent of aiming at a target an inch wide on the other side of the observable universe and hitting the mark.[61]

- *Science is unable to explain why we are persons and not just physical objects.* In February 2001 the Human Genome Project unveiled its landmark report spelling out the three billion letters that make up the human genome. Commenting on it, the British physician and medical journalist James Le Fanu acknowledged that it was an 'impressive achievement', but also 'devastating news' for scientists who had promised that it would reveal all we needed to know about ourselves. He then went on, 'The holy grail, the dream that science would soon tell us something significant about what it means to be human, has slipped through our hands—and we are no wiser than before. *The human genome ... can tell us absolutely nothing about the really important things in life*'[62] (emphasis added).

- *Science is unable to explain why the mind exists and functions as it does.* We will look at this in a later chapter, but need to take note here of this comment by the English biochemist and Templeton Prize winner Arthur Peacocke (1924–2006): 'Science can investigate all the physical aspects of the brain, but there is still something about the mind—and therefore about who you really are—that it cannot get at.'[63]

- *Science is unable to explain ethical principles.* It can study the results of human behaviour, but can say nothing about honour, love, truth, virtue, justice or goodness. It cannot tell us how to distinguish between right or wrong—or why we should choose one rather than the other. We will dig deeper into this in another chapter, but take note here of the fact that the English geneticist (and atheist) J.B.S. Haldane (1892–1964) admitted, 'Science can't give an answer to the question, "Why should I be good?"'[64] In *The God Delusion,* Richard Dawkins admits, 'We can all agree that science's entitlement to advise us on moral values is problematic, to say the least.'[65] Richard Feynman is convinced that the sciences 'do not directly teach good or bad'[66] and that 'ethical values lie outside the scientific realm'.[67]

- *Science is unable to answer life's deepest questions.* The Swiss physician Paul Tournier (1898–1986), the pioneer of person-centred psychotherapy, came to the following conclusion: 'Everybody today is searching for an answer to those problems to which science pays no attention, the problem of their destiny, the mystery of evil, the question of death.'[68] Sir John Eccles (1903–1997), the Australian neurophysiologist who won the 1963 Nobel Prize in Physiology or Medicine elaborated: 'Science cannot explain the existence of each of us as a unique self, nor can it answer such fundamental questions as "Who am I? How did I come to be at a certain place and time? What happens after death?" These are all mysteries beyond science.[69] The Welsh geneticist Steve Jones says, 'Science cannot answer the questions that philosophers—or children—ask: why are we here, what is the point of being alive, how ought we to behave? ... These questions may be interesting, but scientists are no more qualified to comment on them than is anyone else.'[70]

- *Science is unable to show that God does not exist.* It is sometimes argued that as God cannot be proved by any scientific hypothesis we can take it that he does not exist, but it is easy to demolish this argument. The very statement, 'God cannot be proved by any scientific hypothesis' cannot be proved by any scientific hypothesis. Does this mean that the statement does not exist? Peter Atkins let the cat out of the bag in the course of the Oxford University debate mentioned earlier. Before letting fly with both barrels at religion in general and Christianity in particular he inserted this significant escape clause: 'I have to admit from the outset that science cannot disprove the existence of God.' Richard Dawkins also concedes that 'science has no way to disprove the existence of a supreme being'.[71] As the Scottish molecular biologist Andrew Miller says, 'It is certainly not a scientific matter to decide whether or not there is a God.'[72]

The Austrian physicist Erwin Schrödinger (1887–1961), who won the 1933 Nobel Prize for Physics, summed up his view on the limits of science: 'I am very astonished that the scientific picture of the real world around me is very deficient. It gives us a lot of factual information, puts all of our experience in a magnificently consistent order, but it is ghastly silent about all and sundry that is really near to our heart, that really matters to us. It cannot tell us a word about red and blue, bitter and sweet, physical pain and physical delight; it knows nothing of beautiful and ugly, good or bad, God and eternity. Science sometimes pretends to answer questions in these domains but the answers are very often so silly that we are not inclined to take them seriously.'[73]

The phoney war

On the BBC Television programme *Soul of Britain*, Richard Dawkins claimed, 'I think science really has fulfilled the need that religion did in the past, of explaining things, explaining why we are here, what is the origin of life, where did the world come from, what life is all about … science has the answers.'[74] But as we have already seen in this chapter, it would be difficult to cram more error into a single sentence. Science cannot explain why we are here, it cannot explain the origin of life, it cannot explain where the world came from, and it cannot explain what life is all about. Science is the ongoing process of discovering truth about the natural world, but its reach is strictly limited to that field. When asked in the film *The Unbelievers* about the purpose of life, Dawkins replied, 'Well there is no purpose, and to ask what it is is a silly question.' Peter Atkins goes even further and claims, 'Science can show that there is not a purpose in the universe, and is not going to waste its time worrying about it.'[75] If I stood at the foot of Ben Nevis, Britain's highest mountain, at midnight and shone a torch upwards, I would not be able to see the summit, but this would hardly be proof that the summit was not there. It would simply mean that it was beyond the torch's reach. A tin opener is a very useful instrument in the kitchen, but it can hardly power a jetliner. As Francis Collins puts it, 'If God exists, then he must be outside the natural world, and therefore the tools of science are not the right ones to learn about him.'[76]

If science is unable tell us whether there is a creator who gives meaning to life, where can we turn? In the Christmas 2013 edition of *Radio Times*, the English television presenter Michael Palin (who was also a member of Monty Python) wrote, 'I don't disbelieve.

I am an agnostic with doubt,' then added, 'If you're going to understand the world, you've got to be prepared to be open to questions of faith.'[77] Yet Peter Atkins says there is no point in going there. In the course of a 1998 Oxford debate he called religion 'outmoded and ridiculous' and claimed that it 'was not possible to believe in gods and be a true scientist.'[78] This takes us back to one of the ideas we identified earlier in this chapter and which says that faith and the scientific method are mutually exclusive. But this is not the case. In fact, the principles of modern scientific thinking were laid down not by men who embraced scientism and rejected faith, but by outstanding scientists who worked on the assumption that God created an ordered universe that made its scientific explanation possible. As the British mathematician and philosopher John Lennox puts it, 'Far from belief in God hindering science, it is the motor that drove it.'[79]

The 1663 Charter of the Royal Society, a Fellowship of the world's most eminent scientists and the oldest scientific academy in continuous existence, states, '[The Royal Society's] studies are to be applied to further promoting by the authority of experiments the sciences of natural things and of useful arts, to the Glory of God the Creator, and the advantage of the human race.' The manifesto of the British Association for the Advancement of Science, drawn up in 1865 and signed by 617 scientists, including many with outstanding credentials, had no difficulty in holding that there was no clash between their religious beliefs and their scientific discoveries. The original document can be seen in the Bodleian Library at Oxford.

The English physicist and mathematician Sir Isaac Newton (1643–1727) remains one of the most influential scientists of all time. His most famous work, *Philosophiæ Naturalis Principia Mathematica* (Latin for 'Mathematical Principles of Natural Philosophy') was first published in 1687 and has been called 'a book that transformed the course of modern science'. In it, Newton wrote, 'Without all doubt this world ... could arise from nothing but the perfectly free will of God.'[80]

Before and after Newton, there is a 'Who's Who' of ground-breaking scientists who put God at the centre of their worldview. These include the following:

The English philosopher, scientist and politician Francis Bacon (1561–1626), who devised what is now known as the scientific method.

The German scientist Johannes Kepler (1571–1630), universally recognized as the father of physical astronomy.

The French mathematician, philosopher and scientist Blaise Pascal (1623–1662), a genius who by the age of sixteen had written a book on conic sections reckoned to be the greatest advance in geometry for 2,000 years.

The Irish chemist Robert Boyle (1627–1691), described on his tombstone as 'the father of chemistry', and best known for Boyle's Law, which established the relationship between the pressure, temperature and volume of a mass of gas.

The English naturalist John Ray (1627–1705), listed in *The Dictionary of Natural Biography* as 'the father of English natural history'.

The Swedish scientist Carl Linnaeus (1707–1778), who drew up a detailed classification system of plants and animals and became known as the father of biological taxonomy.

The English chemist and physicist Michael Faraday (1791–1867), the foremost experimental scientist of his day, who discovered electro-magnetic induction.

The English physicist James Joule (1818–1889), whose work formed the basis of The First Law of Thermodynamics.

The French chemist and microbiologist Louis Pasteur (1822–1895), best known for discovering the principles of vaccination, microbial fermentation and pasteurization.

The Scottish mathematical physicist William Thomson (1824–1907), who published 661 papers on scientific subjects, patented seventy inventions, was made Baron Kelvin of Largs, and established The Kelvin Temperature Scale, universally used today.

The Scottish scientist James Clerk Maxwell (1831–1879), now recognized as the father of modern physics.

These are no more than a few examples of a 'hall of fame' that went on to span the whole of the twentieth century, and is being added to in the twenty-first century. It makes nonsense of Peter Atkins' claim that no 'true scientist' could believe in God, and does the same to Richard Dawkins' statement that any connection between religion and science is 'a shallow, empty, hollow, spin-doctored sham'.[81] No honest historian of science would give these claims house room. The American palaeontologist and evolutionary biologist Stephen Jay Gould (1941–2002) came to this conclusion: 'Unless at least half my colleagues are dunces, there can be … no conflict between science and religion.'[82]

All scientists work on the understanding that in the natural world there is truth to be discovered, understood, analysed and used. They see order, not chaos, and can rely on predictability in such a way as to make their investigations with confidence. Scientists who believe in God go one step further and believe that all truth discovered by science is God's truth, embedded in nature. Scientists with no faith in God must surely struggle to equate the order they see with their contention that it came about in some random way. Writing in *The Spectator*, the English journalist Melanie Phillips drew her readers' attention to the fact that 'contrary to popular myth' Western science was based on the claim that 'the universe was the product of a rational Creator, who endowed man with reason so that he could ask questions about the natural world.'[83]

If Phillips is right, she is confirming that all scientists—including those who deny that God even exists—depend on him in order to do their work. If the laws that God has put into place to govern the universe were not consistent, no science could be done. Even scientists who do not believe that these laws are designed by God never treat them as if they were unpredictable coincidences, but as part of reality that is 'out there' and can be trusted. As John Benton explains, 'They assume that we and whatever the universe came from speak the same language in a way that is not true for other creatures ... Put another way, scientists assume that scientific law can be expressed, communicated and understood through human words.'[84] To illustrate this, he writes, 'If there were no regularities, if randomly water sometimes flowed uphill and rhinos bred rabbits, there would be no pattern to study and scientific prediction would be impossible. But reality is not like that. There is order and pattern.'[85]

This order and pattern opens the door for science to be so amazingly successful. If the universe was not ordered and predictable, science would not be possible. Yet for all of its brilliant successes, science has no answer to the question as to whether life has any meaning. We will need to look elsewhere—and we can begin by looking upwards.

The cosmic clue

'Space is big. Really big. You just won't believe how vastly, hugely mind-bogglingly big it is. I mean, you may think it's a long way down the road to the chemist, but that's just peanuts to space.'

These may be the best-known words in the English author Douglas Adams' multi-media phenomenon *The Hitchhiker's Guide to the Galaxy*—and he can hardly be accused of exaggerating. If planet Earth was the size of the full-stop at the end of this sentence, the moon would be five-eighths of an inch away, the sun just over nineteen feet and the nearest star 1005 miles. Those numbers and proportions are staggering enough, but like that trip to the chemist they are 'peanuts'. Keeping to the same scale, we would still be 467,600,000 miles from the Andromeda Galaxy. Yet this is the nearest galaxy to ours (the Milky Way). The Extreme Deep Field (XDF) image obtained by the Hubble Space Telescope suggests there are at least 175 billion other galaxies in the known universe, stretching out some fourteen billion light years (a light year is about six trillion miles) from Earth in every direction. Two hundred years ago most scientists believed that the Milky Way was the entire universe and that only about 100 million stars existed. Today, we know differently—and space really is 'vastly hugely mind-bogglingly big'. The Sun, a million times the size of Earth, bears the same relation to the size of the known universe as a single grain of sand does to all the world's beaches.

This should lead us to ask the inescapable question posed by the German mathematician and philosopher Gottfried Leibniz (1646–1716): 'Why is there something rather than nothing?'[86] This opens out into other questions we need to ask if we are serious about getting to grips with the issue of whether life on planet Earth has any meaning: How did the universe come into existence? Why is it the way it is? Where did the laws of nature come from? Why is there such amazing order and design? Is this a clue that there is a meaning to life? In *The Hitchhiker's Guide to the Galaxy* a superior race builds a supercomputer able to calculate the meaning of 'life, the universe and everything'. After seven-and-a half million years it comes up with the answer: '42'. Douglas Adams was often asked why he chose that number, and he replied that it was a joke: 'I sat at my desk, stared into the garden and thought "42 will do". I typed it out. End of story.'

We can do better than that and will begin by looking at two of the best-known theories about the existence of the universe.

The first is that it has always existed, an idea that is generally called the Steady State Theory. This seems to be what Bertrand Russell had in mind when he said, 'I think the word "universe" is a handy word in some connections, but I don't think it stands for anything that has a meaning ... I should say that the universe is just there, and that's all.'[87] Elsewhere he claimed, 'There is no reason why the world could not have come into being without a cause; nor, on the other hand, is there any reason why it should not have always existed. There is no reason to suppose that the world had a beginning at all.' As he said this in a lecture to the South London Branch of the National Secular Society on 6 March 1927, I imagine he had a sympathetic hearing, but today's astronomers laugh the idea out of court. The American astrophysicist and radio astronomer Arno Penzias, who shared the 1978 Nobel prize for Physics and co-discovered cosmic background radiation, which helped to produce the Big Bang theory, says, 'The creation of the universe is supported by all the observable data astronomy has produced so far.'[88] Hubble discoveries have settled that question, and have also shown that the known universe is expanding outwards in every direction, with the galaxies moving farther and farther away from us and from each other.

This discovery triggered off a massive game-changer, because by rewinding the process and taking time backwards instead of forwards, astronomers could see the universe getting smaller and smaller, with the galaxies getting closer to each other and to us. Eventually, all the mass, energy, and space-time in the universe would have been compressed to an infinitely dense, dimensionless point, usually called a 'singularity'. This fits perfectly with the Second Law of Thermodynamics, which (put at its very simplest) says that as the universe's available energy is 'running down' it must have begun in a highly ordered, energy-packed state. Albert Einstein had problems squaring this with his Theory of Relativity, but after he had accepted the American astronomer Edwin Hubble's invitation to visit the Palomar Observatory at Mount Wilson, California in 1931 and looked at the evidence through its massive telescope, he emerged to tell the media, 'I now see the necessity of a beginning.'

The second idea is that the universe is self-created. Theories about spontaneous generation can be traced as far back as the writings of the Greek philosopher Aristotle (384–322 BC) and over the centuries scientists and others have applied it to many different forms of life. As we saw in Chapter 1, Stephen Hawking has given the theory the ultimate accolade. In *The Grand Design* he claims 'Because there is a law such as gravity, the universe can and will create itself from nothing. Spontaneous creation is the reason there is something rather than nothing, why the Universe exists, why we exist.'[89] If he is right, there can obviously be no meaning to life, and there is no point in trying to find one—but is he right? I am neither a physicist nor a philosopher, but it seems obvious to me that there are a number of fundamental flaws in his claim. We can look at four of them here.

Firstly, it is self-contradictory. It begins by giving credit for the creation of everything to the law of gravity, but then says that before there was anything there was 'nothing'. But how could the universe have been created out of nothing if self-creation depended on the laws of nature, including the law of gravity? If gravity and the laws of nature triggered the creation of the cosmos, we would have to abandon the idea that everything began with nothing, and would also have to explain who or what created those laws; was it 'nothing'? Can 'nothing' create anything, let alone the elegant and dependable laws that govern the universe?

Secondly, as the British author C. S. Lewis (1898–1963) pointed out, the laws of nature can never create anything: '*In the whole history of the universe the laws of nature have never produced a single event.* They are the pattern to which every event must conform, provided only that it can be induced to happen ... the source of events must be sought elsewhere.'[90] (emphasis added). Earlier he had said that imagining the laws of nature could create anything 'is like thinking that you can create real money by simply doing sums'.[91] Even if we went along with Stephen Hawking's theory we would still be left with the question, 'Why and how do the laws of nature exist?'

Physical laws are unable to create anything. All they can do is describe how things happen or predict how they will happen. Peter Atkins makes the baffling claim that 'space-time generates its own dust in the process of its own self-assembly'.[92] He calls this his 'Cosmic Bootstrap' principle, but as John Lennox comments, 'Nonsense remains nonsense, even when talked by world-famous scientists.'[93] This comment would also apply to the equally baffling claim by Atkins that the entire universe, with all its amazing interlocking order, is 'an elaborate and engaging rearrangement of nothing'.[94]

Thirdly, the idea turns logic on its head, because for something to create itself it would need to exist in order to do the creating. Bringing something into existence is an action (and in the case of the universe a mind-bogglingly big one!), but if the universe did not exist before it brought itself into existence how could it create anything, let alone itself? Since nothing can create itself, there has to be a first, uncreated cause.

Fourthly, the theory of spontaneous generation clashes with the First Law of Thermodynamics (sometimes known as the law of conservation of mass and energy) which says that while mass can be converted into energy, and energy into mass, it can neither be self-created nor totally destroyed.

Reviewing the Hawking television programme *A Brief History of Mine* in *The Daily Telegraph*, Michael Deacon writes about trying to get his mind around Hawking's claim that 'The universe just came into existence all by itself'. He explains that he found it 'a vain struggle', because 'If the universe just came into existence all by itself, that means that before the universe there was nothing. And if there was nothing, there were no materials with which to create the universe. Which means that …'[95] One thing is certain: if the universe did come into being 'all by itself' we are wasting time looking for a meaning to life on one of its tiny planets.

David Hume, who remains one of the most important men in Western philosophy, was a full-blown sceptic with no religious axe to grind, yet in *Dialogues Concerning Natural Religion*, first published in 1779, three years after his death, he wrote these words:

'Look around the world: Contemplate the whole and every part of it: You will find it to be nothing but one great machine, subdivided into an infinite number of lesser machines, which again admit of subdivisions to a degree beyond what human faculties can trace and explain. All these various machines, even their most minute parts, are adjusted to each other with an accuracy which ravishes into admiration all men who have ever contemplated them. The curious adapting of means to ends, throughout all nature, resembles exactly, though it much exceeds, the productions of human contrivance—or human designs, thought, wisdom and intelligence.'[96] Later in the same book he pressed the point home: 'A purpose, an intention, or design strikes everywhere the most careless, the most stupid thinker; and no man can be so hardened in absurd systems, as at all times to reject it.'[97] The language may be old-fashioned, but it is important to grasp what Hume is saying.

In his eulogy at Douglas Adams' funeral on 17 September 2001, Richard Dawkins declared, 'The world is a thing of utter inordinate complexity and richness and strangeness that is absolutely awesome. I mean the idea that such complexity can arise not only out of such simplicity, but probably absolutely out of nothing, is the most fabulous extraordinary idea. And once you get some kind of inkling of how that might have happened, it's just wonderful. And … the opportunity to spend seventy or eighty years of your life in such a universe is time well spent as far as I am concerned.'

His first sentence is sublimely true, but can we really believe that our highly complex universe came into existence 'absolutely out of nothing'? The English scholar Keith Ward, a Fellow of the British Academy, shows where this kind of thinking leads:

'One day there might be nothing. The next day, there might be a very large carrot. Nothing else in existence whatsoever, all alone and larger than life, a huge carrot. If anything is possible, that certainly is. The day after that, the carrot might disappear and be replaced by a purple spotted gorilla. Why not? … Why does this thought seem odd, or even ridiculous, whereas the thought that some law of physics might just pop into existence does not? Logically, they are exactly on a par.'[98]

The influential German philosopher Immanuel Kant (1724– 1804) wrote, 'In the world we find everywhere clear signs of an order which can only spring from design.'[99] We could say that the ordered structure of the universe is just an idea we have come up with, or something we have tried to impose on what we find as we explore our planet and get a sense of its place in the universe.

Yet the remarkable order we see is obviously not something we have either made up or brought about, nor can we find any natural explanation or reason as to why it should exist. But what we do find is so amazing that it makes no sense to sweep it under the carpet, shrug our shoulders and move on. As Richard Dawkins rightly says, 'Humans have a great hunger for explanation',[100] and the more we have become aware of the size, composition and complexity of the universe the greater our longing to know why it should be as it is, and whether this tells us anything about the meaning of life.

Paul Davies puts it like this: 'Modern physics has shown that there is something truly extraordinary about the way the laws of physics fit together. It is not just any old universe; it is a very special, fine-tuned arrangement of things', then adds, 'The laws of physics dovetail with such an exquisite consistency and coherence that *the impression of design is overwhelming*'[101](emphasis added). Elsewhere, with no religious agenda, he says, 'It is hard to resist the impression that the present structure of the universe, apparently so sensitive to minor alterations in the numbers, has been rather carefully thought out.'[102] The English preacher and author Melvin Tinker sums it up: 'The universe is not random and chaotic. We live in a universe which has all the hallmarks of a cosmos—the well designed, intricate, purposeful motions of planets, not the haphazard meanderings of rocks thrown around by chance.'[103]

Fine-tuned facts
It has long since been pointed out that if the depth of earth's oceans, the angle at which it is tilted on its axis (23.4 degrees), its rotational speed (just over 1000 miles an hour), its land-water ratio (30%-70%), its average distance from the sun (just under 93 million miles), and a number of other factors were not precisely as they are our planet could not sustain life of any kind, let alone human life. The conditions in our solar system and planet need to

be just right. Without an atmosphere of oxygen, none of us would be able to breathe, and without oxygen there would be no water. Without water there would be no rainfall for our crops, while other elements such as hydrogen, nitrogen, sodium, carbon, calcium, and phosphorus are also essential for life.

Yet these all exist, and scientists have produced statistics that point to an amazing degree of fine-tuning in the universe. Here are just a few of the many facts and comments that could be quoted.

- Francis Collins says that the chances of the fifteen physical constants (physical qualities generally believed to be universal in nature and constant in time) existing with precisely the right values to give us a stable universe is 'almost infinitesimal'.[104]

- It has been said that if you covered the United States with small coins piled so high that they reached to the moon, repeated this 1,000 times, then put a small mark on one of the coins and asked a blindfolded person to pick it out, the chances of them doing so at the first attempt would be the same as the possibility of the finely-tuned universe coming into being by accident.

- There are four fundamental forces of nature—gravity, electromagnetism, the strong nuclear force and the weak nuclear force. If their relationship to each other was not precisely as it is the sun would not exist. For example, the Australian theoretical physicist Brandon Carter calculates that if gravity were different by a mere one part of 10^{40} (1 followed by forty zeros) not only would the sun not exist, but neither would 'any form of life that depends on solar-like stars for its sustenance'.[105] If the strong nuclear force were two per cent weaker, protons and neutrons would not stick together. If it were 0.3 per cent stronger, hydrogen (which all biological systems need) could not exist.[106]

- Stephen Hawking admits, 'The whole history of science has been the gradual realization that events do not happen in an arbitrary manner, *but that they reflect a certain underlying order*' (emphasis added).[107] Writing about the precise balance of the fundamental forces, he admits, 'The remarkable fact is that the values of these numbers seem to have been finely adjusted to make possible the development of life.'[108] Elsewhere he says that if the universe's original rate of expansion had been smaller by one part in a hundred thousand million million, 'the universe would have collapsed before it ever reached its present size'.[109]

- The American astrophysicist and Nobel laureate George Smoot says that if the universe had come into existence with equal amounts of matter and antimatter 'a vast annihilation event would have occurred'.[110] If this had happened, we would obviously not be here to discuss it!

- It has been calculated that the odds against the unplanned formation of our fine-tuned universe is 1 in 10,000,000,000[124], the kind of figure that, according to the English astronomer Sir Fred Hoyle (1915–2001), 'suggests that a superintellect has monkeyed with physics'[111]—his way of saying that such a thing never happened.

- The Canadian astrophysicist Hugh Ross estimates that the chances of human life originating in this scenario are less than one chance in a trillion trillion trillion trillion trillion trillion trillion trillion trillion trillion trillion trillion, odds 'defying the laws of probability'.[112]

In March 2014, a team of American scientists announced that operating a £12 million telescope at the South Pole they had found conclusive evidence for the existence of gravity waves, colossal ripples in space-time that were formed in a staggering moment of inflation one trillionth of a trillionth of a trillionth of a second after the Big Bang. *The Daily Telegraph* science journalist Michael Hanlon called it 'a length of time shorter than it would take Starship Enterprise (a spacecraft featured in the famous Star Trek film and television series) to cross from one side of a grain of sand to another.'[113] Yet towards the end of his article Hanlon said that 'on a more profound level, we do not know what the purpose, if any, of our universe is; or what role if any, life like ours plays in it'— and closes by saying, 'Quite the most remarkable thing about our universe is that we can begin to understand it at all.'[114]

What has all of this to do with our question about the meaning of life? *Everything!* There is growing evidence that intelligent life on earth demands a unique arrangement of stars, planets and galaxies—exactly the ones we know are in place. If the universe came into existence by chance or accident, there can be no rhyme or reason to it and no plan or purpose in it. Yet if there is no meaning in the existence of the universe, how can there be any meaning in human life, wherever it is to be found? Anything that sprang into life on our planet (or any other planet or star for that matter) would merely be adding to a series of fantastic flukes. As C. S. Lewis put it, 'Either there is significance in the whole process of things as well as in human activity, or there is no significance in human activity itself … You cannot have it both ways. If the world is meaningless, then so are we.'[115] Hugh Ross agrees: 'If the universe is simply uncreated, eternally self-existent or randomly self-assembled, then it has no purpose and consequently we have no purpose.'[116]

Some people are attracted to the idea of a multiverse (or meta-universe), which suggests there is a finite or infinite number of universes (sometimes called parallel universes) other than our own, but looking there for answers to our question is just kicking the can down the road. The existence of multiple universes would need even more explanation than the existence of the one we know. What is more, as God could create as many universes as he liked, how can the multiverse theory rule him out? Stephen Hawking can say only that 'a great many universes were created out of nothing' and that 'they arise naturally from physical laws'.[117] There is not a shred of evidence for this, and in any case the parallel universes notion gets us nowhere nearer an answer to our question about the meaning of life. In her article for *The Spectator*, Melanie Phillips wrote, 'Richard Dawkins told me that he was "not necessarily averse" to the idea that life on earth had been created by a governing intelligence—provided that such an intelligence had arrived from another planet. How can it be that our pre-eminent apostle of reason appears to find little green men more plausible as an explanation for the origin of life than God?'[118]

There are many millions of different species (distinct life forms) on the earth, with thousands of new ones being listed every year. Humankind is the most advanced of all species, yet if its ancestry can ultimately be traced back to an accident, seeking to give it any serious meaning is as futile as trying to make sense out of nonsense, or to say that 'xhyfcd' can be made to spell 'wheelbarrow'. As the English academic Kathleen Jones (1922–2010) pointed out, 'If as [Dawkins] insists, the origin of the universe was an accident that happened to nothing, all the complex discoveries of astrophysics and quantum mechanics would be totally meaningless. They would all have happened by chance, out of whirling atoms that came from nowhere … So who invented atoms? Come to think of it, who invented chance?'[119]

Creation and meaning

Oceans of ink and acres of space are spent on discussing things such as the Big Bang theory and the age of our planet, but the fundamental question goes beyond these: *is the known universe the result of an intelligent act of creation, or is it the result of a combination of chance events?* If it is not the product of supreme reason, where can we look to find a solid basis for the meaning of life, or for giving human beings value, dignity and purpose? It is impossible to find any valid human meaning in a meaningless universe.

Over the centuries, countless people have pointed us towards such a basis. The Roman philosopher Cicero (106–43 BC) wrote, 'What could be more clear or obvious when we look up to the sky and contemplate the heavens, than that there is some divinity or superior intelligence?'[120] Nicolaus Copernicus (1473–1543) the Polish mathematician and astronomer who stunned the scientific world of his day by proving that the sun, rather than the earth, was at the centre of the universe, said that our world 'has been built by the best and most orderly workman of all'.[121] The American scientist Allan Sandage (1926–2010), one of the twentieth century's most influential astronomers (he was the first to identify quasi-stellar radio sources now known as quasars) took another step: 'I find it quite improbable that such order came out of chaos. There has to be some organizing principle. God to me is a mystery but is the explanation for the mystery of existence—why there is something rather than nothing.'[122]

If all the elements in the universe, human or otherwise, are unconnected, where can human life find meaning or purpose? If no meaning was put into the universe, none can be found there. If God does not exist we are in serious trouble, as we are living on a planet spinning at well over 1,000 miles an hour and orbiting the sun at over 69,000 miles an hour, as part of a galaxy that is moving through space at nearly 2,725,000 miles an hour—and nobody is in charge. On the other hand, if all the elements are connected, we can properly ask why this is the case. Small wonder that Abraham Lincoln (1809–1865), the sixteenth President of the United States, said, 'I can see how it might be possible for a man to look upon the earth and be an atheist, but I cannot conceive how he can look up into the heavens and say there is no God.'[123]

Arno Penzias says this about his research: 'The best data we have [for the Big Bang] are exactly what I would have predicted had I nothing to go on but the five books of Moses, the Psalms, and the Bible as a whole.'[124] This is a remarkable testimony from a distinguished expert in the field, and C. S. Lewis gave a fine-tuned version of the same testimony: 'No philosophical theory which I have yet come across is a radical improvement on the words of Genesis, that "In the beginning God made heaven and earth".'[125] If we set aside the idea that the universe is self-created or exists by chance, we would need five elements to bring it about—time, intelligence, energy, space and matter. Now look again at Lewis' quotation of the opening words of the Bible. 'In the beginning' speaks of time; 'God' speaks of intelligence; 'made' speaks of energy; 'heaven' speaks of space; and 'earth' speaks of matter. Is this just a coincidence? It is also worth noting that it was not until the nineteenth century that scientists claimed evidence that the universe had a beginning, something the Bible has been saying for thousands of years.

The English scientist Andrew Parker, selected by The Royal Institution in 2000 as one of the top eight in the nation to be a 'Scientist for the New Century', is an evolutionary biologist who does not believe in God. Yet when he looked carefully at what the Bible says about creation he came to this conclusion: 'Without expecting to find anything, I discovered a whole series of parallels between the creation story on the Bible's first page and the modern, scientific account of life's history ... The more detail is examined, the more convincing and remarkable I believe the parallels become ... The opening page of Genesis is scientifically accurate but was written long before the science was known. How did the writer of this page come to write this creation account ... I must admit, rather nervously as a scientist averse to entertaining such an idea, that the evidence that the writer of the opening page of the Bible was divinely inspired is strong. I have never before encountered such powerful, impartial evidence to suggest that the Bible is the product of divine inspiration.'[126]

Nobody was there to see the universe come into being, nor can we conduct any experiment that gets within light years of duplicating what took place. It would seem reasonable to say that if it was created our only way of knowing anything about this would be if its creator was to tell us—and in its opening words (C. S. Lewis quoted them loosely) the Bible claims that he does: 'In the beginning, God created the heavens and the earth.'[127] There is no single word in Hebrew (the language in which the early part of the Bible was originally written) that matches our English word 'universe', but *hassamayim we'et ha'ares* (translated 'the heavens and the earth') tells us that God created everything that exists outside of himself. Elsewhere, the Bible underlines this by stating, 'By him all things were created, in heaven and on earth, visible and invisible, whether thrones or dominions or rulers or authorities—all things were created through him and for him.'[128] As the American scholar Douglas Kelly explains, '"All things" include the various ranks of angels, and every form of life from whales and elephants to viruses. "All things" include every form of energy and matter, the speed of light, nuclear structure, electromagnetism and gravity, and all of the laws by which nature operates.'[129] Richard Dawkins told a

BBC radio audience that the idea of creation 'doesn't do justice to the grandeur of the truth,'[130] and elsewhere writes, 'The universe presented by organized religion is a poky little medieval universe, and extremely limited,'[131] but both statements are at odds with the facts.

(The paragraph you have just read has the first direct quotations from the Bible, and there will be others in later chapters. If you have genuine questions about the Bible's authority and relevance, you may want to read the Appendix before you go any further. Alternatively you may want to do this when you have reached the end of the book).

The Bible says that the universe reveals God's 'invisible attributes, namely his eternal power and divine nature', and that those who refuse to recognize this are 'without excuse.'[132] In London's St Paul's Cathedral, the tomb of its architect, Sir Christopher Wren, has the Latin inscription, 'Reader: if you seek his monument, look around you.' God points us to creation and says the same kind of thing. As the Welsh author Stuart Olyott puts it, 'Nobody can plead that he is ignorant of the existence of God. It can clearly be seen that there is an Unseen.'[133] This ties in with the Bible's claim, 'The heavens declare the glory of God, and the sky above proclaims his handiwork.'[134] George Washington Carver (1864–1943), the outstanding American scientist, botanist, educator and inventor, who was only the third American in history to have a national monument erected in his honour, believed that in the wonders of the natural world God is pointing us to himself: 'I love to think of nature as an unlimited broadcasting system through which God speaks to us every hour, if only we will tune him in.'[135]

As Sir John Houghton, puts it, 'The order and consistency we see in our science can be seen as reflecting orderliness and consistency in the character of God himself.'[136] Does it take any more faith to believe this than to believe that the amazing order, harmony and beauty we see in the natural world is a gigantic fluke, that life itself sprang into existence by chance, that logic is sheer luck and that the vast amount of information in living things had no intelligent source?

The cosmos has no scientific reason for existing, and the universal, elegant and consistent laws of nature are amazingly and precisely suited to allow life on our planet. How can these be explained in natural terms? The Bible's explanation for them is reflected in words inscribed on the entrance to the Cavendish Laboratory at Cambridge University when it was opened in 1874: 'The works of the Lord are great.' Keith Ward has no doubt that 'God is the best final explanation there can be for the universe.'[137]

On her tenth birthday Richard Dawkins wrote to his daughter, encouraging her to think for herself. In the course of an impressive letter he said, 'Next time somebody tells you something that sounds important, think to yourself: "Is this the kind of thing that people probably know because of evidence? Or is it the kind of thing that people only believe because of tradition, authority or revelation?" And next time somebody tells you that something is true, why not say to them: "What kind of evidence is there for that?" And if they can't give you a good answer, I hope you'll think very carefully before you believe a word they say.'[138] Those who are asked why they claim that the universe was created by God, and why this is a clue to there being a meaning to life can give 'a good answer'.

The American astronomer, physicist and cosmologist Robert Jastrow (1925–2008), the first Chairman of NASA's Lunar Exploration Committee, called himself 'an agnostic, and not a believer', yet in *God and the Astronomers* he admitted 'Now we see how the astronomical evidence leads to a biblical view of the origin of the world.'[139] Later in the same book he wrote about the result of trying to rule God out of our world: 'For the scientist who has lived by his faith in the power of reason, the story ends like a bad dream. He has scaled the mountains of ignorance; he is about to conquer the highest peak; as he pulls himself over the final rock, he is greeted by a band of theologians who have been sitting there for centuries.'[140]

The theory

'We are here because one odd group of fishes had a peculiar fin anatomy that could transform into legs for terrestrial creatures; because the earth never froze entirely during an ice age; because a small and tenuous species, arising in Africa a quarter of a million years ago, has managed, so far, to survive by hook and by crook. We may yearn for a "higher" answer, but none exists.'[141]

This summary of human history seems to rule out any possibility of finding any meaning to life. It was written by Stephen Jay Gould, one of the world's most frequently quoted scientists on a subject that millions of people believe is the explanation of what we are and how we got here: *evolution*. Gould did not buy into all the ideas commonly taught about evolution today, but he agreed with most of them, and certainly saw humankind as evolution's state of the art production.

The theory of evolution is so deeply embedded today that Richard Dawkins calls it 'a fact that is proved utterly beyond reasonable doubt'. Elsewhere he claims, 'It is absolutely safe to say that if you meet somebody who claims not to believe in evolution, that person is ignorant, stupid or insane.' [He added that what he disliked about those who believed in creation (by God) was that they were so intolerant—but we will let that go!] He underlines his claim by suggesting, 'No qualified scientist doubts that evolution is a fact, in the ordinarily accepted sense in which it is a fact that the Earth orbits the Sun. It is a fact that human beings are cousins to monkeys, kangaroos, jellyfish and bacteria.'[142] In saying this, he is being economical with the truth, because countless highly qualified professors, academics, researchers and other experts in the fields of biology, physics, chemistry, mathematics, geology, anthropology and other disciplines raise serious objections to evolutionary theory.

The theory took off in 1859 with the publication of a book by the English naturalist and geologist Charles Darwin (1809–1882). The book's full title was *On the Origin of Species by Means of Natural Selection or the Preservation of Favoured Races in the Struggle for Life* (mercifully now referred to as *The Origin of Species*). The word 'evolution' did not appear in the book until the sixth edition, but by the time Darwin wrote *The Descent of Man* in 1871 his complete theory was in place: humankind had appeared 'not according to some ordered plan but as the result of chance operating among the countless creatures by nature's unlimited tendency towards variation'.[143] As the English writer and researcher Ian Taylor explains, 'The idea that life on earth originated from a single-celled organism and then progressed onwards and upwards in ever-increasing complexity to culminate in man himself is what the theory of evolution is all about.'[144] Nobody can seriously question the fact that perfectly natural processes produce marked changes within a given type or group. These changes are what we could call 'horizontal' rather than 'vertical', and over long periods of time they can result in huge variations in the size, colour and other characteristics of the plants or animals concerned. We can even accelerate these changes by crossbreeding or by the genetic engineering of animals such as dogs, horses and birds—but however big the changes we can help to bring about *they remain dogs, horses and birds.*

These 'horizontal' changes are known technically as *microevolution*.Darwin's so-called 'general theory', known technically as *macroevolution*, included 'vertical' changes and claimed that there is no limit to evolutionary processes. This theory says that all living species, from worms to wolves, carrots to crocodiles, grass to gorillas—and hummingbirds to humans— are not the result of any creative design, but are the outworking of unguided natural processes over many millions of years. This would mean that all living things can be traced back to the first spark of life that somehow arose in non-living elements on our planet at some point in prehistory. Darwin hedged his ideas around with so many questions that phrases like 'we may suppose' occur over 800 times in *The Origin of Species* and *The Descent of Man,* but his theory has been promoted so strongly in the media and elsewhere that it is now taken for granted as giving an accurate description of exactly how we came to be what we are.

A good summary of this was set out when a tiny zircon crystal was found on a sheep ranch in Western Australia in 2001 and was said to be the oldest piece of our planet. In February 2014 *The Daily*

Telegraph ran an article on this,[145] illustrated by a column giving the following timeline:

4.54 billion years ago. Earth is formed from debris in the solar system.

4.4 billion years ago. The first zircon crystals form, showing Earth is beginning to cool.

3.8 billion years ago. Molecular life begins with bacteria.

900 million years ago. First multicellular life develops.

530 million years ago. First vertebrates appear.

250 million years ago. Dinosaurs become the dominant species.

200 million years ago. An asteroid wipes out dinosaurs and earliest mammals evolve.

6 million years ago. Hominids diverge from closest relatives, the chimpanzee and bonobo.

Macroevolutionists frequently shuffle these numbers around as different discoveries are assessed, and in this case they relate them to a piece of crystal that measures some 200 x 400 microns, about twice the diameter of a human hair. Yet the implications are so far-reaching in our search for the meaning to life that we need to trace the evidence and see where it leads. The American lawyer Charles Colson (1931–2012) made the point very well: 'So where did we come from? This is the most crucial question humans can raise, because the answer not only determines what it means to be human and why we are here, but it also affects every area of human endeavour. There is a raging debate among scientists and philosophers over this question, whether life began by chance or by design. So focus carefully on where the evidence leads you, for the question is not just about science; it's about *you*—whether *your* life began by chance or design.'[146]

Darwin's pond

In trying to find a starting point for his theory Darwin imagined that there might have been 'some warm little pond, with all sorts of ammonia and phosphoric salts, light, heat, electricity, etc. present', together with 'a protein compound chemically formed ready to undergo still more complex changes'.[147] One has only to read those words carefully to see that they hardly get our search off to a promising start! In 1983, an award-winning American television programme used a brilliant sequence of computer-generated graphics in trying to get the same message across, but the script was hardly an improvement in spelling things out. It spoke of 'a mass of cosmic dust and particles' on a planet that was then 'almost completely engulfed by the shallow primordial seas'. Powerful winds 'gathered random molecules from the atmosphere' and deposited some of them in the seas, where 'tides and currents swept the molecules together', until 'somewhere in this ancient ocean the miracle of life began' and from these one-celled organisms 'all life on earth began'.[148] No evidence was offered to back up this story, which reads more like science fiction than science.

Although countless experiments have been conducted to see how it might have been possible for the first spark of life to have arrived in this way, the most anyone has done is to produce a few amino acids, which are almost infinitely less complex than the simplest protein molecules essential for life. Drawing attention to this, Phillip Johnson, the American founder of the Intelligent Design movement, makes this comment: 'There is no reason to believe that life has a tendency to emerge when the right chemicals are sloshing about in a soup. Although some components of living systems can be duplicated with very advanced techniques, scientists employing the full power of their intelligence cannot manufacture living organisms from amino acids, sugars and the like. How then was the trick done before scientific intelligence was in existence?'[149] Paul Davies makes the same point: 'Nobody knows how a mixture of lifeless chemicals spontaneously organized themselves into the first living cell ... How did stupid atoms spontaneously write their own software?'[150] He asks a good question, and in trying to answer it speculation is no substitute for information. When Richard Dawkins calls people who promote the idea of Intelligent Design 'a well-organized and well-financed group of nutters'[151] he is generating more heat than light, and doing nothing to solve the problem. To say that life somehow arose from non-life is on a par with saying that something accidentally came from nothing. It would surely seem safer to suggest that intelligent life came about when an intelligent source inserted genetic information into matter that had no life of its own? Francis Crick (1916–2004), the English molecular biologist, biophysicist and neuroscientist best known for his co-discovery in 1953 of the double helical structure of the DNA molecule, wrote, 'An honest man, armed with all the knowledge available to us now, could only state that in some sense the origin of life appears at the moment to almost be a miracle, so many are the conditions which would have had to have been satisfied to get it going.'[152] The key word here is 'almost', because as he had what he called 'a strong inclination towards atheism' Crick had to be careful to rule out the possibility of creation by God.

Another scientist who once took the same line was the English scholar Antony Flew (1923–2010). Known at one time as the world's most notorious atheist, he changed his mind and in 2007 wrote a book titled *There is a God*. In it, he wrote about a symposium at

New York University at which he announced that he now believed in the existence of God. Asked if recent work on the origin of life pointed to the activity of a creative Intelligence, he replied, 'What I think the DNA material has done is that it has shown, by the almost unbelievable complexity of the arrangements which are needed to produce (life), that intelligence must have been involved in getting these extraordinarily diverse elements to work together. It's the enormous complexity of the number of elements and the enormous subtlety of the ways they work together. The meeting of these two parts at the right time by chance is simply minute. It is all a matter of the enormous complexity by which the results were achieved, which looked to me like the work of intelligence.'[153] The German-born British biochemist and Nobel Prize winner Ernst Boris Chain (1906–1979) is often quoted as saying that the principle of a divine purpose in DNA 'stares the biologist in the face wherever he looks' and that 'the probability for such an event as the origin of DNA molecules to have occurred by sheer chance is just too small to be seriously considered'.

The British engineer and physicist Alan Hayward (1923–2008) explained the problem and asked the right kind of question: 'The very first bacterium must have had at least three components working together as a team: nucleic acids, enzymes, and a cell wall. The problem is which came first—the chicken, the egg, or the hencoop? Nucleic acid cannot be formed without the aid of enzymes. Some enzymes can only be manufactured by other enzymes, and these other enzymes can only be manufactured by nucleic acid. Cell walls are only made by enzymes, and the enzymes cannot do their job unless they are kept in place by the cell wall. So how on earth did it all start?'[154] In spite of this, *Encyclopaedia Britannica* says, 'It is not unreasonable to suppose that life originated in a watery "soup" of prebiological organic compounds and that living organisms arose later by surrounding quantities of these compounds by membranes that made them into "cells". Yet to call this scenario 'not unreasonable' is itself unreasonable, as experts in many relevant fields have pointed out.

James Coppedge (1920–2004) the American Director of the Center for Probability Research in Biology in California, put the odds against a single protein molecule (essential for life) coming into existence by chance as 1 in 10^{161}. We can illustrate that number in this way: If there were ten universes for every atom in our universe, the number of atoms in all ten universes would be 10^{161}. The British-Australian molecular biologist Michael Denton writes, 'It is surely premature to claim that random processes could have assembled mosquitoes and elephants when we still have to determine the actual probability of the discovery by chance of one single functional protein molecule!'[155]

Sir Fred Hoyle wrote, 'The likelihood of the formation of life from inanimate matter is 1 to a number with 40,000 noughts after it ... It is big enough to bury Darwin and the whole theory of evolution.'[156] To emphasize his point, he asked us to imagine a vast number (1 with fifty zeros after it) of blind people, each with a Rubik's cube, all solving the problem simultaneously, before adding, 'You then have a chance of arriving by random shuffling, at just one of the many biopolymers on which life depends. The notion that not only the biopolymers but the operating program of a living cell could be arrived at by chance in a primordial organic soup here on the Earth is evidently nonsense of a high order.'[157]

The American biologist R. E. Dickerson points out, 'The evolution of the genetic machinery is the step for which there are no laboratory models; hence we can speculate endlessly, unfettered by inconvenient facts.'[158]

The English organic chemist A. E. Wilder-Smith (1915–1995), who was at one time a convinced evolutionist, wrote, 'It is emphatically the case that life cannot arise spontaneously in a primeval soup ... Furthermore, no geological evidence indicates an organic soup ever existed on this planet. We may therefore with fairness call this scenario "the myth of the pre-biotic soup".'[159]

After a careful study of the subject Michael Denton came to this conclusion: 'Considering the way the prebiotic soup is referred to in so many discussions of the origin of life as an already established reality, it comes as something of a shock to realize that there is absolutely no positive evidence for its existence.'[160] This knocks a serious dent in the idea—as it is sometimes put—that we can draw a line 'from the goo, through the zoo, to you'.

Darwin could have known nothing about biochemistry, microbiology or DNA, but we now know that even *Mycoplasma genitalium*, the bacterium with the smallest known amount of genetic information, has 580,000 base pairs on its 482 genes.[161] We also know that all the DNA data needed to specify the design of a complete human being is packed into a unit weighing less than a few thousand-millionths of a gram, and several thousand million million times smaller than the smallest piece of functional machinery used by man. The DNA coding staggers the imagination. It has been said that it would take a stack of books that would encircle the earth 5,000 times to contain the information in a mere pinhead of DNA. Another estimate suggests that all the information needed to specify the design of every living species that has ever existed on our planet could be put into a teaspoon, with enough room left over for the contents of every book ever written.[162]

In *Evolution: A Theory in Crisis*, Michael Denton, who calls himself an agnostic, writes, 'Molecular biology has shown that even the simplest of all living systems on the earth today, bacterial cells, are exceedingly complex objects. Although the tiniest bacterial cells are incredibly small, weighing less than 10^{-12} grams, each is in effect a veritable micro-miniaturized factory containing thousands of exquisitely designed pieces of intricate molecular machinery, made up altogether of one hundred thousand million atoms, far more complicated than any machine built by man and absolutely without parallel in the non-living world.'[163] Later, he fleshes this out: 'To grasp the reality of life as it has been revealed by molecular biology, we must magnify a cell a thousand million times until it is twenty kilometers in diameter and resembles a giant airship large enough to cover a great city like London or New York. What we would then see would be an object of unparalleled complexity and adaptive design. On the surface of the cell we would see millions of openings, like the port holes of a vast space ship, opening and closing to allow a continual stream of materials to flow in and out. If we were to enter one of these openings we would find ourselves in a world of supreme technology and bewildering complexity. We would see endless highly organized corridors and conduits branching in every direction away from the perimeter of the cell, some leading to the central memory bank in the nucleus and others to assembly plants and processing units. The nucleus itself would be a vast spherical chamber, resembling a geodesic dome inside of which we would see, all neatly stacked together in ordered arrays, the miles of coiled chains of the DNA molecules.'[164] Does this sound like the product of weather conditions in a 'warm little pond'? Even as an agnostic, Michael Denton's research leads him to say, 'The complexity of the simplest known type of cell is so great that it is impossible to accept that such an object could have been thrown together suddenly by some kind of freakish, vastly improbable, event. Such an occurrence would be indistinguishable from a miracle.'[165]

The sheer amount of information in the simplest cell backs up Denton's comment and this alone is enough to torpedo the idea that it could just 'happen' in some kind of prebiotic soup. As Denton adds, 'Between a living cell and the most highly ordered non-biological system, such as a crystal or a snowflake, there is a chasm as vast as it is possible to conceive.'[166]

Harry Rubin, Professor Emeritus of Cell and Developmental Biology at the University of California, Berkeley, says, 'Life, even in bacteria, is too complex to have occurred by chance.'[167] As Werner Gitt, one-time director and professor at the German Federal Institute of Physics and Technology puts it, 'There is no known law of nature, no known process and no known sequence of events which can cause information to originate by itself in matter.'[168] Richard Dawkins claims, 'As a lover of truth, I am suspicious of strongly held beliefs that are unsupported by evidence.'[169] He will find no evidence in Darwin's pond for his strongly held belief that life originated by accident.

Links?

Undeterred by this, the theory of macroevolution presses on and says that from one complete, self-contained, self-replicating life form (today's best guess is some kind of bacterium) increasingly complex forms appeared and eventually developed into every living thing that has ever existed on our planet. The obvious fact that this would take a vast amount of time is brushed aside by those who claim, 'Time is the hero of the plot. Given enough time, anything can happen—the impossible becomes probable, the improbable becomes certain,'[170] but in this chapter we have already seen that the odds against even getting the whole process kick-started rules out this idea as an escape route. The other fatal weakness in the theory is the idea that the original life form was self-replicating. Richard Dawkins offers this solution: 'Nobody knows how it happened, but somehow, without violating the laws of physics and chemistry, a molecule arose that just happened to have the property of self-copying—a "replicator".'[171] The words 'just happened' are surely a flimsy basis for such a massively important claim? He admits elsewhere that such a thing would have been 'exceedingly improbable'[172] but then smuggles into it the idea that 'given enough time, everything is possible.'[173] But where in all of this is his insistence on the need for evidence? No wonder Robert Shapiro (1935–2011), who was Professor Emeritus of chemistry at New York University, called it 'mythology rather than science'.[174] This is not an encouraging basis on which to claim that life has any meaning.

Macroevolution says that over millions of years the first single-celled organisms became more complex, though at that stage they were invertebrates, that is to say they had no spinal column or backbone. After another 1,000 million or so years, invertebrates became vertebrates, such as fish. In another thirty million years these evolved into amphibians, capable of living on land as well as in water. These eventually evolved into reptiles, such as snakes, lizards, crocodiles and tortoises. Then, over millions more years, some of these evolved into birds; those without legs developed them and added wings. Birds then evolved into four legged, furry animals, from which ape-like mammals came into being. These evolved into apes, then finally into humans. This fascinating scenario is now taken for granted, so that in the American television premiere of *Ape Man: The Story of Human Evolution*, the presenter told viewers, 'If you go back far enough, we and the chimps share a common ancestor. My father's father's father's father, going back maybe half a million generations—about five million years—was an ape.'[175] Richard Dawkins caps this and says, 'It is the plain truth that we are cousins of chimpanzees, somewhat more distant cousins of monkeys, more distant cousins still of aardvarks and manatees, yet more distant cousins of bananas and turnips.'[176] The British-American author Christopher Hitchens (1949–2011), another passionate atheist, claimed that we evolved 'from sightless bacteria.'[177]

What is needed to back up these claims is evidence, and the best place to find it would clearly be in the fossil record. Darwin was frustrated by the absence of any fossils that showed links between different groups, as he realized that according to his theory there should be masses of them. The absence of these intermediate links was 'the most obvious and serious objection' to his theory, but he decided this must be due to 'the extreme imperfection of the geological record'[178]—in other words, a lack of suitable fossils. Some time later he wrote to a friend and conceded that 'imagination must fill up the very wide blanks.'[179]

Today's hard-core evolutionists are right to point out that vastly greater numbers of fossils have been unearthed since Darwin's day—yet they have still not proved the 'molecules to man' case. The American biologist and palaeontologist Niles Eldredge, on the staff of the American Museum of Natural History, writes, 'The search for "missing links" between various living creatures, like humans and apes, is probably fruitless, because they never existed as distinct transitional forms … *no one has yet found any evidence of such transitional features*' (emphasis added).[180] Elsewhere, he says palaeontologists claim that the history of life supports the idea of gradual evolution, 'all the while knowing that it does not.'[181] Stephen J. Gould goes so far as to say that the extreme rarity of transitional forms in the fossil record 'persists as the trade secret of palaeontology.'[182]

Referring to the last of these 'missing links', Steve Jones writes, 'A chimp may share 98% of its DNA with ourselves but it is not 98% human: it is not human at all—it is a chimp. And does the fact that we have genes in common with a mouse or a banana say anything about human nature? Some claim that genes will tell us what we really are. The idea is absurd.'[183]

Phillip Johnson summarizes the situation well: 'Instead of a fact we have a speculative hypothesis that says that living species evolved from ancestors which cannot be identified, by some much-disputed mechanism which cannot be demonstrated, and in such a manner that few traces of the process were left in the record— even though that record has been interpreted by persons strongly committed to proving evolution.'[184]

Jumped-up apes?

In recent years, evolutionists have leaned on a new approach. If genes underwent radical alterations (mutations), natural selection could make use of the best of them and, given sufficient time, could produce new and better forms. In particular, natural selection could make use of countless tiny changes over millions of years that would mean 'the survival of the fittest' and eventually turn an ape or ape-like creature into a human being. This scenario is what leads Richard Dawkins to claim, 'We are jumped-up apes and our brains were only designed to understand the mundane details of how to survive in the Stone Age savannah.'[185]

The question of our origin is obviously and hugely important, for if we get the wrong answer to this, everything else falls to pieces, and we would have no hope of ever discovering the meaning to life. The idea that Dawkins puts forward runs into several road blocks. Firstly, a living cell is not just physical matter, but is packed with genetic information. As he rightly says, 'It is information, words, instructions ... If you want to understand life, don't think about vibrant, throbbing gels and oozes, think about information technology.'[186] Secondly, changes in the course of genes being passed on are extremely rare, about one in every ten million duplications of a DNA molecule. Thirdly, ninety-nine per cent of these changes are harmful. We could liken them to typing errors, which means they would not result in better versions of what came before. Fourthly, no animal lives long enough to allow the millions of tiny mutations needed to make a significant contribution to turning one creature into an entirely different one.

There is a fifth and ultimate roadblock. As almost the entire genetic code is similar in apes and humans, it is claimed that this is a very small gap, one that could be bridged by millions of years of evolution. But this misses the point that as the human genome contains about three billion units of information, the difference between apes and humans represents about 150 million units of additional genetic information. Now for the roadblock: *nobody has ever found a single case of a mutation adding any information.* The American biophysicist Lee Spetner, who taught information and communication theory at America's Johns Hopkins University, illustrates where this puts the 'apes to humans' theory: 'Whoever thinks macro-evolution can be made by mutations that lose information is like the merchant who lost a little money on every sale but thought he could make it up on volume ... The failure to observe even one mutation that adds information is more than just a failure to find support for the theory. It is evidence against the theory.'[187]

There are some ways in which other creatures are 'superior' to man—an agrodiaetus butterfly has 268 chromosomes, a carp 194, an African hedgehog 88, a wolf 78, and a donkey 52, while humans have only 46—yet there is no natural bridge from animal to man. There is a massive difference not only between life and non-life but—as we will see in a later chapter—between human beings and all other living creatures. As someone has said, there is 'a vast gulf in scientific, literary, artistic, cultural and technological achievements between humankind and all other animals … What is surprising is that chimpanzees, despite being genetically so similar, are so vastly different from us: no libraries, no art galleries, no technology, no science, no symphony orchestras, no religion.'[188] Macroevolution reduces everything to nature and natural processes and we need to bear this in mind in trying to answer our question about the meaning of life. The American historian of science and of evolutionary biology William Provine, who calls himself 'a total atheist', spells out where macroevolution leads: 'Let me summarize my views on what modern evolutionary biology tells us loud and clear … There are no gods, no purposes, no goal-directing forces of any kind. There is no life after death … There is no ultimate foundation for ethics, *no meaning to life* …'[189] (emphasis added). The Australian ethicist Peter Singer (described by *The New Yorker* as the most influential philosopher alive)[190] agrees: 'Life began, as the best available theories tell us, in a chance combination of molecules; it then evolved through random mutations and natural selection. All this just happened; it did not happen for any purpose.'[191]

Questions

A worldview governed by macroevolution affects every part of human life, and if we are merely biological accidents we are faced with a huge raft of questions. We will look at some of them later, but here are a few obvious ones:

- If we are an accidental collection of biological bits and pieces that came together with no aim in mind, why do we even imagine that life may have any meaning?

- If our lives are the meaningless product of physics, chemistry and biology and our minds are just accidental by-products, how can we rely on anything we think?

- How can our claim to intelligence mean anything if it did not have an intelligent source?

- If, as Richard Dawkins says, we are merely 'gene machines', blindly programmed to preserve the selfish molecules known as genes[192] why do we claim to have rights to such things as justice and freedom?

- What gives us greater value, significance or importance than fish, birds, animals or plants?

- Why do we have a moral dimension, a built-in sense of right and wrong?

- Where did conscience come from, and where does it get its power?

- If the survival of the fittest is our ultimate purpose, why should we care for the senile, the chronically sick, the starving or those with special needs?

- Why are we the only species preoccupied with death and what may lie beyond it?

Claiming to believe in a process of unplanned evolution is one thing, but consistently living with all its implications is another matter. Can we seriously and consistently live as if we owed our existence to millions of mindless accidents, as if there was no rational or moral order, and as if we were ultimately nothing more than manure in the making? Evolution can give humankind no higher status than that of an accidental by-product of the laws of nature. It can offer no clues as to the meaning of life.

A recognition that this is the case may lie behind an answer Richard Dawkins gave in response to a question put to him at the end of 2005, by The Edge Foundation, a science and technology think tank and website: 'I believe that all life, all intelligence, all creativity and all "design" anywhere in the universe is the direct or indirect product of Darwinian natural selection'. It seems at first glance that he was declaring macroevolution to be an open and shut case, but it is important to note the question to which he was responding: 'What do you believe is true *even though you cannot prove it?*' In a speech at Washington University, St. Louis, Missouri, he said of evolution, 'We don't need evidence. We know it to be true,'[193] yet elsewhere he admits, 'We must acknowledge the possibility that new facts may come to light which will force our successors of the twenty-first century to abandon Darwinism or modify it beyond recognition.'[194]

The restless search

In his book *Hasidism and Modern Man*, the Austrian-born Jewish philosopher Martin Buber (1878–1965) told a delightful story about a very forgetful man who, whenever he got up in the morning, forgot where he had left his clothes the night before. Things got so bad that he dreaded going to sleep—until one day he hit on a solution. As he undressed that night he took a notepad with him and wrote down exactly where he left each item of clothing. Getting up the following morning he consulted the notes he had made. The first said, 'Trousers—on chair', so he put them on. The next said, 'Shoes—under the bed', so he put them on. He carried on in the same way until he was fully dressed, then said to himself, 'Now, where am I?' He checked his notes, but there was no answer to his question.

Millions of people ask the same kind of questions as they try to find a meaning to life. Bearing in mind what we have seen in the last two chapters, these come thick and fast. If the entire universe has no explanation, how can my life have any? If there is such amazing order in the universe, should there not be some in my life? If the first spark of life in the world came about by accident, how can I be sure that I have any meaning or value? If I am nothing more than a gene machine, what sense is there in trying to find any other purpose in my life? The British writer Andrew Knowles asks the same kind of questions: 'Am I really a random coincidence, adrift in a cosmic accident, meaning nothing, going nowhere? Surely I have a dimension that animals and vegetables lack? After all, a carrot is oblivious of the size of Jupiter. A cow cares nothing for the speed of light. But I am in a different class. I observe and appreciate. I create and choose. I criticize. Sometimes I even criticize myself.'[195]

In the American Tribal Love-Rock Musical *Hair* the song 'Where do I go?' asks,

Why do I live, why do I die?
Where do I go?
Tell me why, tell me where?
Tell me why, tell me where?
Tell me why?[196]

People have been asking questions like these for as far back as we have been able to dig into our history. Nearly 2,500 years ago the Greek philosopher Plato (427–347 BC) even went so far as to describe man as 'a being in search of meaning'. The Norwegian theologian Ole Hallesby (1879–1961) claimed, 'One of the characteristics of human life, among others, is that it must discover the meaning of life … Man himself must know what it means to be a man ... and this is what men have been working at down through the ages as far back as we have historical records.'[197] Rheinallt Williams tells us why we should not be surprised at this: 'Human nature, like material nature, abhors a vacuum ... for if to be shovelled underground, or scattered on its surface, is the end of the journey, then life in the last analysis is a mere passing show without meaning, which no amount of dedication or sacrifice can redeem.'[198] Man's longing to know the meaning of life is such that to meet the demand for the German author Eckhart Tolle's book *A New Earth: Awakening to Your Life's Purpose,* in 2008 Penguin was printing a million copies a week.

Many people say they are willing to settle for the fact that life is nothing more than 'a passing show', but do they honestly live as if this were the case? Franz Kafka, rated as one of the twentieth century's most influential authors, wrote of a world smothered in bureaucracy, 'The conveyor belt of life carries you on, no one knows where. One is more of an object, a thing, than a living creature.' The English author Cicely Isabel Fairfield (1892–1983), better known as Rebecca West, claimed, 'I do not believe any facts exist, or, rather, are accessible to me, which give any assurance that my life has served an eternal purpose.'[199] The American palaeontologist George Gaylord Simpson (1902–1984) denied the possibility of human life having any purpose when he wrote, 'Man is the result of a purposeless and natural process that did not have him in mind.'[200] In his first and best-known novel, Jean-Paul Sartre had one of his characters question his right to exist at all: 'I existed like a stone, a plant, a microbe ... I was just thinking ... Here we are, all of us, eating and drinking to preserve our precious existence, and ... there is nothing, nothing, absolutely no reason for existing.'[201] Elsewhere, Sartre came to the conclusion that as there was no explanation for the existence of anything, man must accept the fact that he has been dumped into a meaningless universe and is caught between 'the absurdity of life's origin and the fear of life's extinction'.[202]

William Provine takes the same line: 'The universe cares nothing for us and we have no ultimate meaning in life'.[203] When the English neurobiologist Colin Blakemore was being grilled in a 1993 edition of BBC Radio 4's programme *In the Psychiatrist's Chair*, one of the final questions put to him was, 'So if I were to ask you … what do you feel is the purpose of your life, the point of your life, what would you say?' Although he has been hailed as one of the most influential scientists in the United Kingdom, Blakemore replied, 'I don't feel that life has a purpose in the sense that you could ask a question, "Why are we here?" It doesn't have a purpose in the sense that there are goals to be achieved … When it has ended, as far as I'm concerned, there is nothing left.'

In 1995 Peter Atkins wrote an *Independent* article headed, 'A desolate place to look for answers' and sub-titled, 'The meaning of life in our universe is not as perplexing as it is depressing'. The article ended, 'Where did it come from? From nothing. Where is it going? To oblivion. How is it getting there? By purposeless decay into chaos. And the cosmic purpose? I leave you to draw your own conclusion'.[204] The American philosopher Thomas Morris (who personally takes a very different line) tells us where Atkins and those who think like him leave us as we try to find a meaning to life: 'Life itself has no meaning. Your life has no meaning. My life has no meaning. Existence is without meaning of any kind. There is a void of significance to everything. There is no purpose in life. No plan. No reason. There are no ultimate values that we are here to embrace or embody. And nothing is finally of any importance whatsoever … In a reality consisting only of matter in motion, it's hard to see what the ultimate status of anything as different from an atom as a meaning would be. And if we think that we can give anything meaning, we are fooling ourselves ... Any attempts to create meaning are themselves nothing more than empty, meaningless gestures in a universe that just doesn't care.'[205]

Asked about the purpose of life in a 1995 issue of *The Observer* (in which he was introduced as 'increasingly our most militant atheist') Richard Dawkins replied that this was a silly question, with the same status as 'What is the colour of jealousy?'[206] Elsewhere he complained, 'We humans have purpose on the brain' and called this 'a nearly universal delusion'.[207] Yet as Stephen Hawking says, 'People have always wanted answers to the big questions. Where did we come from? How did the world begin? What is the meaning and design behind it all? The creation accounts of the past now seem less credible. They have been replaced by a variety of superstitions, ranging from New Age to Star Trek.'[208] The Australian journalist and broadcaster Jon Casimir says, 'There is no meaning of life' and that looking for one is like 'trying to find a lost sock in the cosmic laundromat'.[209]

In the Introduction to *The Good Life*, Charles Colson asked the right questions and admitted that the answers are not always obvious: 'What makes life worth living? Why am I here? What's my purpose? How can my life be meaningful? These are questions on everyone's mind, both at times of crisis and underneath the surface of daily events. For most of us, life is messy and confusing, filled with paradoxes. We wake up in the night, worrying about our jobs, our kids, or the best laid plans, which suddenly unravel due to the pressures of living in our high-tech, fast-moving world. One day we seem to have things under control; the next day we get steamrollered by events ... If you haven't experienced this, please write me; you would be the first person I know to have life all together.'[210] This explains why in January 2014 The Prince's Trust, a leading UK youth charity founded in 1976 by The Prince of Wales, reported that seventy-five per cent of young adults it polled said they had nothing to live for. This is tragic, and suggests that our modern culture is not meeting the needs of a younger generation. Does it make any sense to go through life without believing that there must be some meaning or purpose to it? —and without making any attempt to find out what that meaning or purpose might be?

For some people, the meaning of life is tethered to their emotions. Sir Ranulph Fiennes, the English adventurer and author, was the first man to reach both the North Pole and the South Pole by surface, and climbed to the summit of Mount Everest when he was sixty-five years old. Asked for the meaning of life, he replied, 'To me life has many meanings depending what mood I'm in at the time,'[211] but does it make sense to marry together meaning and mood? A person for whom everything is going well may give a positive and optimistic answer, but what answer might we get from a harassed housewife overwhelmed by family responsibilities, a businessman fighting a losing battle in the rat race, a person who has just been told they have terminal cancer, a man whose wife and children have died in a car crash, a married couple getting further into debt every month, a drug-dependent teenager, an alcoholic, a homeless refugee, or someone in prison for a crime they never committed? Their mood may indicate how they *feel*, but it tells us nothing about what their lives mean.

Winners—or losers?

If we all ask Charles Colson's questions, where can we look for answers to them and find meaning for our lives? John Benton writes, 'We are taught from an early age that the only things which matter, the only things which exist, are the things you can taste, touch, hear, smell and see. Death is the end, and therefore we must adopt the philosophy of "Eat, drink and be merry for tomorrow we die." So we are brainwashed into believing that success in life means business success, academic success, sporting success. The question as to whether a person is loving, patient, kind and loyal is viewed as largely irrelevant. "How much does he earn?" "What grades did he get?" These are the questions our society operates on, and that sort of attitude is producing a hard, lonely and cut-throat world.'[212]

We can easily find examples of this. Countless people in their teens and twenties envy their sporting heroes and believe that matching their success would bring lasting meaning to life—to say nothing of financial and other fringe benefits. But is this the case?

The English rugby union player Jonny Wilkinson's greatest claim to fame came in the final of the 2003 Rugby World Cup between England and Australia. The game was tied 17–17 as it moved into extra time, when Wilkinson kicked a magnificent drop goal to give England a 20–17 victory. He was voted the BBC Sports Personality of the Year and the 2003 International Rugby Board's International Player of the Year, and was awarded an OBE (Order of the British Empire) in the 2004 Honours List. After his last game in Britain, when he captained the winning team in the final of the 2014 Heineken Cup, he was lauded as 'the most decorated player of his generation'.[213] Yet six years after the World Cup-winning kick in Australia he made this significant confession to *The Times*: 'I had already begun to feel the elation slipping away from me during the lap of honour around the field. I couldn't believe that all the effort was losing its worth so soon. This was something I had fantasized about achieving since I was a child. In my head I had reached the peak of the mountain and now all that was left was to slowly descend on the other side. I'd just achieved my greatest ambition and it felt a bit empty.'[214]

The German tennis player Boris Becker became Wimbledon's youngest-ever men's champion at the age of seventeen and eventually reached the top of the world rankings. Yet later he wrote, 'I won Wimbledon twice, once as the youngest player. I was rich. I had all the material possessions I needed: money, cars, women, everything ... I know this is a cliché. It's the old song of the movie and pop stars who commit suicide. They have everything, and yet they are so unhappy ... I had no inner peace. I was a puppet on a string.'[215]

The English athlete Kriss Akabusi, who won gold medals at World and European Championships, tells a similar story: 'I was in a situation where I had everything. I'd got much more than I needed, but it wasn't giving me happiness. There was no meaning and purpose to my life. I was rushing around trying to be famous— and I was getting famous. I was trying to get rich—and I was getting rich. But I wasn't very happy with my life or with my relationships.'[216]

The award-winning 1981 film *Chariots of Fire* has a scene in which just before the final of the 100 metres sprint in the 1924 Olympic Games in France, the English athlete Harold Abrahams says to team member Eric Liddell, 'You know, I used to be afraid to lose. Now I am afraid to win. I have ten seconds to prove the reason for my existence, and even then I am not sure I will.'

Today's headlines are full of success stories in business and professional life, but other truths often lie behind the headlines. The American tycoon Lee Iacocca engineered two Ford cars before becoming CEO of the Chrysler Corporation, the Portfolio website calling him the eighteenth greatest American CEO of all time. Yet in his retirement he said, 'Here I am in the twilight years of my life, still wondering what it's all about … I can tell you this, fame and fortune is for the birds.'[217]

Charles Colson testified, 'After I got out of the marines, I scrambled up the ladder, finishing law school at night while working for a U.S. Senator. Then, when I was only thirty, I cofounded a law firm that would become very successful. Eight years later I was seated in the office next to the President of the United States … Yet at the peak of my power I found the so-called good life empty and meaningless.'[218]

TIME magazine called the American best-selling author, financial adviser, fundraiser and motivational speaker Suze Orman one of the world's most influential people. Yet when the author of *The 9 steps to financial freedom* had become so wealthy that she could take holidays on a private island she said, 'I had more affluence that I'd ever dreamt of. Yet I felt sad and empty—and at a loss. For if money didn't equal happiness, I had no idea what did.'

The English author Jack Higgins (real name Harry Patterson) is the millionaire author of over sixty novels, including his 1975 blockbuster *The Eagle Has Landed*, yet says that if there is one thing he would like to have known as a small boy it would be this: 'When you get to the top, there's nothing there.'[219]

The English novelist Barbara Taylor Bradford, whose twenty-nine novels have sold nearly ninety million copies, told *The Daily Telegraph* in 2013, 'If I'm going to be defined by the building in which I live and the possessions I have, then I've accomplished nothing in my life.'[220]

The glitter and glamour of the entertainment world might seem a way to find meaning and fulfilment in life but here again there are those honest enough to admit not everything that shines spells success. In a 1989 *Reader's Digest* article 'The Key to Lasting Happiness' the writer pointed out, 'These rich, beautiful individuals have constant access to glamorous parties, fancy cars, expensive homes, everything that spells "Happiness". But in memoir after memoir, celebrities reveal the unhappiness beneath all their fun: depression, alcoholism, drug addiction, broken marriages, troubled children, profound loneliness.'[221]

The Australian film star Errol Flynn (1909–1959) was world-famous for his swashbuckling roles, but in his autobiography *My Wicked, Wicked Ways*, he wrote, 'There I was, sitting on top of the world, I had wealth, friends, I was internationally known, I was sought after by women. I had anything money could buy. Yet I found that at the top of the world there was nothing. I was sitting on a pinnacle, with no mountain under me.'[222]

The American actor Larry Hagman, famous for his part as J. R. Ewing in the chart-topping television soap opera *Dallas*, admitted, 'I have a lot of money, but there still seems a void in my life.'[223]

The Irish singer, songwriter and political activist Bob Geldof was granted an honorary knighthood by Queen Elizabeth II for his outstanding success in raising millions of pounds for famine relief in Ethiopia and elsewhere in Africa through concerts such as Live Aid and Band Aid. In 2012 his personal wealth was estimated as £32 million, yet after one of the concerts he asked a fellow organizer, 'Is that it?', a question that became the title of his autobiography.

The American musician Kurt Cobain, best known as the lead singer, guitarist and primary song writer of the grunge band Nirvana, committed suicide in 1994 when he was just twenty-seven years old. A biographer commented, 'His whole approach to performance was a scream for attention. It must have been galling to achieve his ambition and realize it still wasn't enough ... What Cobain never knew was contentment.'[224]

The English musician, singer and songwriter John Lennon (1940–1980), a founder member of the Beatles, the most commercially successful band in the history of popular music, wrote, 'We thought the angle was to get famous and be rich, so we got famous and rich and it's nowhere ... We always thought there was some kind of goal, an end to it, because we were naïve enough to think there was some end product in it ... So where were we? Rich and famous and nothing at all going on in our minds.'[225]

The Tanzanian-born British musician Freddie Mercury, best known as the lead vocalist and songwriter of the rock band Queen, was often called one of the greatest popular singers of all time. Shortly before he died in 1991 of an AIDS-related disease he said, 'You can have everything in the world and still be the loneliest man, and that is the most bitter type of loneliness. Success has brought me worldwide idolization and millions of pounds but it has prevented me from having the one thing we all need—a loving relationship.'[226] The lyrics of Queen's song 'The show must go on' include the question, 'Does anybody know what we are living for?'

The American singer and pop music icon Britney Spears earned $58 million in 2012 alone, yet complained, 'If there's nothing missing in my life, then why do these tears come at night?'[227]

Tomfoolery?
These are just a few examples of the many we could give to press home one single point: finding ultimate meaning in life is not a matter of possessions, popularity or pleasure. Ravi Zacharias is 'absolutely convinced that meaninglessness does not come from

being weary of pain; meaninglessness comes from being weary of pleasure'.[228] Elsewhere he writes, 'When the pleasure button is repeatedly pressed and can no longer deliver or sustain, the emptiness that results is terrifying.'[229] Sixteen centuries earlier, the African theologian Augustine of Hippo (354–430), whose writings have had a massive influence ever since, wrote, 'I looked for pleasure, beauty and truth not in [God] but in myself and his other creatures, and the search led me instead to pain, confusion and error.'[230]

Unfortunately, most people get towards the end of life before they realize this—and then find themselves unable to put things right. In 1967 an elderly man who had once been a student at Edinburgh University wrote an anonymous letter in the university's *Student* newspaper. Headed 'An old fogey's lament', it warned students then at the university of the danger of life slipping quickly by without a focused meaning:

'All our life long, we have been living in dread of creeping old age and death. Now that we have reached the senile state, we can assure you, young fellows, that it isn't all funny. Our genitors would have saved us an awful lot of misery if they had refrained from pulling us out of nothingness... only to force us back to where we came from, after this perfectly useless sojourn in a mad world. Only when you reach the last stage of your earthly passage do you begin to realize that life is just a senseless, useless, stupid adventure, seeing that once you are dead you revert back to the condition of non-existence as if you had never lived at all. Dreams and future planning create the illusion that life is worth living and struggling for. And it is only when you reach the terminus that you begin to realize that life is tomfoolery from beginning to end ... Whether you pop off after 100 minutes, 100 hours or 100 years of earthly existence, what difference does it make?'[231]

The fundamental mistake that countless people make is to pin the meaning of life to whatever works for them, or at least to whatever makes them feel better; life is simply there to be used up. As Charles Colson said, 'Our modern consumerist age is deluded to think that life consists of meeting our animal needs: eating, drinking, money, power, sex and leisure.'[232] Is it sensible to settle for this? If so, how can we claim to have greater dignity or significance than cows, camels or cockroaches? C. S. Lewis is surely right when he says, 'We are half-hearted creatures, fooling about with drink and sex and ambition when infinite joy is offered us, like an ignorant child who wants to go on making mud pies in a slum because he cannot imagine what is meant by the offer of a holiday at the sea. We are far too easily pleased.'[233]

When we are not enjoying life's daily grind, we imagine that a radical change might help—a change of house, a change of job, a change of car, a change of partner, a change of spouse, anything that might turn things around. The last of these is the most tragic. As the English author Vaughan Roberts says, 'We do not seem to be able to make our relationships last. We live in a throw-away culture. When the toaster stops working we just throw it away and get the new model. We do the same with lovers, which leaves many people feeling as if they are on the scrap heap.'[234] In 1996 *The Sunday Times* reported that 150 'Quick Court' kiosks had been ceremonially unveiled in Arizona. When a person pressed a button a voice asked, 'Are you absolutely certain this marriage can't be saved?' If the person concerned then pressed 'Yes', the divorce papers were printed out. This had to be rubber-stamped in court, but as *The Sunday Times* reporter commented, 'So in the time it takes to prepare a pepperoni pizza, your marriage has been terminated.'[235]

For untold millions of people enjoying life is its entire purpose and the only motive they have. For such people, meaning is spelled 'happiness' and they are prepared to try anything that might bring this about. In 2014 a paper entitled 'Suffocation of Marriage' was released by a professor at Northwestern University, Illinois. In it, he suggested that committing adultery could be the key to a successful marriage. He called it 'an openly consensual non-monogamous relationship'. This could 'relieve monotony' and fulfil 'higher needs like self-expression and self-actualisation'.[236] Yet none of this frantic search for meaning in life by satisfying physical or emotional needs gets us anywhere. Interviewed for *The Observer,* the celebrated American film director and screenwriter Robert Altman (1925–2006) looked back on a brilliant career and admitted, 'None of it—gambling, money, winning or losing—has any real value. It is simply a way of killing time, like crossword puzzles … I am sitting here today in this bleak atmosphere in the middle of winter, making this silly movie, and to me it is an adventure. I have no idea what it will be like. But even if it works, it will all be for nothing. If I had never lived, if the sperm that hit the egg had missed, it would have made no difference to anything.'[237]

Responding in *The Times* to a Church of England minister who was concerned that most people in his parish lived out 'their sordid little lives without reference to God', the English journalist and author Libby Purves reacted with a challenging article in which she wrote this: 'The phrases of the age are "quality of life", "live life to the full" and "lifestyle". The worst insult is "get a life". We pore over newspaper day-in-the-life-of celebrities and wonder if we would be better off if we moved to the country, went to the gym, or dressed only in white and ate raw celery … We scheme to get a few extra years and then worry about whether we will enjoy them. Meanwhile, we are uncomfortably aware that our daily lives are a bit short on intimations of immortality, so we seize on anything which promises a quick glimpse of the Beyond: it could be sex and drugs and rock 'n' roll, an exercise adrenalin high, a dose of sloppy diluted Buddhism. A mantra, an isolation tank … Anything to disguise from ourselves the fact that, secretly, most of us do indeed lead 'sordid little lives' … We are all, when we can spare the time from the coarse, squalid, selfish business of getting through the day, looking for a way out and up.'[238] She could hardly have made the restless search for a meaning to life any clearer. Another British journalist, Jenny McCartney, told *The Sunday Telegraph* readers, 'Here, in the UK, it can sometimes feel as if our culture floats like a cheerful raft of trash on a sea of nonsense.'[239]

The bottom line

A stunning testimony written about 3,000 years ago trumps every example given in this chapter of the truth that possessions, positions and power can never give life any satisfying meaning. The man concerned ruled over a nation during its golden age of prosperity and influence. His personal wealth was greater than that of all other known kings in the world. He surrounded himself with all the trappings of power and maintained an impressive standing army. He was a skilled diplomat, a brilliant architect (he masterminded massive building projects, one of which employed nearly 190,000 men) and a prolific writer and poet, with over 1,000 songs and 300 proverbs to his name. People flocked to him from other countries to catch some of his wisdom and some of his sayings—such as 'Pride comes before a fall'—are still used today. To condense the credits, this man—Israel's King Solomon—has been said to possess 'the greatest mental, material and political resources ever combined in one man.'[240]

Now comes the crunch. He began one of his best-known works, preserved for us in the Bible in a book titled Ecclesiastes, by declaring, 'Vanity of vanities! All is vanity.'[241] The original Hebrew

word translated 'vanity' is used elsewhere in the Old Testament
(the first of the Bible's two main divisions) about something that
is brief, unsubstantial, futile, frail, pointless and meaningless. It
is used to describe man's life as being like a cloud that 'fades and
vanishes'[242] and in another context about 'a leaning wall' and 'a
tottering fence'.[243] Solomon used the word thirty-seven times in
twelve chapters, and his message is as relevant in today's world as
when he first wrote it.

After his opening statement he went on to elaborate on the
way he indulged in his possessions, pastimes and pleasures,
including farming, gardening, writing, drinking and music, always
relentlessly searching for happiness. In his own words, 'Whatever
my eyes desired I did not keep from them. I kept my heart from
no pleasure'.[244] Yet when he had soaked himself in every pleasure
his vast wealth could buy we find him facing the facts: 'Then I
considered all that my hands had done and the toil I had expended
in doing it, and behold, all was vanity [meaninglessness] and a
striving after wind, and there was *nothing to be gained under the
sun.*'[245] I have emphasized that last phrase because in the same
book he uses the words 'under the sun' twenty-nine times, and
this tells us exactly what he is getting at. In the context in which he
uses it, the phrase living 'under the sun' means living without any
reference to God. Solomon had not only tried that, he had gone
at it full-pelt, and at the end of the day admitted that it got him
nowhere. As the English author Gareth Crossley puts it, 'He looks
back upon the time and energy expended and concludes that it has
all been pointless, a sheer waste of time. Wherever he has turned
his attention, the result has eventually been the same: nothing has
any point, whether power, popularity, prestige or pleasure.'[246]

When a person's life is self-centred, what they see is all they
get. The American television and social media personality Kim

Kardashian makes the bizarre claim that issuing daily photographs of herself on the social networking service Instagram is for her 'the purpose of life'.[247] Solomon had everything going for him except the one thing that mattered most—a worldview centred on God. The German pastor and theologian Dietrich Bonhoeffer (1906–1945), who was hanged by the Nazis, once wrote, 'If you board the wrong train, it's no use running along the corridor in the opposite direction.'[248] Leaving God out of one's life is a tragic example of boarding the wrong train, as it guarantees failing to find life's ultimate meaning.

The first pointers

The Danish author and poet Hans Christian Andersen (1805–1875) wrote a famous short story called 'The Emperor's New Clothes' that is worth repeating here. A vain emperor who loved wearing showy clothes hired two men who promised him the finest suit it was possible to make. They told him it would be made of a special fabric that would render it invisible to anyone who was either unfit for their position or 'hopelessly stupid'. The emperor saw this as a way of finding out which of his ministers he could safely dismiss and which he should retain. What he did not know was that the two tailors were swindlers. They allegedly called for the finest fabrics and pretended to work long hours designing and making the suit. As the work went on, several of the Emperor's ministers went to visit the tailors at work, but dared not say they could see nothing emerging, as this would mean them losing their jobs. When the Emperor visited the tailors he told everyone he thought the (invisible) suit was coming along beautifully.

When the tailors reported that the suit was finished they pretended to dress the Emperor, then sent him out to lead a big parade through the town. Everyone who knew about the promise the tailors had made commented how impressive the Emperor looked in his new clothes, as they were afraid to be called stupid or unfit for purpose. Everything seemed to be going as the Emperor and the dishonest tailors had hoped, until a child cried out, 'But he isn't wearing anything at all!'

The phrase 'The Emperor's Clothes' has long since become an English idiom to illustrate various things, including a worthless claim to which no one will admit the obvious truth, and it fits in here. We saw in the last chapter that looking for the answer to the question, 'Is there a meaning to life?' has nothing to do with the things we possess or achieve. Anyone who claims that wealth, fame, power or pleasure clothes their life with meaning is being as foolish as the Emperor. We need to look elsewhere to find life's meaning, but before we do it will help if we remind ourselves what we saw in Chapter 3.

Following the clue

In that chapter we saw that if the arrangement of stars, planets and galaxies that astronomy is discovering is a gigantic fluke there can be no purpose to anything on earth, let alone human life. Suggesting that the universe came about by chance gets us nowhere. Letting a bull loose in a china shop will not result in beautifully designed tableware, and giving chance a blank cheque produces questions, not answers. The American theologian R. C. Sproul easily explains why the existence of the universe by chance can be ruled out: 'Chance is given credit for creating the universe.

However, such a prodigious feat is beyond the capabilities of chance. Why? Chance can do nothing *because it is nothing*. Chance is merely a word that we use to explain mathematical possibilities. It is *no thing*. It has *no power*. It cannot produce, manage or cause anything because it is nothing.'[249] As John Benton puts it, 'The account of chance is overdrawn at the bank of credibility.'[250]

Could you be persuaded to believe that the book you are now reading had no author, publisher or printer? Are you even dabbling with the possibility that it suddenly (or slowly) came into existence out of nothing? Are you toying with the thought that all of its letters, words, sentences, paragraphs, pages and chapters fell into place by chance—and that in the same random, unguided way the hundreds of Endnotes chime perfectly with the references in the body of the text, and the cover design ties in with the book's title? Every book has an author, every song has a composer, every painting has an artist, every building has an architect; the universe has a creator.

In *The Salmon of Doubt: Hitchhiking the Galaxy One Last Time*, Douglas Adams wrote, 'If you try and take a cat apart to see how it works, the first thing you have on your hands is a non-working cat.'[251] In Chapter 3 we looked at some of the discoveries suggesting that, far from being a haphazard collection of spatial junk, the universe is teeming with evidence of order and design. As the English theoretical physicist and theologian John Polkinghorne points out, 'We are so familiar with the fact that we can understand the world that most of the time we take it for granted. It is what makes science possible. Yet it could have been otherwise. The universe might have been a disorderly chaos rather than an orderly cosmos.'[252] The American scientist Owen Gingerich, a senior Astronomer Emeritus at the Smithsonian Astrophysical Observatory, says, 'It seems to me that a universe that just is and we happen to be here as part of this incredible, astonishing complexity without any sort of purpose or ultimate meaning makes it a sort of macabre joke and I find it difficult to accept that … it simply makes a lot more sense to me to think that somehow there is ultimate purpose and reason behind it.'[253]

The universe might have been such that we could never get to grips with any of it, yet we find that our minds seem somehow to be in synch with the laws that govern our universal habitat. As the English author Jonathan Skinner says, it seems that 'God made the external laws of the universe totally compatible with the internal software of our minds.'[254] In looking for the reason for the universe it makes no sense to look for it within the universe itself. The Austrian-British philosopher Ludwig Wittgenstein (1889–1951) hit the nail on the head when he wrote, 'The solution of the riddle of life in space and time lies outside space and time.'[255] Let me illustrate on a much smaller scale. My study is at the front of my house and I can see my car (I have no garage) twenty feet away as I write these words. If I were to dismantle every part of it and describe them all I would still be no nearer finding out why it exists. Instead, I would be left staring at a 'dead car' to match Douglas Adams' 'dead cat'. An orderly cosmos suggests that intelligence was involved in putting it together. As Keith Ward says, 'If there is a vast intelligence behind the universe, it is reasonable to think that it has brought the universe into being for a purpose.'[256] If we can discover what that purpose might be, we will have gone a long way towards answering our question.

In 1973, Brandon Carter came up with the phrase 'anthropic principle' (*anthropos* is the Greek word for 'human') to define the theory that the entire universe is fine-tuned to sustain intelligent life, and in particular human life, on our planet. I have written about this elsewhere[257] and the issue is highly relevant to the question we are trying to answer in this book.

In *Nature's Destiny: How the Laws of Biology Reveal Purpose in the Universe*, Michael Denton writes, 'In the discoveries of science, the harmony of the spheres is also now the harmony of life. And as the eerie illumination of science penetrates evermore deeply into the order of nature, the cosmos appears increasingly to be a vast system finely tuned to generate life and organisms of biology very similar, perhaps identical, to ourselves. All the evidence available in the biological sciences supports the core proposition of traditional natural theology—that the cosmos is a specially designed whole *with life and mankind as a fundamental goal and purpose*, a whole in which all facets of reality, from the size of galaxies to the thermal capacity of water, have their meaning and explanation in this central fact'[258] (emphasis added). In his contribution to *Why I am not an Atheist*, the Scottish author Alex MacDonald makes the point very well: 'What is there is not just something, it is this incredibly ordered and beautiful *and human* universe. It is ordered in the sense that we can discover uniformity in it and frame scientific laws about it. It is beautiful, in that we can appreciate the beauty of the natural world *and of human beings*. But it is also *a kind of human universe*, and even in science there is the development of ... the idea that things seem to be fitting together *in relation to human beings*. And this is what we discover: that the world is there for our benefit and that there are all sorts of things *that fit together for us*. We discover and invent all sorts of things from the universe. We develop our life and culture from it. It all seems to fit together. Now this poses a huge question: why should it be so? The universe does not seem to be random and utterly meaningless' (emphasis added).[259]

Linking the evidence for a designed universe and the idea of there being a purpose to our lives, Paul Davies concludes, 'If physics is the product of design, the universe must have a purpose, and the evidence of modern physics suggests strongly to me that *the purpose includes us*' (emphasis added).[260] John Polkinghorne agrees: 'We live in a universe whose constitution is precisely adjusted to the narrow limits which alone make it capable of being our home.'[261] Owen Gingerich suggests, 'Whether atheist or theist, a thoughtful person can only stand in awe of the way the universe seems designed as a home for humankind.'[262] Why should this be the case? Is the human race nothing more than one small part of a gigantic fluke? It makes more sense—and nudges us towards finding a meaning to life—to believe that the ordered universe we know has been specifically and purposely designed by an intelligent Creator to sustain life in general and human life in particular.

The American Nobel Prize-winning physicist Charles Townes (he discovered the maser, which led to the laser) points us in this direction: 'In my view, the question of origin seems to be left unanswered if we explore from a scientific view alone. Thus, I believe there is a need for some religious or metaphysical existence.'[263] Arno Penzias, who matches Townes' honour as a Nobel prize-winner, comments, 'Astronomy leads us to a unique event, a universe that was created out of nothing, one with the very delicate balance needed to provide exactly the right conditions required to permit life, and one which has an underlying, one might say "supernatural" plan.'[264] Yet another Nobel Prize winner, the American physicist Arthur L. Schawlow (1921–1999), goes further, 'It seems to me that when confronted with the marvels of life and the universe, one must ask why and not just how. The only possible answers are religious ... I find a need for God in the universe and in my own life.'[265]

John Lennox makes this link between the ordered vastness of the universe and the significance of our lives: 'The starry heavens show the glory of God, yes; but they are not made in God's image. You are. That makes you unique. It gives you incalculable value. The galaxies are unimaginably large compared with you. However, you know that they exist, but they don't know that you exist. *You are more significant, therefore than a galaxy.* Size is not necessarily a reliable measure of value, as any woman can tell you as she looks at the diamonds on her finger and compares them with lumps of coal'(emphasis added).[266] Here are five pointers to show that Lennox is right.

Body language

The first piece of evidence is *our physical make-up*. The English philosopher C.E.M. Joad (1891–1953), best known for his many appearances on the BBC Radio programme *Brains Trust*, famously said that an average human body consists of enough fat for seven bars of soap, enough iron to make one medium-sized nail, enough sugar to sweeten seven cups of tea, enough lime to whitewash one chicken coop, enough phosphorous to tip 2,200 matches, enough magnesium to provide one dose of salts, enough potash to explode one toy cannon, and enough sulphur to rid an average-sized dog of fleas. He may well have been right, but even so, that is hardly the full story! Nor is it enough to describe us, as someone did, 'an ingenious assembly of portable plumbing'.[267] The English preacher and author David Watson (1933–1984) made a neat point: 'Tell the television audience that Miss World is 'nothing but a complex bio-chemical mechanism,' and I think most of them will disagree. Or, if you like, put a beautiful computer in place of Miss World and see if you get the same viewing audience!'[268]

The human frame is an engineering marvel, with 200 bones, 600 muscles and 100 joints, all designed to work in perfect harmony with each other. The tendons that anchor the muscles to the bones are so strong that they could stand a stress of eight tons per square inch.

The human hand has been called 'the most perfect and precise instrument in a world bristling with the mechanical wonders of the atomic age'.[269] Powerful enough to wield a sledgehammer, yet delicate enough to conduct microsurgery, it has over 652,000 nerve endings.

The human ear has the equivalent of 24,000 'strings' and 20,000 'keys', compared to 240 strings and eighty-eight keys on a grand piano.

The human eye, able to process 500,000 messages simultaneously, has a tiny retina with 130 million rod-shaped cells and six million cone-shaped cells, performing different functions. It also has ducts producing just the right amount of fluid to clean it in one five-hundredth of a second.

The human heart automatically beats about 100,000 times a day, pumping blood through 80,000 miles of blood vessels. Every day an average person's blood cells travel an accumulated distance of 168 million miles, equivalent to 6,720 times the earth's circumference.

The human brain accounts for only about two per cent of the average person's body weight yet has about 100 billion nerve cells, each one with up to 100,000 connections with other parts of the brain, which can process sufficient data over an eighty-year lifetime to fill 1,255,580,357,143 DVDs. By contrast to the human brain, no computer can decide to re-programme itself, be instinctively creative or discover meaning. No computer knows it is a computer or wishes it was something else. No computer can relax, daydream, be amused or frustrated, become bored, or angry, or fall in love. No computer can contemplate the reason for its existence—or consider the possibility of the existence of God.

The human liver has over 500 essential functions, including the production of bile, the storage of sugars, vitamins and minerals, the maintenance of hormone balance and the manufacture of over 1,000 different enzymes.

The human kidneys weigh only 240–280 grams, yet have a million functioning units, which flush out toxic materials and surplus water, leaving vital fluids in the bloodstream.

The human lungs, which maintain life by inhaling oxygen and exhaling carbon dioxide, have 300 million tiny air sacs which if spread out would cover an area the size of a tennis court.

The entire human frame is covered by its largest organ, the skin, which has three integrated layers of flexible waterproofing and houses a complex air-conditioning system with six miles of ducts which allow sweat out without letting water in.

Richard Dawkins is hugely impressed by facts like these: 'When a biologist looks at particular organs or organisms, an eye or a brain, what he sees is a machine, which has every indication of being designed for a purpose. In that sense, living things quite obviously do have a purpose. But natural selection manages to explain how they came into being without there being an ultimate purpose. There is admittedly a strain between the thought of blind chance and design. For living beings are not only designed, they are supremely well designed, beautifully designed and far more complicated than any man-made machine.'[270] He goes on to say (though with no evidence to back it up) that 'the blind forces of physics could, given enough time, build these highly complicated machines'.[271] Elsewhere, he says, 'Natural selection is the blind watchmaker, blind because it does not see ahead, does not plan consequences, has no purpose in view. Yet the living results of natural selection overwhelmingly impress us with the illusion of design and planning'.[272] He gives no explanation of how blind 'designers' might work, but he rules out divine creation, admits that natural selection would need 'some luck to get started'[273] and invents a word—'designoid'—to describe objects that he claims are not really designed but merely give the impression that they are.[274]

Inventing words to fit one's own ideas shows imagination, but hardly provides information. In total, a human body has trillions of cells, of more than 100 different types, and according to the American chemist, biochemist and educator Linus Pauling (1901–1994) a single cell is 'more complex than New York City'.[275] How did these trillions of cells come about, and why do they operate as they do? On the BBC Radio 4 programme *Start the Week*, the English geneticist Alison Woollard was asked how these billions of cells knew exactly what to do. She replied, 'This is a question that has vexed biologists for so long. We have about forty trillion cells in the average human body, and all of these cells do different things. So our heart cells do different things from our skin cells, for example. So cells must know what to do. And we know that cells know what to do because of the proteins they produce, and that they produce proteins because of the DNA sequence that they have inside all of our cells. But the real conundrum is the fact that all of our cells contain exactly the same DNA, the same genome. So how is it that cells can interpret this information in different ways, in order for cells to do the right thing at the right time and in the right place?'[276] She raised a massive question—and could only answer it with another question—but surely interpreting information and doing 'the right thing at the right time' suggest that there is meaning in what is going on?

An individual human body comprises some 10,000 trillion trillion atoms arranged in a specific and unique way. Those atoms are strings of genes that form genomes, and each person has nearly 40,000 genes in the double helix structures that form DNA. Is this a biological accident or the product of natural forces that have no purpose? If so, any idea of finding the meaning to life disappears. But what if the three dynamic Bible words 'God created man'[277] are true? C. Everett Koop (1916–2013), who was widely regarded as the most influential Surgeon General in American history, made it clear where he stood on the issue: 'If I didn't believe that I had a God who was solid and dependable, a God who makes no mistakes, I couldn't continue what I'm doing. I never operate without having a sub-conscious feeling that there's no way this extraordinarily complicated mechanism known as the human body just happened to come up from slime and ooze ... When I make an incision with my scalpel, I see organs of such intricacy that there simply hasn't been enough time for natural evolutionary processes to have developed them.'[278] Isaac Newton has been reported as saying, 'In the absence of any other proof, the thumb alone would convince me of God's existence.' Elsewhere he asked, 'Was the eye contrived without skill in optics, and the ear without knowledge of sounds?'[279] A Boeing 747 airliner has over six million separate parts and the technicians making and maintaining it know how every one of them works—but does this mean that the American aviation pioneer William Boeing (1881–1956) the founder of The Boeing Company, never existed? Francis Collins has no difficulty in linking his faith with cutting edge science: 'The God of the Bible is also the God of the genome. He can be worshipped in the cathedral or in the laboratory. His creation is majestic, awesome, intricate and beautiful.'[280]

Even without knowing the amazing facts that science has now revealed to us, one of the Bible's authors had no doubt about the explanation for his physical attributes and cried out to God, 'For you formed my inward parts; you knitted me together in my mother's womb. I praise you, for I am fearfully and wonderfully made. Wonderful are your works; my soul knows it very well.'[281]

The sense of self

Secondly, *we are both conscious and self-conscious.* When a student in a philosophy class asked her professor, 'How do I know I exist?' he replied, 'And whom shall I say is asking?' We want to know who we are and where we fit into the world in which we find ourselves.

This is a massive conundrum for those who rule God out of the picture. The American philosopher Jerry Fodor admits, 'Nobody has the slightest idea how anything material could be conscious.'[282] The Zambian-born British philosopher A. C. Grayling, who calls himself an atheist, a secularist and a humanist, is equally baffled: 'One of the greatest mysteries facing science and philosophy is the phenomenon of consciousness … how do we explain the existence of belief, memory, reason?'[283] Francis Crick writes, 'There is no easy way of explaining consciousness in terms of known science; how can you explain the redness of red in terms of physics and chemistry?'[284] The American neuroscientist Sam Harris, one of the so-called 'Four Horsemen of New Atheism', admits that the question of finding a link between consciousness and matter 'has not been settled'.[285] His fellow 'horseman' Richard Dawkins admits that consciousness is 'the most profound mystery facing modern biology'[286] and that 'we don't yet really have any idea how it evolved and where it fits into a Darwinian view of biology'.[287] In his television programme *The Meaning of Life* Stephen Hawking tried to brush the problem aside by saying, 'Eventually, awareness became so sophisticated that one animal became aware of itself—and that is what we are, self-aware animals that evolution has equipped to be conscious.'[288] How or why this fascinating development took place was left hanging in mid-air.

Human consciousness is a 'given' and the fact that we can find no natural way to explain it opens the door to there being a supernatural one, one that would in turn point to human life having unique meaning. The Polish-born British mathematician and biologist Jacob Bronowski (1908–1974) claimed that man 'is not different in kind from any other forms of life', that 'living matter is not different in kind from dead matter', and that 'man is part of nature, in the same sense that a stone is, or a cactus, or a camel,'[289] but our self-consciousness proves the opposite. After all, if a camel could say, 'I am a camel,' it would no longer be a camel. As the English author Joe Boot says, 'If we were a part of nature ... we would know it! Just as a dog does not ask why it is not a bear or a brick, we would not ask what it means to be human, what is right and wrong, where we are from and where we are going.'[290] When in the course of his 1967 Reith Lectures, a series of annual radio lectures commissioned by the BBC, the English social anthropologist Edmund Leach (1910–1989) claimed, 'There is no sharp break between what is human and what is mechanical', but the fact that he could think and say such a thing is evidence that he was wrong. If we are nothing but machines, *how can we claim that anything we do has meaning?* Yet we assume meaning in virtually everything we do. We make choices, we have friends, we enjoy things, we marry, we make love, we share ideas, impressions and possessions, we care for those in need, we give to charitable causes, we value truth, justice, friendship, compassion and sympathy. A machine can do none of these things.

Given the choice of rescuing a parrot or a helpless child from a fire threatening to destroy a house, no right-thinking person would choose the parrot—but why? Why would we all agree that saving the child would be the right thing to do and that saving the parrot would be the wrong thing to do? C. Everett Koop says that we are distinct from all other creatures in the world in that, 'We are able to know what is around us; the subject can know the object.'[291] C. S. Lewis drives the point home: 'One of the things that distinguishes man from the other animals is that he wants to know things, wants to find out what reality is like, simply for the sake of knowing.'[292] As human beings we are uniquely curious about the meaning of life and of the world in which we live.

A cut above

Thirdly, *we have a deep-rooted conviction that as human beings we have unique dignity.* We know instinctively that we are more than biological accidents. Even the strongly atheistic *Second Humanist Manifesto* speaks of 'the preciousness and dignity of the individual'—but where do preciousness and dignity come from? As the American philosopher and theologian Francis Schaeffer (1912–1984) wrote, 'If man has been kicked up by chance out of what is only impersonal, then those things that make him man—hope of purpose and significance, love, notions of morality and rationality, beauty and verbal communication—are ultimately unfulfillable and are thus meaningless.'[293] At a Prayer for America rally held in Yankee Stadium, New York on 23 September 2001, eleven days after the 9/11 terrorist attack, the actor James Earl Jones spoke for us all when he declared, 'We reaffirm our faith in the dignity of every individual.' So did US President Barack Obama, when at a ceremony in France in 2014 to mark the 70th anniversary of the 1944 D-Day invasion of Europe that turned the Second World War in the Allies' favour, he spoke of 'our commitment to … the inherent dignity of every human being'.

Our sense of dignity is so ingrained that it extends even to the human body after death. A friend of mine who was a medical student told how, at the end of a particular semester, all the students were required to attend a service led by the university chaplain prior to disposing of the cadavers they had dissected. This was a way of recognizing the dignity of those who had agreed to their dead bodies being used by medical science. Yet as my friend pointed out, he had spent a year as a biology student cutting up snails, fish, pigs and other creatures, but it would never have entered anyone's head to mark the disposal of their remains in this way.

The last English king to die in battle was Richard III, who was killed at the Battle of Bosworth Field in 1485. His body was buried in a crude grave in Greyfriars Friary, in Leicester, but its exact location was lost when the friary was demolished. Over 500 years later, his remains were found under a car park. In the course of a furious row over where they should be reinterred, the Leader of Leicester City Council said, 'He deserves to be buried with dignity and honour in Leicester Cathedral.' Whilst the Bishop of Leicester, the Rt Revd Tim Stevens, said of the reinterment planned for March 2015: 'Our cathedral has been consistently committed to providing a fitting, dignified and memorable ceremony for the reinterment of King Richard.'[294]

In 2014 the Paralympian athlete Oscar Pistorius stood trial in South Africa for the murder of his girlfriend Reeva Steenkamp. When Gert Saayman, the pathologist who carried out the post-mortem examination on the victim, went to the witness stand he asked that because of the graphic nature of the evidence he was about to give all live broadcasts of the trial be switched off to protect 'the dignity of the deceased'. The judge, Thokozile Masipa, agreed.

On 17 July 2014, Malaysia Airlines Flight MH17, a scheduled passenger flight from Amsterdam to Kuala Lumpur, was shot down while flying over a part of eastern Ukraine controlled by pro-Russian rebels, with the loss of 298 lives. During the storm of controversy surrounding the security of the crash scene and the recovery of the victims, UK Foreign Secretary Philip Hammond protested, 'It's a fundamental principle of human decency that the victims and their possessions should be treated with dignity.'[295]

When terrorists demolished the twin towers of New York's World Trade Center on 11 September 2001, only 18 of those trapped were rescued alive, 2,753 victims perished. Yet so profound is our sense of human dignity that over the next thirteen years the city's Medical Examiner's Office, using ground-breaking forensic techniques, successfully identified 21,906 fragments of human remains (some less than one inch long) and returned them to the families of those concerned.[296]

R. C. Sproul is right when he says, 'We want our lives to count. We yearn to believe that in some way we are important. This inner drive is as intense as our need for water and oxygen. We argue about religion and politics, abortion, homosexuality, nuclear weapons and welfare programmes. We bicker about a host of things, but at one point we are all in harmony: every person among us wants to be treated with dignity and worth.'[297] The atheist Peter Atkins claims that the human race is 'just a bit of slime on a planet,'[298] but not even he lives as if this is true, and his atheism comes unstuck at this point. The atheist claims that life begins as an accident and will end in annihilation, yet never lives as if his life means nothing. Where is the logic in this? We have an inner conviction that we are not only unique but valuable, and not just a random collection of bits and pieces. Andrew Knowles makes a good point: 'I am a mystery. I wake up in the morning. I find myself the sole occupant of a complex, sensitive and extremely useful body. I am also the proud owner of an intricate, imaginative and highly resourceful brain. Everything about me is unique: my face, my fingerprints, my "self". I am alive. I develop. I grow. So does a vegetable. But I am more than a vegetable. Vegetables don't fall in love, or read the paper, or go on holiday ... I am a body with a brain; an animal. But—I am more than an animal. Animals don't peer through telescopes, or send birthday cards, or play chess, or cook.'[299] If human beings are essentially no different than other creatures, how can we claim to have any more value—or rights—than porcupines, pigs or pilchards? This is where atheists' arguments unravel. As Ravi Zacharias says, 'Atheism walks with its head down, earthbound, which is why it grasps nothing of eternal value. It must admit its predicament: without God, there is no meaning to life.'

At the 86th Academy Awards (known as The Oscars) presented in Hollywood in March 2014 by the Academy of Motion Picture Arts and Sciences, *12 Years a Slave* won the Best Picture Award. The film is about a free African American man who is sold into slavery, and it powerfully develops the tensions that arose during his life after that. The film's English director Steve McQueen won the award for Best Director, and in the course of his acceptance speech he said, 'Everyone deserves not just to survive, but to live.' This was loudly applauded, and it ties in exactly with something Martin Luther King (1929–1968), the American leader of the African-American Civil Rights Movement, said when accepting his Nobel Prize for Peace in 1964: 'I refuse to believe the notion that man is mere flotsam and jetsam in the river of life.' Statements like these are at odds with the idea that we are nothing more than accidental by-products of nature. Nor do they fit the American author Leslie Paul's opinion in his book *The Annihilation of Man* that 'All life is not more than a match struck in the dark and blown out again.

The final result ... is to deprive it completely of meaning.'[300] Albert Camus admitted that this ruins the whole human journey: 'To lose one's life is no great matter; when the time comes I'll have the courage to lose mine. But what's intolerable is to see one's life being drained of meaning, to be told there's no reason for existing. A man can't live without some reason for living.'[301]

Believing in man's creation by God points the way to explaining our unique sense of dignity, and the Bible's fundamental statement on the subject is crystal clear: 'So God created man in his own image, in the image of God he created him; male and female he created them.'[302] Being created 'in the image of God' has nothing to do with size, weight, shape or any other physical characteristics, as 'God is spirit'[303] and has no physical or material properties. It means that man was created with personality, with powers of thought, feeling and will that go far beyond the brute instincts of other creatures. It also means that man is meant to relate to God in a way that is not true of any other living thing on the planet, to know, appreciate, enjoy and worship him. This is what sets us apart from all other life forms and gives us a coherent reason for believing that a human being has more value than a virus.

Mind matters

Fourthly, *we are rational.* We not only think, but can think sensibly, using logic to assess theories, possibilities and suggestions. We can accumulate facts, and remember and evaluate vast amounts of information on an endless variety of subjects. We process data, develop ideas, exercise our imagination and make rational decisions. We use verbal language to express our feelings, ideas, suggestions and conclusions. The Hungarian-born British author and journalist Arthur Koestler (1905–1983) claimed, 'The emergence of symbolic language, first spoken and then written, represents the sharpest break between animals and man.'[304] We can develop theories and concepts, and use technology to transform our lifestyles, and we have developed mathematical language to discuss issues ranging from the nature of the universe to statistics useful in daily life. As John Benton points out, 'Beavers may build dams, but men develop quantum mechanics, paint the Mona Lisa and fly to the moon! To say that animals and man are the same is like saying that coal and diamonds are the same. They are, yet they aren't, are they? There is something essentially different.'[305]

Francis Crick says, 'Your joys and your sorrows, your memories and your ambitions, your sense of personal identity and free-will, are in fact no more that the behaviour of a vast assembly of nerve cells and their associated molecules. As Lewis Carroll's Alice might have put it, "You're nothing but a pack of neurons."'[306] But if this is the case, how can anything we are, think or do have meaning? Why do we put any value on such realities as human love, sympathy, kindness and generosity?

If our thoughts are the result of nothing more than the laws of physics shuffling atoms around in our brains, why should we believe that anything they produce is true or has any sensible meaning? How can we give our thoughts any moral, ethical or spiritual value? How can we gain accurate knowledge about anything? Why is thinking about anything of any more significance than a leaf falling from a tree? Even an atheist like J.B.S. Haldane admitted, 'It seems to me immensely unlikely that mind is a mere by-product of matter. For if my mental processes are determined wholly by the motions of atoms in my brain I have no reason to suppose that my beliefs are true ... and hence I have no reason for supposing my brain to be composed of atoms.'[307] No normal person acts on the assumption that there is no meaning to what their mind is telling them.

The forgotten factor

Fifthly, *we have an aesthetic dimension,* an important pointer that is often ignored or underestimated. Beauty is one of three fundamental values (truth and goodness are the other two) by which we judge the worth or value of things we see or hear. In doing this we take notice of such things as form, texture, colour, order or design—for example in nature, works of art, music or poetry. We have brought the issue of truth into every chapter so far—even though it has been said that in some circles talking about truth is 'about as popular as a teetotal sermon at a local pub'.[308] We will look at the issue of goodness in the next chapter; here, we will concentrate on beauty.

The sceptic David Hume wrote, 'Beauty is no quality in things themselves: It exists merely in the mind which contemplates them'.[309] Richard Dawkins agrees, and while acknowledging that, 'The real world, properly understood in the scientific way, is deeply beautiful and unfailingly interesting',[310] he claims that beauty 'is not an absolute virtue in itself'.[311] This approach says that there is no such thing as objective beauty, then just dumps it into a whirlpool of personal opinions. Yet a thing is not beautiful because people have certain feelings about it. The well-known saying, 'Beauty is in the eye of the beholder' is simply not true—or at least is not the whole truth, as nothing gains or loses its beauty or its true value as a result of how people judge it. The British philosopher E. R. Emmet (1909–1980) put the matter straight: 'Beauty in a sense is something that is there, that whether an object is beautiful or not is a matter of fact and not a matter of opinion or taste, and that value judgements about beauty are true or false, right or wrong'.[312]

Last year, a friend and I had nearly finished playing a round of golf at Langland Bay Golf Club on the Gower Peninsula, South Wales when a rainbow suddenly appeared, perfectly framing the bay and the village behind it. It takes something special for golfers to abandon their clubs and reach for their cameras, but that rainbow succeeded. Now for a question: would the rainbow have been beautiful if we had not seen it? Are rainbows that appear in totally uninhabited places not also beautiful? Does a masterpiece in an art museum lose its qualities, or change in any way, when the day's last visitor leaves, the lights are switched off and the doors are locked? Does colour not exist because people blind from birth have never seen it? The English philosopher Richard Swinburne answers the questions: 'The beauty of the beautiful does not depend upon being recognized. How could it? For recognition of beauty, as of anything else, depends upon the existence of the feature beforehand and independently of being recognized.'[313] I have only a limited grasp of the technical reasons why rainbows appear, but at Langland Bay my response was at a deeper level than a scientific understanding of what I was seeing. As John Polkinghorne says, 'Beauty slips through the scientist's net.'[314]

What has our appreciation of beauty to do with human life having meaning? In the first place it points to the fact that we are unique. At Langland Bay, none of the sheep, cows or other animals in the surrounding fields seemed to take the slightest notice of the rainbow, nor do we know of any animal that stops to admire flowers, marvel at clouds or appreciate a spectacular sunset. Taking pleasure in these things seems to be something that humans alone are capable of doing. It also suggests that we have a unique relationship with the rest of creation. John Polkinghorne goes even further and says, 'It has been our experience that the laws of nature are always expressed in equations of unmistakable mathematical beauty.'[315] Even as an atheist, Francis Crick fine-tunes the point and writes about 'the intrinsic beauty of the DNA helix', calling it 'a molecule that has style'.[316] The world-renowned American cataract eye surgeon James P. Gills, adds his testimony: 'Each cell expresses an extraordinary and incomparable complexity, beauty really, of form, and function.'[317]

What is the source of this beauty? It is very difficult to make a case for it being 'just one of those things' or yet another accidental by-product of nature. The English molecular biologist Denis Alexander rightly claims, 'If the universe has no ultimate purpose, as atheism suggests, then the universal experience of being moved by works of great music or by other great acts of human creativity is difficult to explain.'[318] The agnostic British philosopher Anthony O'Hear admits that our sense of beauty 'cannot usefully be analysed in biological or evolutionary terms'[319] and that 'from a Darwinian perspective, truth, goodness and beauty and our care for them are very hard to explain,'[320] yet he goes on to admit that nowhere is our sense of being 'at home in the world' more strongly suggested than 'in our experience of beauty.'[321]

C.E.M. Joad, who abandoned his atheism late in life, wrote that goodness, truth and beauty are not just 'pieces of cosmic furniture lying about, as it were, in the universe without explanation, coherence or connection, but are revelations of a unity that underlies them,' and even added that they are 'the ways in which God reveals himself to man.'[322] *In Truth Decay* the American philosopher Douglas Groothuis quotes this remarkable testimony by a Russian Ph.D. student for whom the beauty of some mathematical equations about the universe led to him abandoning atheism: 'I was in Siberia and I met God there while I was working on my equations. I suddenly realized that the beauty of these equations had to have a purpose and design behind them, and I felt deep in my spirit that God was speaking to me through these equations.'[323]

John Lennox says the same kind of thing when he writes, 'The beauty of the scientific laws reinforces my faith in an intelligent, divine Creator.'[324] This chimes perfectly with the idea that if there is a divine Creator we have more reason to expect that his creation would be beautiful rather than ugly, and with the statement by Aristotle that 'Beauty is the gift of God.' It also reflects the Bible's teaching that in the wonders of the natural world God is pointing us to himself; it speaks of 'the beauty of the LORD'[325] and says, 'He has made everything beautiful in its time.'[326] Elsewhere, we are told of those worshipping God crying, 'Worthy are you, our Lord and God, to receive glory and honour and power, for you created all things, and by your will they existed and were created.'[327] Keith Ward is right to say that 'the idea of the glory and majesty of God is the idea of beauty, power and wisdom which is complete'.[328] So is the American preacher and author John Piper when he writes, 'The holiness of God is the unique, infinite value of his majestic glory. To say that our God is holy means that he is beautiful beyond degree in the magnificence of his glory, and that his value is infinitely greater than the sum of the value of all created things.'[329] This explains why, as his creatures, we have an aesthetic dimension; in recognizing beauty we are responding as we should to who God is, and to what he has created (or enabled us to design, using materials he has created). Our recognition of beauty points to a meaning that goes far beyond our personal preferences. It is difficult to believe that so much beauty came into existence without any kind of input by a power sensitive to beauty.

Bertrand Russell poured scorn on the possibility that human life had any meaning or purpose by dismissing man as 'a curious accident in a backwater'.[330] Some accident! Some backwater!

Why are you here?

The strongest pointers

The 1998 film *Antz* begins with the American film producer and playwright Woody Allen telling his psychiatrist, 'I feel insignificant.' When his psychiatrist tells him this means they have made a breakthrough, Allen replies, 'We have?' 'Yes' says the psychiatrist, 'You *are* insignificant.' He was wrong, because nobody is insignificant. As C. S. Lewis wrote, 'There are no ordinary people. You have never talked to a mere mortal.'[331]

In the last chapter we looked at five reasons for believing that our lives have meaning, and it will be worth underlining them here. Our physical make-up is so amazing that only our creation

by God could account for it. As we have already seen, far from
our being thrown together by chance, we were 'formed', 'knitted
together', 'wonderfully made' and 'intricately woven'[332] by one who
leaves nothing to chance and never does anything without having a
purpose in mind. Our self-consciousness is another way in which
we are unique. Whatever their characteristics and abilities, all other
creatures are 'without understanding'.[333] By contrast, we are able to
review our past, assess our present situation, have ambitions and
plans for the future, and think about our place in the bigger picture.
Our dignity is not rooted in anything we possess or achieve, but in
the fact that we are created 'in the image of God',[334] with a unique
relationship to our Creator. Our ability to think, calculate, develop
and assess theories, and come to rational conclusions also reflects
our creation by God, whose 'understanding is unsearchable.'[335]
Finally, our recognition of beauty ties in with the statement
attributed to the American poet Ralph Waldo Emerson (1803–1882)
that beauty is 'God's handwriting'; and our enjoyment in finding it
is part of his intention for our lives. There are many other factors
that point in the same direction as these five; in this chapter we will
look at two of the strongest.

The moral maze

The first is that we have a moral dimension. When C. S. Lewis wrote,
'Human beings, all over the earth, have this curious idea that they
ought to behave in a certain way, and cannot get rid of it'[336] he
hit a hugely important nail on the head. We are not merely what
someone called 'computers made of meat'. We have already seen
that we have self-consciousness, a rational dimension, a sense of
self-worth and an appreciation of beauty. Lewis now takes us to
another level and points out that we are also moral creatures, with
an in-built sense of right and wrong. Even if we try to play this
down we find ourselves behaving as if it is true. It seems to be in
our DNA, and to be something that separates us from every other

species on the planet. People may disagree on how they rate things on the moral scale, but we all have an inherent sense of right and wrong, wherever we draw the line. In 2002, a man in Yorkshire was gouged to death with a screwdriver when he tried to stop thieves stealing a friend's car. Almost the first thing police did was to appeal to professional car thieves to turn them in. In doing this they were banking on the fact that while the thieves had no scruples about stealing cars, they would draw the line at murder.

Yet evolution can give no explanation for the unique moral characteristics of the human race, nor can it say anything about truth, beauty, goodness, love or any of the other values or virtues we prize. In *The Descent of Man*, Darwin was honest enough to admit, 'The moral sense affords the best and highest distinction between man and animals.'[337] William Provine brushes this aside and says that if the evolutionary model is true, looking for inspired moral laws or ultimate meaning in life is hopeless.[338] Writing in *The Scientist* he bites the bullet and adds, 'No inherent or moral laws exist, nor are there absolute guiding principles for human society. The universe cares nothing for us and we have no ultimate meaning in life.'[339]

Other creatures are driven only by instinct, as when preying on other species, protecting their territory, fighting for food, or competing for mating partners. None of this brings a sense of identity into play, nor does it have any moral dimension. Is there any other species that asks where it came from, what it is and where it is going? Do sheep or snakes ever have an identity crisis or a concern about their long-term future? Does any other species have a moral dimension? Do dogs feel pangs of conscience when they foul pavements? Do cats ever repent for killing mice? We all know the answers to those questions and can agree with the English theologian Rod Garner, who makes the same point: 'Rats, after all, as far as we know, show no particular enthusiasm for moral issues and questions of meaning; and chimpanzees, delightful though they are, are not normally to be seen on our streets collecting money for impoverished chimpanzees they will never meet.'[340]

When Voldemort, the fictional anti-hero in the English author J. K. Rowling's famous Harry Potter fantasy series, says, 'There is no such thing as good and evil. There is only power,' we know that he is talking nonsense. We can no more escape the moral issue than we can avoid our own shadow. Everybody lives as if moral laws exist. Whenever we criticize what other people do, we are acknowledging that we are all subject to moral laws. What is more, morality is not a subject we can just discuss and leave it at that. It is something that affects our lives on a daily basis, and in our relationships with each other it is closely tied in to our dignity as human beings, regardless of our age or physical condition. There are those who deny this and who say that being human gives us no exclusive claim to moral rights, but where does this kind of thinking take us? Peter Singer is one such person, and his ideas lead him to say that babies born with severe defects can properly be killed: 'All I say about severely disabled babies is that when life is so miserable that it's not worth living, then it's permissible to give it a lethal injection. Why limit the killing to the womb? Infanticide should not be ruled out any more than abortion.'[341] Many years earlier the English evolutionary biologist Sir Julian Huxley (1887–1975) made another statement along the same lines: 'What anguish to have an imbecile child, or to know that one is oneself afflicted with the taint of insanity! What a waste to spend millions on the education and care of the feeble-minded, if the result is another generation of feeble-minded to care for and educate!'[342]

These are examples of the kind of thing that can happen when God has no place in a person's worldview. A statement widely attributed to the Russian author Fyodor Dostoyevsky (1821–1881), asserts 'If there is no God, then all things are permitted.' In a letter to his fellow author N. L. Ozmidov he wrote, 'Now assume that there is no God, or immortality of the soul. Now tell me, why should I live righteously and do good deeds, if I am to die entirely on earth? ... And if that is so, why shouldn't I (as long as I can rely on my cleverness and agility to avoid being caught by the law) cut another man's throat, rob and steal?'[343]

He makes a good point. Left to ourselves we are morally adrift, with nowhere to anchor our beliefs or our behaviour. As Francis Schaeffer used to say, the person who thinks like that 'has both feet firmly planted in mid-air'.[344] When I was addressing a meeting in Oxford an atheist shouted at me, 'Morality is relative', yet less than twenty-four hours earlier a Korean student at Virginia Polytechnic Institute and State University had killed thirty-two people and wounded twenty-five others in the deadliest shooting incident by a single gunman in United States history. Was what he did relatively evil or absolutely evil? In May 2014 two teenage girls in the Indian village of Katra Sadatganj, about 150 miles east of Delhi, were allegedly gang raped then hanged to death on a mango tree. They belonged to the Maurya caste, one of the lowest in the country. With no lavatory in their home, they had gone into a field to relieve themselves when they were apparently attacked, violated and murdered. The story went viral on the internet, and all around the world political leaders and others spoke of their disgust at this outrage. Nobody suggested it was relative.

R. C. Sproul easily holes relativism below the waterline: 'If everything is relative to everything else, then there is no ultimate reference point. There is no basis for truth. If everything is relative then the statement "Everything is relative" is also relative. It cannot be trusted as a fixed truth. All statements become relative. All laws become relative. Relative to what? To other statements, which are also relative ... If I don't like you and decide to murder you, is that good or bad? Neither. Or both. It's relative. For you and your family—your relatives—it may be considered bad. For me it's good since I've destroyed a personal enemy. In a relativistic court why should a judge find against me? ... In relativism, there are particulars but no universals, relatives but no absolutes. This means that we can have values but no Value, truths but no Truth, purposes but no Purpose. That is, we have no fixed standards by which to measure or to judge values, truth, purpose or beauty. Once we embrace relativism we live in a world of ultimate chaos.'[345]

In a letter to *The Observer* in 1957 Bertrand Russell said that he could not live as if ethical values were a matter of personal taste and admitted 'I do not know the solution.'[346] The English Pete Townshend's song 'The Seeker', written for the rock band The Who and included on their album Meaty Beaty Big and Bouncy,[347] has the line, 'I've got values, but I don't know how or why.' In their song 'Epitaph' the London-based progressive rock band King Crimson includes the words, 'Knowledge is a deadly friend when no one sets the rules; the fate of all mankind I see is in the hands of fools.'[348]

Having at one time been an atheist, C. S. Lewis, who set out to disprove the existence of God on the basis of logical argument, wrote of a pivotal moment when he began to realize that unless God 'sets the rules' there is no explanation for why people set their own moral judgements. It is worth quoting where this led him:

'My argument against God was that the universe seemed so cruel and unjust. But how had I got this idea of *just* and *unjust*? A man does not call a line crooked unless he has some idea of a straight line. What was I comparing this universe with when I called it unjust? If the whole show was bad and senseless from A to Z, so to speak, why did I, who was supposed to be part of the show, find myself in such violent reaction against it? A man feels wet when he falls into water, because man is not a water animal: a fish would not feel wet. Of course I could have given up my idea of justice by saying it was nothing but a private idea of my own. But if I did that, then my argument against God collapsed too—for the argument depended on saying that the world was really unjust, not simply that it did not happen to please my private fancies. Thus in the very act of trying to prove that God did not exist—in other words, that the whole of reality was senseless—I found I was forced to assume that one part of reality—namely my idea of justice—was full of sense. Consequently atheism turns out to be too simple. If the whole universe has no meaning, we should never have found out that it has no meaning: Just as, if there were no light in the universe and therefore no creatures with eyes, we should never know it was dark. *Dark* would be without meaning.'[349]

Lewis' argument against God collapsed when he realized that morality was not subjective (something tied in to personal feelings, tastes or opinions) but objective (something that is 'out there', based on observable and testable facts, regardless of what we believe, think or feel). If we rule God out, we have a universe without purpose, humanity without meaning, and morality with no fixed reference point. Many people settle for this, as it suits their lifestyle. The English author Aldous Huxley (1894–1963) made no bones about it: 'I had motives for not wanting the world to have a meaning; consequently I assumed that it had none, and was able without any difficulty to find satisfying reasons for this assumption ... We don't know because we don't want to know ... Those who detect no meaning in the world generally do so because, for one reason or another, it suits their books that the world should be meaningless ... For myself, as no doubt for most of my contemporaries, the philosophy of meaninglessness was essentially an instrument of liberation, sexual and political.'[350] This was a significant confession. He realized that meaning pointed to morality, and as he preferred immorality he ran away from the God who made moral demands he was unwilling to face and airbrushed meaning out of his worldview. When two of the characters in the novel *The Beautiful and the Damned* by the American author Scott Fitzgerald (1896–1940) discuss whether life has any meaning, one of them says, 'I don't care about truth. I want some happiness.'[351]

Yet conscience, an inner moral monitor, points us in a different direction. As the Russian novelist and historian Aleksandr Solzhenitsyn (1918–2008) put it, 'The line dividing good and evil cuts through the heart of every human being.'[352] We can no more do away with an objective moral law that we can do away with the law of gravity. If there is no single, objective moral authority, we are all free to make up our own. But this would mean that while people may disagree with each other, nobody could say that another person's opinions were wrong. If moral judgements are no more than personal opinions, we are like ships without rudders.

The American psychiatrist Armand Nicholi underlines this: 'If I think stealing a person's money or making love to his wife is alright, is this wrong?'[353] and adds, 'If you disagree with me, who is right? If we have no moral point of reference, what you think is no more right or wrong than what I think.'[354] In matters of personal preference, I may like golf (I do) while you may prefer football; I may like classical music while you may prefer heavy metal; I may like crème brûlée (that will definitely be a 'Yes'!) while you may prefer tiramisu. These personal preferences and tastes may be legitimate, truthful and 'correct', but none of them could be called right or wrong—and neither could personal moral judgements if morality was merely subjective. In 1999, the English author and journalist Will Self told readers of *The Independent* that he was brought up in a world where ethics were a matter of personal taste, like 'a designer label, sewn into the inside lining of conscience'.[355] The fact that people have different opinions about whether something is right or wrong is not proof that there is no ultimate standard; in fact, it is exactly the opposite, and shows that they are all subject to an objective standard. There is a huge difference between preferences and principles, and nobody whose daughter was raped, whose car was stolen, or who in some other way suffered as the result of someone else's behaviour would settle for the first. A young man arguing strongly in favour of free sex soon back-pedalled when Francis Schaeffer asked him for the name and telephone number of his live-in girlfriend!

If there are no objective values, we are free to set our own, but where does that lead? Is theft right for the thief but wrong for the victim?—or the other way around?—or is theft neither right nor wrong? If Peter Atkins is right to call us 'a bit of slime on a planet' we are free of any moral obligation—but so is everybody else, which means that we can have no complaint when anyone causes us pain, loss, harm or grief of any kind. The British atheist philosopher Julian Baggini swallows this whole and claims that in God's absence 'we can choose our own purposes ... and thus be the authors of our own meaning'.[356] But if this were true it would lead to complete chaos in society, with everybody pursuing their own ends regardless of how their behaviour affected others. The Danish philosopher Kai Nielsen makes no bones about it: 'If there is no God ... there is no purpose to life; you weren't made for a purpose'.[357]

Atoms to ethics?

Then where does our sense of right and wrong come from? A popular answer is to claim it is something that evolved as humankind appeared on the world scene and then gradually developed over thousands of years, but even hard-wired evolutionists have torpedoed this idea. The English biologist Thomas Huxley (1825–1895), known as 'Darwin's Bulldog' because of his feisty defence of Darwin's theory of evolution, admitted that evolution 'is incompetent to furnish any better reason why what we call good is preferable to what we call evil than what we had before'.[358] Acknowledging that 'I do have a strongly developed sense of good', Richard Dawkins admits that 'as a biologist I haven't a very well worked-out story where that comes from'.[359] Elsewhere he is forced to concede, 'Much as we might wish to believe otherwise, universal love and the welfare of the species are concepts that simply do not make evolutionary sense'.[360] How could they? If we trace the evolutionary idea from Darwin's 'warm little pond' to the unexplained appearance of life, then to life forms becoming more and more complex, then through amphibians to reptiles, birds, four-legged animals and eventually humans, at what point do accidental accumulations of atoms develop ethics and molecules get ideas about morality?

The English astrophysicist Rodney Holder easily pokes holes in the whole idea: 'If we are nothing but atoms and molecules organized in a particular way through the chance processes of evolution, then love, beauty, good and evil, free will, reason itself—indeed all that makes us human and raises us above the rest of the created order—lose their objectivity. Why should I love my neighbour, or go out of my way to help him? Rather, why should I not get everything I can for myself, trampling on whoever gets in my way? After all, I am nothing but a "gene survival machine", and my sole purpose is to propagate my own genes. The best we can do can be to come to some kind of agreement in our mutual interest along utilitarian lines to live in peace, but if it suits us we shall be free to break any such agreement. Our behaviour could degenerate to that which we see in the animal world'.[361] If we are nothing more than jumped-up apes we can make up our own moral standards as we go along—and thumb our noses at any other jumped-up apes that disagree with us.

The American author Camille Paglia, an atheist and self-styled 'world class intellectual', seems to buy into this. She told *The Daily Telegraph* that 'marriages ought to be formed or dissolved according to personal whim or fancy' and that any woman who was unfortunate enough to be raped should not regard herself as a victim. Paglia's advice to her was 'pick yourself up, dust yourself off, and go on.'[362]

On 12 February 1993, two-year-old James Bulger went with his mother to a shopping mall in Bootle, Liverpool. As his mother's back was turned, two ten year-old boys coaxed him to go with them. After viciously assaulting him they killed him and laid his body across the railway line, where it was cut in two by a goods train. Nine months later, the two boys were convicted of murder at Preston Crown Court. Over the next four years, their minimum jail sentence was variously assessed at eight, ten and fifteen years, but in October 2000, the Lord Chief Justice decided they had been detained long enough. In the furore that followed, *The Daily Mail* agreed and argued they should go free: 'Boys of ten have not yet evolved a proper moral sense. They know that something 'feels wrong' but they do not know why, and could neither explain nor justify it. Those two ten-years-olds were not moral beings.'[363]

Then when, and how, was this 'moral sense' to evolve? On what basis were they to come to make the right decisions? On what basis can anyone do so? In a famous radio debate in 1948, the English priest and philosopher Frederick Copleston (1907–1994) asked Bertrand Russell, 'What's your justification for distinguishing between good and bad or how do you view the distinction between them?' Russell replied, 'I don't have any justification any more than I have when I distinguish between blue and yellow. What is my justification for distinguishing between blue and yellow? I can see they are different.' When Copleston went on, 'Well, that is an excellent justification, I agree. You distinguish blue and yellow by seeing them, so you distinguish good and bad by what faculty?' Russell answered, 'By my feelings.' But if every individual is justified in following his or her feelings in deciding issues of morality, nobody is under any moral obligation to anyone else.

If life arose by natural processes, there is nobody to whom we are morally accountable. If we are no more than survival mechanisms, robot vehicles blindly programmed to preserve our genes, why do we have a moral dimension? Why do we feel responsible for our actions? Why do we say there are moral differences between certain actions and attitudes? If there is nothing more to the world than matter and energy, where do we get concepts of good and evil? Where do we get a sense of right and wrong if we are merely the by-products of events in which morality plays no part?

For Richard Dawkins to say that morality is 'just something that has emerged'[364] gets us nowhere. From where did it emerge?—and *how*?—and *why*? The idea that over the centuries man developed a code of morals out of self-interest falls flat on its face, as it would turn selfishness into a virtue. The notion that morality is tied into what is good for society is easily knocked down by C. S. Lewis: 'If we ask: "Why ought I to be unselfish?" and you reply, "Because it is good for society," we may then ask, "Why should I care what's good for society…?" and then you will have to say, "Because you ought to be unselfish"—which simply brings us back to where we started.'[365] Even the idea that something can be called morally good if it is aimed at producing 'the greatest good for the greatest number' is equally flawed, as it can produce horrific results. Adolf

Hitler (1889–1945), the dictator of Nazi Germany, believed that the extermination of six million Jews, gypsies and others in World War 2—he called them 'human bacteria'—would benefit the entire world, but no right-thinking person would claim that what he did was morally acceptable.

We can be equally certain that science can produce no explanation for morality. We touched briefly on this in Chapter 2, but because science has such a high profile in the modern world we need to batten down this point here. In an unpublished letter to a friend in 1944, Albert Einstein told him that 'every attempt to reduce ethics to scientific formulae must fail'[366] and Richard Dawkins helps us to confirm this. As we saw in an earlier chapter, he says, 'We can all agree that science's entitlement to advise us on moral values is problematic, to say the least.'[367] In *A Devil's Chaplain* he takes this a little further and writes, 'Science has no methods for deciding what is ethical,'[368] while in the course of a 2007 debate at the University of Alabama he admitted, 'I don't know on the whole what is moral.'[369] Yet both statements contradict his earlier claim about the all-sufficiency of science. John Lennox uses one of his favourite illustrations to make the point about the failure of science to define morality: 'Science can tell you that if you add strychnine to someone's drink it will kill them. But science cannot tell you whether it is morally right or wrong to put strychnine into your grandmother's tea so that you can get your hands on her property.'[370]

The American author Paul Chamberlain's book *Can we be good without God?* is built around five people having a long-running discussion about right and wrong, truth and conduct. In the course of this, one of them makes this excellent point: 'To say morality is objective is to say that there exists an objective entity independent of any human being. This entity we could call moral value, or moral truth, or a set of moral principles, or a moral standard if you will. What we call it is not important. What is important is that this moral truth is independent of any person. We don't determine or control it. It does not change from one person to another. Nor does it go away because we don't appreciate it.'[371] When we say that people should do certain things and not do other things, we are assuming (even if we fail to grasp this) that there is a moral law to which everyone is subject.

We can go further. If such a moral law exists there must be a moral lawgiver. As it is impossible to find morality anywhere in nature, moral standards must either be accidental or meaningless— or have a moral and meaningful source outside of nature. The clearest explanation of such a source is the one given in the Bible, which says that all human beings, even those without knowledge of God's written commandments have his law 'written on their hearts'.[372] If there is no transcendent God whose perfection is reflected in absolute moral standards, how can anyone claim that such standards exist, or claim to set standards for the entire human race? In a world without God, what one animal does to another animal is morally irrelevant, whether the animals concerned have four legs, two legs, or none. Francis Collins says, 'After twenty-eight years as a believer, the Moral Law still stands out for me as the strongest signpost to God. More than that, it points to a God who cares about human beings, and a God who is infinitely good and holy.'[373] Elsewhere, he writes, 'This moral law, which defies scientific explanation, is exactly what one might expect to find if one were searching for the existence of a personal God who sought relationship with mankind ...'[374] This points clearly to the fact that our lives have meaning.

There is another important point to make. We have seen there is reason to believe that the universe is the work of an intelligent, moral Creator. This universe is governed by laws, including moral laws, and life can only make sense (in other words, have any ultimate meaning) if we respond in the right way to a moral order that governs the universe in which we live. Morality is best understood as living in tune with the moral code that has been put in place to govern our habitat. If this is the case, it should not be difficult for us to accept that we are all hopelessly out of tune. We will face up to this in the final two chapters of this book.

The God-shaped gap

The second of these powerful pointers is that we have a spiritual dimension—the clearest of all the pointers we are considering in these two chapters. The Russian-born author and publisher Joseph Gaer (1897–1969) wrote, 'As far as we can determine, religion has existed in every society, from the most primitive to the most culturally advanced. The more keys modern science finds with which to open the locked doors of the past, the more we learn about the early days of man on earth, the more evidence there is that all societies in the past had one thing in common —some form of religion.'[375] Sir John Houghton agrees: 'There is general evidence that most human beings, from whatever part of the world and from the earliest times, have exhibited a fundamental belief in a divine being or beings, and in some sort of spiritual world.'[376] No group of humans we have been able to trace in all of history has seemed to be without religious belief of some kind. *The Encyclopaedia of Religion and Ethics* has twelve huge volumes and its Preface calls it, 'An effective instrument for the exploration of the world's thought on the things of the human spirit.' It has articles on all the world's religions and religious beliefs and all its ethical systems, and its General Index alone runs to 660 pages. Many of the movements, beliefs and ideas are bizarre, but even these point to man having a spiritual dimension that he feels driven to express. I have written elsewhere about some of the avenues man has pursued[377] and will concentrate here on showing that our spiritual dimension is a powerful pointer to the fact that our lives have meaning.

Belief in God has always marked man out from the rest of creation. There is no evidence of religion in any other creatures— not even the praying mantis prays! If man had evolved from 'lower' forms of life, we should expect to find the earliest traceable humans in history without any signs of religious belief. Yet this is not the case, and as the American scholar Samuel Zwemer (1867–1952) found, 'Religion is as old as the oldest record and is universal among the most primitive tribes today.'[378] Some estimates say there are as many as 4,200 religious belief systems in the world today. Countless people with no attachment to any particular religious group regularly read their horoscopes, while others turn to Ouija boards, black magic, astrologers, mediums, palm readers and other occult practitioners in their attempts to reach into the spirit world. In his book *In Harm's Way,* a fascinating account of his experience as a war correspondent, the English UNICEF Ambassador Martin Bell writes, 'I came to put much faith in certain routines and rituals which may be considered superstitions, but which none the less worked for me.'[379] Among these he included the wearing of his famous white suit and (slightly less famous) green socks, and carrying items which were 'matters of life and death' because they had to do with the tokens of good fortune. These included 'a silver threepenny bit, a four-leafed, and even a five-leafed clover, a fragment of water-snake skin in an envelope, a brass pixie, countless silver crosses and Saint Christophers, and tapes of [the American country music singer] Willie Nelson'. Commenting on this collection of talismans, Bell says, 'I carry them all … and who can tell which will work and which will not? Better to be safe by accumulation than sorry by preferring one to another.'[380]

Yet for all the religious ideas that man has held, the concept of there being one true God has been by far the most persistent, in spite of it being relentlessly attacked, for one reason or another, by those determined to stamp it out. In the twentieth century alone, Marxist-Leninist Communism declared total warfare against it. The revolutionary leader Vladimir Lenin (1870–1924) declared, 'Every religious idea, every idea of God, every flirtation with the idea of God, is unutterable vileness'[381] and in a letter to the Soviet author Maxim Gorky (1868–1936), sometimes known as the father of Soviet literature, he wrote, 'There can be nothing more abominable than religion.'[382] Persistent propaganda, brainwashing, imprisonment, torture and execution were all used in a vicious atheistic crusade against all believers in God. During the Cultural Revolution in China, beginning in 1966, the atheist dictator Mao Zedong (1893–1976) had his opponents killed at the rate of 2,000 a month. Between 1975 and 1979 the Khmer Rouge movement, under its atheist leader Pol Pot (1925–1998), slaughtered over 1,500,000 Cambodians out of a population of about 8,000,000 in the notorious 'killing fields'. Since then, godless regimes in many countries have repressed, bullied, tortured and killed countless people for no other reason than that they believed in God.

More people were killed because of their faith in God during the twentieth century than in the previous nineteen centuries put together, yet he refuses to go away. The front cover of *TIME* magazine for 8 April 1966 asked, 'Is God dead?' and sparked off its biggest newsstand sales in over twenty years—and a record number of 3,500 letters to the editor. But by 1980 the same magazine was telling its readers, 'In a quiet revolution that no one could have foreseen only two decades ago, God is making a comeback. Now it is more respectable among philosophers than it has been for a generation to talk about the possibility of God's existence.'[383] The American author Paul Johnson underlines this: 'The most extraordinary thing about the twentieth century was the failure of God to die. The collapse of mass religious belief, especially among the educated and prosperous, had been widely and confidently predicted. It did not take place. Somehow, God survived, flourished even. At the end of the twentieth century the idea of a personal, living God is as lively and real as ever in the minds and hearts of countless millions of men and women throughout our planet.'[384] In its millennium issue, *The Economist* published what it called God's obituary, but towards the end of 2007 admitted that it had overstepped the mark.[385] As the British scientist and theologian Alister McGrath, comments in *Why God Won't Go Away*, 'Many are now wondering whether the New Atheism itself is beginning to look and sound a little stale and weary, repeating old arguments dressed up as if they were new and radical.'[386]

While all other creatures seem satisfied when their basic physical needs have been met, human beings are not. Blaise Pascal grasped this and wrote, 'There is a God-shaped vacuum in the heart of every person that cannot be filled by any created thing, but only by God, the Creator.'[387] Elsewhere he wrote, 'He alone is our true good', then added, 'From the time we have forsaken him, it is a curious thing that nothing in nature has been capable of taking his place.'[388] One Old Testament writer cried, 'As a deer pants for flowing streams, so pants my soul for you, O God'[389] and even an atheist like Bertrand Russell admitted, 'The centre of me is always and eternally a terrible pain—a curious wild pain—a searching for something beyond what the world contains, something transfigured and infinite—the beatific vision—God.'[390] Jean-Paul Sartre said much the same thing: 'God is silent, and that I cannot possibly deny—everything in me calls for God and that I cannot forget.'[391] The Bible explains this by saying that God 'has put eternity into man's heart'.[392] C. S. Lewis makes an interesting point about this: 'Creatures are not born with desires unless satisfaction for these desires exists. A baby feels hunger; well, there is such a thing as food. A duckling wants to swim; well, there is such a thing as water. Men feel sexual desire; well, there is such a thing as sex. If I find in myself a desire which no experience in the world can satisfy, the most probable explanation is that I was made for another world.'[393] Augustine was certain that this was the case, and addressed God with the words, 'You have made us for yourself, and our hearts are restless until they rest in you.'[394] In the opening words of his book *Nothing To Be Frightened Of*, the English author Julian Barnes (an atheist turned agnostic) admits, 'I don't believe in God, but I miss Him.'[395] Millions would say the same. Others might relate to the Canadian novelist Douglas Coupland, who in *Life After God* writes, 'Now—here is my secret: I tell it to you with an openness of heart that I doubt I shall ever achieve again, so I pray that you are in a quiet room as you hear these words. My secret is that I need God— that I am sick and can no longer make it alone. I need God to help me give, because I no longer seem capable of giving; to help me be kind, as I no longer seem capable of kindness; to help me love, as I seem beyond being able to love.'[396]

The Bible's explanation of our spiritual dimension is the perfectly straightforward statement we saw in the previous chapter: 'So God created man in his own image, in the image of God he created him; male and female he created them.'[397] Man was not created *with* the image of God but '*in* the image of God'. This does not mean that man is a miniature God, but it is the defining thing that makes a human being human, distinct from all other creatures. Without being made divine, man was created with qualities which enable him to enjoy a living relationship with his Maker. What is more, God gave him these clear instructions: 'Be fruitful and multiply and fill the earth and subdue it and have dominion over the fish of the sea and over the birds of the heavens and over every living thing that moves on the earth.'[398] As Douglas Kelly says, 'The dominion mandate of Genesis teaches man both to respect and to subdue nature so as to shape it in a direction that will reflect the beauty, order and glory of its Creator.'[399] As his representatives, we are stewards of all that God has given to us, responsible for carrying out his wishes and taking care of the planet on which he has placed us—and doing so in a way that reflects his holiness, beauty and goodness in our lives.

It is impossible to imagine how our lives could have a greater purpose. Yet all our thinking about life's meaning is framed by one simple truth that none of us can avoid and that puts all of our thinking about life in context. We need to look at this before we go any further.

The gruesome invader

The Oscar-winning film *Schindler's List* tells how a German businessman Oskar Schindler, although a member of the Nazi Party, became concerned at the appalling persecution of Jews in Poland during the Holocaust in the Second World War. As the story developed, he used many different schemes to employ Jews in his factory, and eventually saved the lives of over a thousand people. At one point in the film, when trying to help friends cope with the random slaughter of their fellow Jews, he delivers this chilling line: *'People die. That's life.'*

You may think it strange, in a book about the meaning of life, to devote a whole chapter to death, but it is impossible to miss the connection. What we call 'living' could just as accurately be called 'dying'. The certainty of death sprawls across the whole of life, and from the moment we draw our first breath we move relentlessly towards our last. Julian Barnes says, 'Death is the one appalling fact that defines life; unless you are constantly aware of it, you cannot begin to understand what life is all about; unless you know and feel that the days of wine and roses are limited, that the wine will madeirize and the roses turn brown in their stinking water before all are thrown out for ever—including the jug—there is no context to such pleasures and interests as come your way on the road to the grave.'[400]

What we think about death is bound to have a profound effect on how we live, and on whether we see life as having any meaning. Bertrand Russell laid out where his atheism took him: 'All the labours of the ages, all the devotion, all the inspirations, all the noonday brightness of human genius, are destined to extinction in the vast death of the solar system, and ... the whole temple of man's achievement must inevitably be buried beneath the debris of a universe in ruins.'[401] Our view of how things end puts everything we do, and how we assess life—and death—into perspective. For example, as the American scholar J. Ligon Duncan III says, 'If you believe that there is no God, and that this world evolved from a primitive protein in the explosion of some primary particle, then death is literally meaningless.'[402] Unless we come to terms with this we will not make any real progress in our search for what the whole business of living and dying means.

Blaise Pascal claimed he had learned to define life backwards and live it forwards; by this he meant that he began by defining death, then lived accordingly. This was good thinking. When we have a destination in mind it makes sense to choose the route we will take. If we ignore the issue of death we will never get a clear view of life.

Ravi Zacharias lays out two clear alternatives: 'If there is no life beyond the grave, then life is defined only in terms of "What makes me happy?" On the other hand, if there is life beyond the grave, then life must be defined from that vantage point.'[403] People have approached the subject in many different ways, and we will look at some of them here.

There are those who have simply tried to airbrush death out of their thinking. Epicurus wrote, 'Death … is of no concern to us; for while we exist death is not present, and when death is present we no longer exist.'[404] The Roman philosopher and statesman Seneca (4 BC–AD 65) agreed: 'There is nothing after death, and death itself is nothing.' The Czech-born British playwright Sir Tom Stoppard has a play in which one of his characters says, 'Death is not anything … It's the absence of presence, nothing more … the endless time of never coming back … a gap you can't see, and when the wind blows through it, it makes no sound.'[405] Interviewed on television's *Sky News,* the English politician Tony Benn (1925–2014) said, 'I'm not afraid of dying. I just feel that at a certain time your switch is switched off, and that's it.'[406]

Forced to accept that death is real, many do everything they can to avoid facing up to it. It is said that King Louis XV of France (1710–1774) told his servants never to mention the word 'death' in his presence. Writing of how the First World War changed people's views about things, the Austrian neurologist Sigmund Freud (1856–1939) wrote, 'We have tried to keep a deadly silence about death.'[407] The award-winning American novelist Philip Roth says that one of his characters lives 'with his back turned to death, the way normal people like us do.'[408] The Irish singer-songwriter Bono (real name Paul David Hewson) told *Q Magazine,* 'I haven't really accepted that there are some things that I can't control. I don't remember agreeing to people dying, people close to me, or even people I don't know—if they're dying for no reason—I can't accept that. I'm no good with death.'[409] The French-born British author W. Somerset Maugham (1874–1965) said 'Dying is a very dull, dreary affair. And my advice to you is to have nothing whatever to do with it.'[410] Even the word 'died' is often replaced in serious conversation by 'passed away', 'moved on', 'no longer with us' or 'gone to pastures new.' To avoid getting too close to the subject, people often use trivial terms and speak of someone having 'kicked the bucket', 'snuffed it', 'bitten the dust', 'popped their clogs' or say that they are 'pushing up daisies' or 'six feet under'.

Others try to fight it off with humour. The English journalist Kate Saunders told readers of *The Daily Telegraph*, 'The grim reaper has begun winnowing among my friends. In the last three weeks I have been to two funerals and received an invitation to a requiem mass … One day, who knows when, it will be me under the pall.' After discussing some of the arrangements she would like made ('Tea and whisky will be served afterwards, but no sandwiches, because it is always the saddest person who ends up making them') she added, 'If I am cremated, I don't intend to sit in a jar on the mantelpiece depressing my husband. What if my urn got broken? I don't much relish the thought of being Hoovered out of the carpet by his second wife. I have therefore decided that my ashes will be scattered in my favourite place—up the noses of certain former employers.'[411] In 2014 the English television presenter Richard Madeley told the same newspaper about the death of his mother seven years earlier. Speaking to him in a Norfolk nursing home forty-eight hours before she died she told him, 'I really should lose some weight for the big event, shouldn't I?'[412] In the same year the family of New Orleans resident Miriam Burbank followed her instructions and at her funeral service propped her body up sitting at a table, wearing sunglasses and carrying a glass of wine in one hand and a menthol cigarette in the other.[413] The funeral director told the press that this kind of thing was not unusual and that his company prided itself in putting the 'fun' into 'funeral'. Statements like this may be amusing to some people, but they do nothing to dispel the reality or the fear of death.

Nowhere to go?

Making (or faking) a light-hearted approach to death is sometimes tied in to the belief or hope that death means annihilation, and that nothing follows. Writing as an atheist, Peter Atkins predicts the universe disintegrating and says that when the sun dies, 'We shall have gone the journey of all purposeless stardust, driven unwittingly by chaos, gloriously but aimlessly evolved into sentience, born unchoosingly into the world, unwillingly taken from it, and inescapably returned to nothing.'[414] The English journalist and broadcaster Claire Rayner (1931–2010), who was at one time President of the British Humanist Association, told television viewers, 'Humanism is precisely that this is all there is. Yesterday was oblivion, before I was born; and tomorrow, after I die, that will be oblivion too.' Mourners at the funeral in 2010 of Malcolm McLaren, manager of the English rock band Sex Pistols, travelled in a bus with the destination sign 'Nowhere'. The American author Ernest Hemingway (1899–1961) took an equally pessimistic line: 'Life is just a dirty trick, a short journey from nothingness to nothingness. There is no remedy for anything in life. Man's destiny in the universe is like a colony of ants on a burning log.' He committed suicide three weeks short of what would have been his sixty-second birthday.

Asked how she would like to be remembered after she died, the Australian journalist Germaine Greer, who describes herself as 'a Catholic atheist', replied, 'Compost. I'd want people to say, "She made good compost."'[415] This is one way of expressing the final article in atheism's creed, which can be summarized like this: we begin as a fluke, live as a farce, and end as fertilizer. In 'A Song of Myself' the humanist American poet Walt Whitman (1819–1892) called death 'the bitter hug of mortality' and wrote,

> I bequeath myself to the dirt to grow from the grass I love,
> If you want me again look for me under your boot-soles.
> You will hardly know who I am or what I mean.[416]

Nothing in that scenario can possibly give life any semblance of meaning. Jean-Paul Sartre settled for this when he wrote, 'Man is a useless passion. It is meaningless that we live, and it is meaningless that we die.'[417] Solomon saw where life 'under the sun' led: 'For what happens to the children of man and what happens to the beasts is the same; as one dies, so dies the other. They all have the same breath, and man has no advantage over the beasts, for all is vanity. All go to one place. All are from the dust, and to dust all return.'[418]

'Who's afraid ...?'

Many more people than would be prepared to admit it are afraid of death. Tom Chivers, the English poet, editor and live literature promoter writes, 'I'm terrified of death, my loved ones', everyone's ... the odds are that 100 years after my death, no-one will really know who I was ... There will come a time when not only will you and I not exist, but no-one exists, no life exists ... and all our loves, works and ambitions, quite literally might as well never have been. Which is pretty depressing ... If you're an atheist and this doesn't scare or depress you, then I admire and envy you. For me, it's an infinite tragedy.'[419] J. K. Rowling says, 'My books are largely about death. They open with the death of Harry's parents. There is Voldemort's obsession with conquering death and his quest for immortality at any price, the goal for anyone with magic ... I so understand why Voldemort wants to conquer death. We're all frightened of it.'[420]

The Bible is not exaggerating when it speaks of those who 'through fear of death were subject to lifelong slavery.'[421] Elsewhere it speaks of men being 'brought to the king of terrors'[422] and it is easy to understand why.

- *There is the fear of the unknown.* We may have been present when someone has died, but have never experienced death for ourselves, and we have an inbuilt dread of the unknown. It is said that on his deathbed Thomas Hobbes spoke of taking 'my last voyage, a great leap in the dark'. Speaking at a 2013 Ways with Words Festival, the English broadcaster and author Melvyn Bragg told his audience, 'We are reaching into the unknown. We are going somewhere and we don't know what the end is.'[423] It may be this fear of the unknown that prompts one of the characters in a piece by Woody Allen to say, 'I am not afraid of dying. I just don't want to be there when it happens.'[424] Many people think the same.

- *There is the fear of the pain, disability or disintegration that might precede death.* People have different pain thresholds, but nobody can look forward to weeks, months or years of suffering, knowing that things can only get worse, and that while increasing amounts of medication may reduce the pain it will also limit their enjoyment of life as it closes down. The English clergyman and poet G. S. Studdert Kennedy (1883–1929), who as an army chaplain ministered to injured and dying soldiers during the First World War, said that anyone who was not disturbed by the problem of pain was suffering from hardness of the heart or softening of the brain. In a 2014 newspaper interview Sir Ian Botham, the iconic English cricketer who in his batting career had stood up to the world's fastest bowlers, confessed that he could not bring himself to visit his father even once during the six months before he died of dementia in hospital; he told the reporter that it would be 'horrendous' to see someone he loved 'being ravaged by this disease'.[425]

- *There is the fear that old age will drain life of its meaning.* The English journalist and television presenter Joan Bakewell writes of many old people, 'They get lonely, they can get depressed. Let's face it, at my age [she was 80 at the time] almost everyone is left with a smattering of disappointed hopes and no time to do anything about it. Too late to climb that mountain, build that dream house. But too late also to make up for broken relationships, damaged bonds, neglected friends ... Ageing deprives us of the sense of purpose that drives us forward through our earlier, and indeed middle years. Suddenly, we aren't going anywhere, aiming for anything specific ... the golden years of flourishing are gone for ever.'[426] Describing a nursing home for the elderly, the English politician David Eccles (1904–1999) wrote, 'Contemplate the colourless, senile, dribbling bodies and ask yourself what can be the meaning of an individual life if there is no kind of time but nature's cycle. What is there to stop you treating these old people, male and female husks, as if they were as disposable as a screw of paper, a beer can or a cellophane bag?'[427]

- *There is the fear that death will end a life that never gave us what we were looking for.* Alister McGrath (a one-time atheist) spelled this out at a meeting of students at Ormond College, in Australia's University of Melbourne. He told them of a time when he had walked through a 'Hall of Mirrors' at a fairground and had seen distorted pictures of himself. He went on, 'Everything seemed to be wrong and out of alignment. And that feeling of distortion often comes back to me as I think about life. The way things are seems to be all wrong. We try to pretend that everything is fine. But deep down we know it's not. Many are frightened about dying. They may not want to talk about it. But the fear is there. Some find it unbearable. And deep in the night, they wonder about death. They wonder if its fear could ever be overcome. Others find themselves longing for something—something which they can never quite define, and which anyway never seems to happen. They thought that this career move, that academic qualification, this relationship, would satisfy their deepest desires. But they don't. There is this deep sense of yearning for something that somehow never seems to come along. And people wonder: is there any way in which this deep and unsatisfied longing could ever be satisfied? Yet there always seems to be another mountain to climb, another river to cross. Something seems to be wrong. And we wonder: can anything be done about it?'[428]

On 22 August 1963, when he was at the peak of his career, the English actor and comedian Kenneth Williams (1926–1988) agonized over whether his life would count for anything and said, 'The madness screaming up inside me. So many awful thoughts—this terrible sense of doom hanging over me. I wonder if anyone will ever know about the emptiness of my life. I wonder if anyone will ever stand in a room that I have lived in and touch the things that were once a part of my life and wonder about me? How could they ever be told? How to explain that I only experienced vicariously, never first hand, that the sharing of a life is what makes a life … Now I am thinking all the while of death in some shape or another. Every day is something to be got through. All the recipes of the past are no longer valid. I've spent all my life in the mind. I have entered into nothing.'[429]

- *There is the fear that death will leave us not only with unfinished business, but with unfinished pleasure.* Included among the many golf related books I have is one titled *1001 Golf Holes You Must Play Before You Die.* I drool and dream every time I open it, but I know that although I have played hundreds of courses all around the world I will never play more than a tiny percentage of the holes beautifully illustrated and enthusiastically described in the book. For over forty years I have lived within fifteen miles of the centre of London, judged by many to be the greatest city in the world and bursting at the seams with historic buildings and objects, but I know that I will never see more than a tiny percentage of them. Yet what if I was to play every one of the holes mentioned in the book and see every historic building and object London has to offer? Would doing so add any meaning to my life? The certainty of death teaches us that life is meant to be more than satisfaction in the here and now. We invest so much time, energy, money, enthusiasm and effort into the business and pleasures of life, all the time knowing with nagging certainty that everything we accumulate, value or enjoy will one day be taken away.

- *There is the fear that death will mean we end life with many of its problems unsolved.* In a 2013 newspaper article headed 'Why does a brush with death make people turn to religion?' the English journalist and former national newspaper editor Charles Moore wrote, 'The chief message of 21st Century Western culture is one of self-empowerment. With technology, money, know-how, rights, medicine, problems can be solved: "You can do it!" Often this is true, but an encounter with really serious things—and nothing is more serious than death—tells you that ultimately you cannot.'[430]

- *There is the fear of what happens to the body after death.* In a piece called 'Repulsion' the English poet Julian Turner writes about what happens to a human body after burial or cremation; its first verse focuses on the fear this produces.

The mind shies away from it—a reflex
like the way two pieces of magnetic chess
pressed base-to-base flip round and stand apart
Anathema, it stops you in your tracks

as you labour on the details of your will
pausing over interment or cremation—
the cold constriction of eternity
boxed up beneath four hundredweight of soil,

your skin blisters, your organs liquefy,
a purge of putrefying froth leaks from
all orifices, every feature lost
as your face swells bursting and your eyes

spring out, your brain begins to drizzle down
your cheeks, your sternum ruptures from the force
of methane and ammonia, swollen
like some absurd and slush-filled flesh balloon,

or else, on rollers as the curtains shut
and just before the piped hymn whines its bars
of *I will fear no evil*, the gas jets roar
at 1,700 degrees Fahrenheit

and you put on a light show for yourself
as your salts go up and the flesh is melted off,

your bones, your bones are burned from white to black
and back to white back again, their powder proof

of your fragility and lastly all
affinity between your parts breaks down
and you are sieved as ash—a pause so long
both options pass before your sorry soul.[431]

One reviewer called the poem 'a memorably horrific meditation on modern mortality'. It certainly makes difficult reading, but it helps to put our search for life's meaning into serious perspective. We fill our lives with thousands of different experiences, only to have every one of them snatched away by death. On his way to the cremation of his first wife, the English barrister, dramatist and author John Mortimer (1923–2009) thought, 'It's hard to believe that so much talent, anger, humour, dash and desperation could be shut in a long and slender box.'[432]

- *There is the fear of meeting God.* Many who never give more than a passing thought to this may do so if they attend a funeral. The words of the service may make them think that meeting God is at least a possibility, and an uncomfortable one at that. The English racing driver Stirling Moss, winner of sixteen Grand Prix events and rated 'the greatest driver never to win the World Championship' was noted for his great courage on the racetrack, yet he told a newspaper reporter, 'I am frightened of death. I know it means going to meet my Maker, and one shouldn't be afraid of that. But I am.' In the 2014 television programme *Billy Connolly's Big Send Off*, the Scottish entertainer said he had met someone who told him, 'If you're a good person and you've done everything right in life, that's what counts.' Connolly replied, 'I think that's what worries me most. That's why I'm scared of spiritual things.'[433]

Facing facts

Much of this chapter has been taken up with people's comments or opinions. We can close it with some straightforward facts about death that will help us to get our question about the meaning life into perspective.

- *Life is brief.* The English clergyman Henry Twells (1823–1900) used this truth to write a poem he called 'Time's Paces' and which is fixed to the front face of the clock case in the north transept of Chester Cathedral. The opening lines run like this:

When as a child I laughed and wept,
Time crept.
When as a youth I dreamt and talked,
Time walked.
When I became a full-grown man,
Time ran.
When older still I daily grew,
Time flew.
Soon I shall find on travelling on—
Time gone.

Twells' lines reflect something the Bible repeatedly emphasises. One writer says, 'Our days on the earth are like a shadow'.[434] Another says, 'My days are swifter than a weaver's shuttle'[435] and 'swifter than a runner'.[436] Another uses different pictures to confess, 'My days pass away like smoke'[437] and 'My days are like an evening shadow; I wither away like grass.'[438] Centuries later a New Testament writer challenged businessmen who were bragging about what they were going to do in the future, and asked them an important question: 'What is your life? For you are a mist that appears for a little time and then vanishes.'[439] This last statement has an important truth hidden behind the English translation.

The word 'appears' translates the original Greek word *phainomene*, which in turn is based on a word meaning 'to shine'. The Bible is telling us life is full of things that attract our attention—but that it soon vanishes. All the hustle and bustle, noise and activity, music and colour, achievements and excitement entertain us for a while— then death wipes them all out.

The American businessman and publisher Malcolm Forbes (1919–1990), the founder of *Forbes* magazine and one of the richest men of his generation, famous amongst other things for his collection of houses, yachts, aircraft and art, coined the phrase, 'He who dies with the most toys wins.' A gravestone in Alta Mesa Memorial Park, in Palo Alto, California has those words etched on the grill of a Mercedes Benz car, but how can the person whose body the gravestone marks be called a winner? Death is a great leveller, and the one with the most toys ends in the same way as the one with none—he dies. The Bible says that 'one's life does not consist in the abundance of his possessions'[440] and adds the undeniable fact that 'we brought nothing into the world, and we cannot take anything out of the world.'[441]

As I write these words, 90,000 people are crammed into London's Wembley Stadium, less than twenty miles away, waiting for this year's FA Cup Final, the annual climax of England's football season, to begin. Following tradition dating back to 1927, the crowd is being led in the singing of a hymn written by the Scottish clergyman Henry Francis Lyte (1793–1847). The opening words are 'Abide with me, fast falls the eventide'; I wonder how many of the 90,000 people at Wembley realize the truth of what they are singing?

- *Death is not only certain, but it could come at any time, by design, disease, decay or disaster.* When a Church of England funeral procession reaches the graveside, the minister, reading from *The Book of Common Prayer*, includes the words, 'In the midst of life we are in death.' Death comes to young and old, rich and poor, good and bad, educated and otherwise, king and commoner. The dynamic young businessman, the glamorous actress, the outstanding athlete, the brilliant scientist, the popular television personality and the powerful politician are all in the same boat—none can avoid the moment when death will bring all their power, possessions and achievements to nothing. The Bible could not be clearer: 'Dust you are, and to dust you shall return.'[442]

- *We still exist after death.* Science tells us that no part of the universe is self-created and therefore nothing can ever be completely wiped out. That includes our bodies. They may not remain in the same state, or function in the same way, but they will always exist. If you beat up an egg to make an omelette the egg still exists, even though there is no way in which a chicken can be hatched from it. The substance of the egg-turned-omelette will never be annihilated, not even after you have eaten it. This law operates everywhere in nature. A few years ago someone I knew died playing golf at my home club. If his playing partners had dashed back to the clubhouse and reported that their friend had 'passed away', nobody would have thought that his body no longer existed. The American theologian Emory Bancroft made the point perfectly: 'Unending existence is an inescapable part of man's heritage as a creature made after the image and likeness of God. He is indestructible. He cannot be annihilated.'[443] As the Dutch-American theologian Louis Berkhof (1873–1957) put it, 'God does not annihilate his work, however much he may change its form. The biblical idea of death has nothing in common with annihilation.'[444] As an outspoken atheist, Christopher Hitchens claimed, 'We have every reason to think that "earthly things" are all that we have, or are ever going to have,'[445] but failed to tell us what even one of the reasons might be.

The Bible takes us an important step further and says that when a person dies, 'the dust returns to the earth as it was, and the spirit returns to God who gave it'.[446] This is a hugely important statement; not only is the human body indestructible, but so is the human spirit or soul. Life has no ultimate meaning unless it continues beyond the blink of time we spend on this planet: the Bible says it does. When God created man 'in his own image'[447] this included his immortality. The Bible teems with the fundamental truth that *death does not mean annihilation, but separation.* Death does not put an end to a person's existence; instead, it brings about an immediate change from bodily existence to bodiless existence. The human spirit does not depend on the body for its existence and continues to be alive after the body has ceased to function.

Reinforcing all of this is the fact that man has an innate sense of immortality, an instinct embedded in human beings for as far back as we have been able to trace, that life goes on beyond the grave. The Prussian statesman Count Otto Leopold, Prince of Bismarck (1815–1898) claimed, 'Without the hope of eternal life, this life is not worth the effort of getting dressed in the morning,'[448] while the English author H. G. Wells (1866–1946) said, 'If there is no afterlife, then life is just a sick joke, braying across the centuries.' The English artist, entrepreneur and art collector, Damien Hirst, who became famous for a series of artworks featuring dead animals, including a shark, a sheep and a cow, preserved in formaldehyde, and whose wealth was put at £215 million in the 2010 *Sunday Times* Rich List, gave a clear hint of human instinct for immortality: 'Why do I feel so important when I'm not? Nothing is important and everything is important. I do not know why I am here but I am glad that I am—I'd rather be here than not. I am going to die and I want to live for ever. I can't escape that fact, and I can't let go of that desire.'[449] Francis Schaeffer wrote, 'All men ... have a deep longing for significance, a longing for meaning ... No man... is content to look at himself as a finally meaningless machine which can and will be discarded totally and for ever.'[450] C. S. Lewis fine-tuned the point in his first book (written under the pseudonym Clive Hamilton) when he said, 'We know that we are not made of mortal stuff.'[451] The longing for life beyond the grave does not prove that such a thing exists, but it does point to the need for us to know whether or not it does, because this would help us to get the whole of life in perspective. Unless there is life beyond the grave, all our concerns about values such as truth, justice, love and meaning are a classic case of rearranging the deckchairs on the Titanic. But *where* does it go on? Some may think that modern man has got beyond the ancient practice of burying with the deceased things they might enjoy or find helpful in the next life, but this is not the case. When her husband died, the highly-respected head of a fine school at which I once spoke placed in his coffin two table games, Scrabble and Humbug, together with a walking guide to England's south coast. She said that as he was 'a sociable chap' he could 'play those games with anyone he might meet'. Gestures like this are well-meant, but one further fact renders them meaningless.

Death is followed by judgement. When the English novelist Barbara Cartland (1901–2000) was asked by *The Sunday Telegraph* whether she was afraid of dying, she replied, 'Not a bit. It will either be better than this life, or nothing at all, in which case there is no point in being frightened.'[452] We have already seen that science, the Bible's teaching and human instinct are all against the notion of 'nothing at all'. For Barbara Cartland, that left the exciting prospect of something 'better than this life'. Most people who think like this are banking on the idea that a God of love holds open house and that to get to heaven all anybody has to do is die. The hugely popular American comedian and actor Robin Williams, who committed suicide in August 2014 after struggling for much of his life with alcoholism, drug abuse and depression, had the same optimistic idea. He once said, 'Death is nature's way of saying, "Your table is ready."'[453]

In a 1925 essay Bertrand Russell offered another escape route: 'I believe that when I die I shall rot, and nothing of my ego will survive',[454] but this is another case of wishful thinking, and the Bible warns us against making this tragic mistake. It tells us, 'The eyes of the Lord are in every place, keeping watch on the evil and the good',[455] that he is 'the Judge of all the earth',[456] that 'it is appointed for man to die once, and after that comes judgement',[457] when 'each of us will give an account of himself to God'.[458] To press home the point that on that day there is no detail 'that will not be known and come to light',[459] Jesus warned that 'on the day of judgement people will give account for every careless word they speak'.[460] That warning is matched by the Bible's statement that as far as heaven is concerned, 'nothing unclean will ever enter it'.[461] God is certainly a God of love, but he is also a God of perfect justice, and we need to be aware of both. As an article in *Punch* put it, 'You can't just have the bits of God you like and leave out the stuff you're not so happy with.'[462]

We make much of the idea that 'justice should be done, and be seen to be done'—and we would want to press for it to be done if someone committed a crime against us. As God is 'righteous in all his ways'[463] what does our conscience tell us when we match our lives against his perfect law? We know that not one of us has kept that. As C. S. Lewis put it, 'People know the law of nature; they break it. These two facts are the foundation of all clear thinking about ourselves and about the universe we live in.'[464] This explains why the British-born Canadian theologian J. I. Packer is right to say, 'No man is entirely without inklings of judgement to come.'[465] The Bible makes it clear that God has revealed himself fully enough in creation to make anyone who rejects this 'without excuse.'[466] That being the case, a wise person will want to think very carefully about their likely fate when they appear before God, mankind's 'righteous judge.'[467]

Try as we might to avoid even thinking about it, death is inescapable. Julian Barnes says, 'You would buy shares in death, if they were available; you would bet on it, however poor the odds.'[468] It is also mysterious and threatening, a hideous invader robbing us of everything we possess, value or enjoy, wrenching us from our families and friends, and wrecking any plans or ambitions we might have for the future. This may be why Barnes says he thinks about death 'at least once each waking day'.[469] Only when we know how to die will we know how to live—but how can we do this? If only we could find one person in human history who faced severe pressures and problems and came through all of them unscathed, knew with absolute certainty why he was born and what the meaning of life is, then, best of all, took on our greatest enemy—death—and overcame this too, we would finally be on track to answer the question with which we started this book.

One man did.

Why are you here?

The Master

As we trawl through the only reliable record we have of his life, a lot of what we read could make some people think he is the last person who could show us that life has meaning, or explain what that meaning is.

He was born in some kind of outhouse about four days' travel from his family home, and soon afterwards had to be smuggled out of the country to escape a massacre of infants by a vicious king who already had the blood of several members of his own family on his hands. When he had returned safely he lived in a town with such a poor reputation that anyone giving it as their address when applying for a job might not even get an interview—we read of someone asking whether anything good could come from there.[470] We know next to nothing about what he said or did for many years after that, except for one incident when his family visited the country's capital city. In the massive crowds that were there for a special festival he got separated from his parents, who were 'in great distress'[471] until they found him three days later.

Unmarried, he left home when he was about thirty years old, and began travelling the country, fulfilling what he said was his life's mission. From then on he had no regular address, and 'nowhere to lay his head'.[472] Early on, he was challenged to prove that he had authority for the remarkable things he was saying and doing.[473] On one return visit to his home town, some people were so furious at him that they 'rose up and drove him out of the town',[474] threatening to throw him over a cliff.

As he travelled around he became the target for all kinds of criticism. He was accused of keeping bad company,[475] of being 'a glutton and a drunkard',[476] of encouraging a small group of followers to break long-established laws,[477] and of not keeping to social conventions.[478] He was charged with 'deceiving the people',[479] and critics said he was 'out of his mind'.[480] Some said he had 'an unclean spirit',[481] while others told him to his face that he was demon-possessed.[482] He so enraged certain people that time and again they hurled stones at him.[483]

The last year

In the last year of his life things became worse. There were times when even his closest followers could not understand what he was saying[484] and were 'utterly astounded'[485] at what he was doing. They began to question his teaching methods[486] and one of them 'took him aside and began to rebuke him.'[487] Many people 'took offence at him'[488] while others fed him trick questions in the hope of confusing him[489] or, even worse, getting him into trouble with the nation's intolerant rulers.[490] His strongest opposition came from the religious authorities, who could see that his teaching about the meaning of life and how it should be lived contradicted what they were saying and threatened to undermine their position. They had him in their sights for a long time and eventually got together with others and 'made plans to put him to death.'[491]

Partly because he attracted large crowds wherever he went, his enemies had been frustrated at every turn, but then got on to an inside track. One of his inner circle did a deal with them and agreed to betray him for a handful of silver coins[492] and at a chosen moment late one night he identified the target by faking a sign of affection.[493] After being arrested by an armed mob, the prisoner was forced to face two trials, the first before religious authorities (Jews) and the other before civil authorities (Romans). Both were held in three stages over a period of nine hours, beginning late at night, and the Jewish trial alone was illegal on several counts. To give just some examples, long-established law ruled that nobody could be arrested and charged based on information given by one of his followers; no arrest could be made at night or as the result of a bribe; trials could not be held during the Jewish feast of Passover; no trial could be held at night; the accused must be allowed legal or other representation; they must not be asked self-incriminating questions; and after hearing the evidence, members of the court must return home and consider it for at least one full day before giving their verdict. These rules were all swept aside in the prosecution's determination to see the prisoner convicted and punished as quickly as possible. Students of the case have pointed out so many illegalities in the religious trial that the Dutch scholar William Hendriksen (1900–1982) wrote, 'In the annals of jurisprudence no travesty of justice ever took place that was more shocking than this one.'[494]

In the course of the first trial, the prosecution team needed witnesses who would confirm that the prisoner deserved the death penalty, but they could find none, even though they persuaded some people to give perjured evidence.[495] Eventually two witnesses gave a garbled version of things the accused had said. The charge of blasphemy had been levelled at him several times in the previous three years;[496] now, his enemies decided to press for punishment. When the presiding officer asked what should be done to him, he was told, 'He deserves death.'[497] Some of those present then 'spit in his face and struck him.'[498]

Early the following morning the prosecutors met to plan their next move. They decided to send the prisoner for trial before the Roman governor, but as they knew the Romans had no interest in the country's religious laws, they switched the charge to treason. After a first hearing the governor announced, 'I find no guilt in him'[499] and decided to send him to the Romans' client king who happened to be in the city at the time. This mockery of a trial turned out to be a non-event, as the prisoner refused to say a word, and was sent back to the governor. He repeated his verdict of Not Guilty, but by now a crowd had been whipped up into a storm of hatred and demanded that he be executed by crucifixion.[500] This was the most humiliating and agonizing form of capital punishment then in use. It was forbidden under Jewish law and abolished by the Romans about 300 years later, but to avoid a riot, the governor, who had tried five times to have the prisoner released, finally caved in and agreed.[501] Literally wiping his hands of the case, he told the crowd, 'I am innocent of this man's blood.'[502] Soldiers then stripped the prisoner naked, spat on him, dressed him up to look like a king, kneeled before him in mock worship, and led him away to be executed in public.[503]

While the victim was hanging on a huge cross, pinned there by nails driven through his hands and feet, his persecutors 'scoffed at him',[504] while passers-by 'derided him'.[505] Three horrific hours later he died. The bodies of crucified criminals remained the property of the Romans, but that evening one of the victim's friends asked for the body and was given permission to remove it. He then placed it in a tomb (a cave cut out of a nearby rock face) which he had bought for his own burial, and closed the entrance to it with a great stone.[506]

In terms of the way we often judge people's importance or influence the victim ranked a long way down the list. There is no evidence that he had any formal education, let alone a university career. He never held public office, was never elected to serve on a committee, or to lead any social group of his peers. There is no record that he ever had a paid career, owned property or held a bank account. He seemed to be more or less penniless, even having to borrow a coin to give an illustration.[507] He never wrote a book, painted a picture, composed any poetry or music, raised an army or masterminded a revolution, and other than that early escape from a massacre, he never went outside his own tiny country.

If there was nothing else to go on, it would seem farcical to put this man forward, out of the sixty billion people in human history, as the only person who can tell us whether life has any meaning, or show us what that meaning is. All we have is the blood-stained corpse of someone who seems to have been a born loser. The American historian Kenneth Scott Latourette (1884–1968) wrote, 'So far as the casual spectator late on the afternoon of the execution could have seen, [his] work had ended in failure.'[508] But the story does not end there …

Day 3

The corpse was laid in the cave on a Friday evening; *on Sunday morning it was no longer there*. When friends went there early on that day to complete the embalming process they got the shock of their lives—the body had gone. Because the deceased had attracted so much attention over the previous three years, the Roman governor had ordered the stone closing the entrance to the cave to be secured with his official seal (breaking it would attract the death penalty). For added security he put a squad of soldiers in place to guard it.[509] Yet there is no record of anybody denying that by Sunday morning the body was no longer there. The English academic Sir Norman Anderson (1908–1994), one-time Director of the Institute of Advanced Legal Studies at the University of London, claimed, 'There was no point in arguing about the empty tomb. Everyone, friend and opponent, knew that it was empty. The only questions worth arguing about were why it was empty and what its emptiness proved.'[510] The Hungarian-born British scholar Géza Vermes (1924–2013), a world-famous authority on Jewish history, a Fellow of the British Academy, honoured by the United States House of Representatives in 2009 for 'inspiring and educating the world', agreed: 'In the end, when every argument has been considered and weighed, the only conclusion acceptable to the historian … must be that the women who set out to pay their last respects … found to their consternation, not a body, but an empty tomb.'[511]

A few weeks later an even greater bombshell hit the city—his followers took to the streets to announce that the man who had been persecuted, brutalized, executed and buried had come back to life and had met with them several times. His name was Jesus, often known as Jesus of Nazareth (to link him with his home town) and his resurrection from the dead is the historical heartbeat of the Christian faith. It is also crucially important in our search for the meaning to life.

It is not difficult to imagine that the social media of the time (rumour and gossip) went into overdrive over what may have happened. Bloggers would have had a field day, and there have been more conspiracy theories on the issue than surrounded the assassination of US President John F. Kennedy in 1963. I have written elsewhere about some of these[512] and will only summarize them here.

- *The body was removed by a person or persons unknown.* There is not a shred of evidence for this. Why would they? One can imagine thieves might do so if a rich man had been buried there, thinking that he may have had valuable items placed with him. Yet (as we will see in a moment) the grave-clothes were still there, so why would they steal the naked corpse of a penniless 'criminal'? As Sir Norman Anderson wryly put it, 'A Jew of that period could scarcely be suspected of stealing bodies on behalf of anatomical research.'[513] And how would they have overcome the armed guard?

- *The Roman authorities removed it.* They obviously had the opportunity, but what would be the point? When Jesus' followers began to claim that he was alive, all the Romans had to do was to open the tomb and produce the body. This would prove that the resurrection story was nonsense.

- *The Jewish authorities removed it.* In their case, there was a motive. They knew that Jesus had not only spoken of being rejected by them and eventually executed—but had also stunned everybody by saying that he would come back from the dead 'after three days'.[514] When his followers began to tell the crowds that he had done exactly as he prophesied, all the authorities had to do was keep the body safe *for four days*, then produce it. This would not only prove that Jesus had been a liar but that his followers were preaching nonsense. It would also have buried the

Christian church there and then. There is not a scrap of evidence that they did.

- *His followers stole the body*. This theory is even more far-fetched. Their friend's body was in the best possible place. It had not been thrown on a public rubbish dump, as the bodies of crucified criminals often were, but was safely in the burial place of someone who was not only one of their number, but 'a respected member of the Council'.[515] There is also the fact that they were terrified of being next in the authorities' firing line. When the death sentence had been carried out they were in no mood to launch a commando raid on the cave. Instead, they hid themselves behind locked doors 'for fear of the Jews'.[516] How could these frightened followers have plucked up the courage to tackle an armed Roman guard? Why is there no record that they did so?

- *When his followers went to embalm the body they went to the wrong tomb*. This is an imaginative idea, but it leaks like a sieve. The women who went to embalm the body were there when it was buried a few days earlier—they 'saw the tomb and how his body was laid'[517]—so they were unlikely to forget where it was. My wife's body lies in a grave surrounded by thousands of others, but there is never the risk that I will not be able to find it. At least five friends went to Jesus' tomb on that Sunday morning, and there may have been others who wanted to check it out. Are we to imagine these people dashing around in a frantic search for a tomb which not one of them could find? Even if that was the case, all they had to do was to ask the friend who owned the tomb. Was he also suffering from short-term memory loss?

- *Jesus never died*. This theory says that while hanging on the cross Jesus went into a coma and was still in this state when he was placed into the tomb. It took over 1,800 years for this idea to come to life, but it never gets to its feet. When the Roman governor was asked for permission to remove the body from the cross he asked the execution squad to make sure Jesus was dead. A soldier confirmed this, then to make absolutely sure he 'pierced his side with a spear, and at once there came out blood and water'.[518] This satisfied the governor (and should satisfy us) but if Jesus was merely comatose, in spite of all that he had gone through, why did none of the friends who carried him to the tomb notice that he was still breathing? If he was in a coma when placed in the tomb, how did he recover, wriggle his way out of the tightly-wound grave-clothes, push aside the great stone closing off the cave, break the governor's seal and overpower the security guards? One more thing: when his friends went to the tomb on the Sunday morning they 'saw the linen cloths lying there, and the face cloth, which had been on Jesus' head, not lying with the linen cloths but folded up in a place by itself'.[519] Assuming that he had managed to extricate himself from these wrappings, why would he leave them behind (taking the trouble to fold up the head covering neatly) before walking away when he had nothing else to wear? Of all the alternative theories trying to explain away the resurrection of Jesus, this is surely the most absurd?

Evidence

In some 2,000 years since Jesus was executed and buried, nobody has been able to show that the tomb was not empty, or explain *why* it was empty, unless he rose from the dead. There is powerful evidence that he did.

- *Hundreds of people claimed that they had seen him.* Six independent witnesses record eleven separate appearances in the course of forty days. These were not hallucinations; the distinguished English surgeon Arthur Rendle Short (1880–1953), described in *The Times* as 'a clear thinker, with quick perception',[520] said that the resurrection appearances 'break every known law of visions'.[521] Nor did Jesus' followers see a ghost, because they had talked with him,[522] touched him[523] and shared several meals with him.[524] On one occasion he appeared to over 500 people at the same time. When one follower wrote about this some time later, he said that most of these were 'still alive'.[525] This means that at the time of writing hundreds of people could have been asked to describe exactly what had happened.

- *His followers were transformed.* As we saw earlier, immediately after his death they were terrified of being persecuted, and hid behind locked doors, but after he had met with them and commissioned them to tell the world about him they fearlessly took to the streets. As a result, they were arrested, imprisoned and tortured, but nothing could stop them. When their leaders were executed, others immediately took their places. Why do this if they knew they were lying, and the body of Jesus was rotting away somewhere? The American philosopher Peter Kreeft makes the point well: 'Liars always lie for selfish reasons. If they lied, what was their motive, what did they get out of it? What they got out of it was misunderstanding, rejection, persecution, torture and martyrdom. Hardly a list of perks!'[526] Meeting with Jesus after his resurrection changed these men from frightened rabbits to roaring lions. Men are sometimes willing to suffer and die for something they believe to be true, *but never for something they know to be false.* If Jesus' followers had made up the story, they could have come up with the idea of a spiritual resurrection, but as Ravi Zacharias says, 'Instead, they went the hard way by talking about the resurrection of the actual physical body, which, if not true, was an enormous risk to take should the body have ever been detected.'[527] Sir Norman Anderson said that defeated cowards turning into men that no persecution could silence is 'a psychological absurdity'.[528]

Two particular believers make the evidence even more impressive. One was a man called Peter, who was one of Jesus' inner circle of friends. When Jesus was on trial, and someone accused Peter of being one his followers, he denied three times that he had ever had anything to do with him.[529] Yet after the resurrection Peter became a leading spokesman for those first believers, refusing to back down even when the authorities threatened to kill him.[530] Tradition says that he was eventually sentenced to death by crucifixion, and that he asked to be crucified upside down, as he did not count himself worthy of being executed in exactly the same way as Jesus. Does this sound like the man who knew that the resurrection was a lie that he and others had concocted?

The other was a man called Saul, a passionate Jew who set out to destroy the Christian church, seeing it as a direct threat to the nation's traditional religion. We find him 'breathing threats and murder'[531] against its members, persecuting them with what he himself called 'raging fury',[532] and endorsing the decision to stone one of them to death.[533] Yet some time later, under his adopted name of Paul, the church's greatest persecutor became its greatest preacher. He put the dynamic change in his life (which according to tradition was also to end in execution) down to something that happened long after the headline-grabbing event of Jesus' resurrection: 'he appeared also to me.'[534] Sir Norman Anderson went so far as to say that the transformed lives of those early believers was 'far and away the strongest circumstantial evidence for the resurrection'.[535]

- *The Christian church came into existence.* Those few first believers were the founders of what has since become the largest religious body the world has ever known. In spite of greater opposition, more persecution, and more martyrs than any other grouping in history it has continued to grow for 2,000 years and today has billions of members living in every country in the world—and it all began with the resurrection of Jesus. Kenneth Scott Latourette claimed that but for this 'the death of Jesus, and even Jesus himself, would probably have been all but forgotten'.[536] If that were the case, the Christian church would not exist today.

Over the centuries the Christian church has rightly been criticized for some of the appalling things done in its name, but these have never reflected the character or the teaching of Jesus, its founder. Forged currency gives us no reason for rejecting the real thing. On the other hand, the Christian church has a matchless record of things it has done to benefit humanity. No revolution in history can compare with the one produced by the resurrection of Jesus from the dead. The Christian church has been the greatest force for good the world has ever known. Its influence in the field of education, in meeting the needs of the sick, the disadvantaged, the homeless, widows and orphans, and the victims of war, violence and 'man's inhumanity to man' is without parallel.

Sceptics have tried for 2,000 years to airbrush the resurrection from history, but they have been unable to do so, and leading experts in the field of evidence have had no hesitation in confirming its truth. The American lawyer and jurist Simon Greenleaf (1783–1853), one of the principal founders of Harvard Law School, once set out to disprove the resurrection, but eventually became convinced that those first believers were right: 'It was … impossible that they could have persisted in affirming the truths they have narrated, had not Jesus actually risen from the dead, and had they not known this fact as certainly as they knew any other fact.'[537] The American-born British lawyer and politician John Singleton Copley (1772–1863), who became the 1st Baron Lyndhurst, was one of the greatest minds in British legal history, and was three times Lord High Chancellor of Great Britain. In a document found among his private papers after his death he delivered this powerful verdict: 'I know pretty well what evidence is; and I tell you, such evidence as that for the resurrection has never broken down yet.'[538] Sir Lionel Luckhoo (1914–1997) the Guyana-born politician, diplomat and lawyer, once listed in *The Guinness Book of Records* as the world's most successful lawyer, was equally certain: 'I say unequivocally the evidence for the resurrection of Jesus Christ is so overwhelming that it compels acceptance by proof which leaves no room for doubt.'[539] No wonder Vaughan Roberts says, 'As I examined the evidence for the resurrection for the first time, I came to see that it was far easier to believe that Jesus had risen than to believe the alternatives—it is amazing what you have to believe to not believe.'[540]

Speaking at the University of Cape Town, South Africa, I had a long conversation with a committed atheist. Called away to fulfil another engagement, I asked him a final question: 'What do you think of Jesus Christ?' I have never forgotten his reply: 'I'm not sure, but I do know that everything depends on whether or not he rose from the dead.' He was dead right! It is said that the last words of the distinguished American historian Jaroslav Pelikan (1923–2006) were, 'If Christ is risen, nothing else matters—and if Christ is not risen, nothing else matters.' He was also right, as we are about to see.

Identity

Jesus is the most controversial person in history. All his recorded words and actions have been analysed and interpreted (or misinterpreted) and debated by countless experts and others over the centuries. Yet the most controversial issue about him is not what he taught, but who he is, not his ideas, but his identity. One Bible statement centred on the resurrection says three important things about this: it says that he 'was promised beforehand', was 'descended from David according to the flesh and was declared to be the Son of God in power ... by his resurrection from the dead'.[541]

- The statement that 'he was promised beforehand' refers to prophecies recorded in the Old Testament and made hundreds of years before he was born. Central to these was the promise that God would one day break into history by sending someone—a Messiah—who would meet man's deepest spiritual need. When Jesus read one of these prophecies in his local place of worship he followed it by saying, 'Today this Scripture has been fulfilled in your hearing'.[542] It was an astonishing claim to make—but here were facts to back it up. In the life of Jesus some 300 Old Testament prophecies were fulfilled and these were recorded by at least a dozen writers over a 350 year period, the latest of which was at least 400 years *before* he was born. These included his birth, his character, his teaching and his power. Even more remarkably, twenty-nine of them were fulfilled in the twenty-four hours leading up to his death. These included saying that he would be deserted by his followers,[543] wrongly accused,[544] ill-treated,[545] executed with criminals,[546] and crucified,[547] a form of execution never carried out by the Jews. It was also prophesied that he would not retaliate when he was bullied and tortured,[548] that he would pray for his executioners,[549] that his body would be pierced,[550] and that as he was being executed people would gamble for his clothing.[551] Every one of these prophecies was fulfilled to the letter. One man fulfilling 300 prophecies made at least 400 years before he was born demands an explanation. So does the fact that Jesus is identified as 'Christ' (the New

Testament word for 'Messiah') about 600 times in the New Testament.

- The statement that he was 'descended from David according to the flesh' establishes that he was truly human, and not an android, a hybrid, or some kind of alien life form that landed on earth from outer space. The David concerned was the second king of Judah and Israel, and the Old Testament prophets declared that the Messiah would be a Jew from the tribe of Judah, and from a family line in which David would be a key figure (Jesus is called 'son of David' fourteen times in the New Testament). This would exclude almost the entire human race. Amazingly, the Old Testament narrowed it down even further and also prophesied that the Messiah would be born in the Judean town of 'Bethlehem Ephrathah'.[552] There were two Bethlehems, one in Judea, the other seventy miles away in Zebulon. The New Testament confirms that the prophecy was precisely fulfilled: 'Jesus was born in Bethlehem of Judea'.[553]

His mother's name was Mary, and we can follow his development as a 'baby',[554] a 'child'[555] and a 'boy'.[556] As an adult he got tired,[557] 'hungry'[558] and thirsty.[559] He not only 'rejoiced',[560] but knew what it was to be 'very sorrowful'.[561] Temptation is one of the obvious marks of being human, and Jesus was 'tempted as we are'.[562] These facts show that he was truly human, and Jesus underlined his humanity by calling himself 'Son of man' about eighty times.

- The statement that he was 'declared to be the Son of God in power … by his resurrection from the dead' takes us an important step further. He did not become the Son of God at his resurrection, nor even at his conception. He was the Son of God *before* he stepped into human history and became the son of his human mother Mary.[563] Although he had a birth, he had no beginning. Instead, as he told a religious leader, he 'descended from heaven'.[564] He was miraculously conceived in the womb of a virgin—but could this not have been a unique case of parthenogenesis (in which embryos or seeds develop in the womb without fertilization of the male of the species)? There is a very simple answer to the question. In the genetic make-up of human beings, the male has 'x' and 'y' chromosomes, and the female has 'x' and 'x'. This means that if Mary's conception had been a one-in-sixty-billion event in human history, there would have been no 'y' chromosome involved, and the baby would have been female. When the American television and radio host Larry King, was asked who in all of history he would most like to interview he replied, 'Jesus Christ'. When asked, 'And what would you like to ask him?', King replied, 'I would like to ask him if he was indeed virgin-born. The answer to that question would define history for me.'[565] The Bible gives us the answer to King's question. It tells us the birth of Jesus fulfilled a prophecy that 'the virgin shall conceive and bear a son.'[566] Even before Jesus was born, his mother was told by an angel that 'the child to be born will be called holy—the Son of God.'[567] Jesus is called 'Son of God' about fifty times in the New Testament and had no hesitation in claiming the title.[568]

In the musical *Jesus Christ Superstar,* the actress playing Mary Magdalene sings of Jesus, 'He's a man, he's just a man', but this is at best a half-truth. Jesus was not only a man, he was also God in human flesh and form. In John Lennox's great phrase, 'God coded himself into humanity.'[569] He was not mainly God and partly man, nor was he mainly man and partly God. Instead, he was both fully God and fully man, as fully human as if he was not divine, yet as fully divine as if he was not human. As J. I. Packer puts it, 'Here are two mysteries for the price of one—the plurality of persons within the unity of God, and the union of Godhead and manhood in the person of Jesus ... the Almighty appeared on earth as a helpless human baby, unable to do more than lie and stare and wriggle and make noises, needing to be fed and changed and taught to talk like any other child. And there was no illusion or deception in this: the babyhood of the Son of God was a reality. The more you think about it, the more staggering it gets.'[570] In one of the Bible's clearest statements about Jesus we are told that 'in him the whole fullness of deity dwells bodily'.[571]

Time and again Jesus made statements to underline the fact that he was divine. His close friends were not philosophers or theologians, but down-to-earth working men for whom seeing was believing, but when one of them said to him, 'Show us the Father, [that is, God] and it is enough for us', Jesus replied, 'Have I been with you so long, and you still do not know me, Philip? Whoever has seen me has seen the Father.'[572] As the English author John Marsh says, 'The surprising thing is not that Jesus talked about God, or even that he talked about him as much as he did, but rather the way he talked about him, and in particular the way in which he talked about his relationship with him.'[573] When people asked him to describe his relationship to God, Jesus had no hesitation in replying, 'I and the Father are one.'[574] Two thousand years after the event sceptics question whether Jesus really meant that he was claiming to be divine, but his enemies, who were up close and personal at the time, had no doubt as to what he meant. They immediately 'picked up stones ... to stone him' for blasphemy, 'because you, being a man, make yourself God.'[575] C. S. Lewis put it perfectly when he said, 'God has landed on this enemy-occupied planet in human form',[576] and the American astronaut Jim Irwin (1930–1991), the lunar module pilot on the successful Apollo 15 mission, was not exaggerating when he said, 'Jesus walking on the earth is more important than man walking on the moon.'[577]

Indications

His resurrection from the dead was the most dramatic proof in
the New Testament that Jesus is both God and man, but there are
others. The quality of his life speaks volumes. Although he was
'tempted as we are' he was absolutely faultless. He was 'without
sin';[578] he 'knew no sin';[579] he was 'without blemish or spot';[580] he
was 'holy, innocent, unstained, separated from sinners'.[581] When
Jesus asked his opponents, 'Which one of you convicts me of
sin?'[582] there were no takers—and there are still none today. The
man who betrayed him admitted, 'I have sinned by betraying
innocent blood'[583] and even the way he died was so impressive
that the soldier in charge of the execution cried out, 'Certainly this
man was innocent.'[584] He was not only the finest; he was flawless,
a perfect role model of integrity, goodness, kindness, sympathy,
purity, patience and love. As the English preacher and author
Michael Green puts it, 'The life of Jesus ... is so superb, and yet so
unexpected, that no person could have made it up.'[585]

Many of his actions clearly pointed to his deity. One of the New
Testament writers claimed that if all the things Jesus did were
recorded 'I suppose that the world itself could not contain the
books that would be written.'[586] We need not take that literally to
know why he said it. It has been suggested that Jesus performed
more miracles in one day than occurred in all the centuries covered
by the Old Testament—and that might be the case. We read of him
calming a storm that threatened to drown his followers,[587] feeding
over 5,000 people with five loaves and two fish,[588] healing people of
'every disease and every affliction',[589] including the blind, the deaf,
the dumb, the lame, the leprous and the paralyzed. He cast out evil
spirits and healed 'all who were oppressed by the devil'.[590] He even
demonstrated his power over death by bringing at least three dead
people back to life, including a man who had been buried four days
earlier.[591]

Another thing he did marks him out as being both God and man; he forgave the sins of people he had never met before and who had not sinned against him personally.[592] If Jesus was merely a man, how could he do that? If a stranger told me of a sin or crime he had committed, I would have no right to forgive him and assure him that the slate was wiped clean. C. S. Lewis makes the point perfectly: 'We can all understand how a man forgives offences against himself. You tread on my toe and I forgive you, you steal my money and I forgive you. But what should we make of a man, himself unrobbed and untrodden on, who announced that he forgave you for treading on other men's toes and stealing other men's money? ... Yet this is what Jesus did. He told people that their sins were forgiven, and never waited to consult all the other people whom their sins had undoubtedly injured. He unhesitatingly behaved as if he was the party chiefly concerned, the person chiefly offended in all offences. This makes sense only if he really was the God whose laws are broken and whose love is wounded in every sin. In the mouth of any speaker who is not God, these words would imply what I can only regard as a silliness and conceit unrivalled by any other character in history.'[593] Those listening to Jesus understood this: 'Why does this man speak like that? He is blaspheming! Who can forgive sins but God alone?'[594] They knew perfectly well that all sin is against God, and only he can remove the guilt and pardon the sinner. They failed to see that Jesus had every right to do so.

The French artist, illustrator and sculptor Paul Gustave Doré (1832–1883) once lost his passport while travelling. At the next international border he explained his problem to an immigration official and assured him that he was who he claimed to be. The official handed him a piece of paper and a pencil and said, 'Prove it!' Doré quickly produced such a brilliant sketch that the official had all the evidence he needed. The things Jesus did point powerfully to his identity.

Implications

Everything we have seen in this chapter points to some important implications as far as our search for the meaning of life is concerned, and these are pinned to the fact that Jesus knew exactly why he came into the world.

He came to show us what God is like. The Bible tells us that 'God is light, and in him is no darkness at all'[595] and Jesus said, 'I am the light of the world.'[596] It is difficult to miss the connection. We saw in Chapter 6 that 'God is spirit,'[597] which explains why 'no one has ever seen God', yet in the same sentence we are told that Jesus 'has made him known.'[598] We are able to see 'the light of the knowledge of the glory of God in the face of Jesus Christ.'[599] Jesus is eternally God, and remained fully divine throughout his earthly life, yet he was also truly and completely human. God is not cosmic dust or atmospheric energy, but is personal, as we can tell from his actions.[600] The American scholar Peter C. Moore goes so far as to say, 'The ultimate fact about the universe is a personal God.'[601] In Jesus we see a human illustration of God's character.

He came to do God's will and so fulfil his purposes. He told people, 'I have come down from heaven, not to do my own will but the will of him who sent me,'[602] and in the next two chapters we will focus on exactly what this was. On another occasion he taught his followers, 'My food is to do the will of him who sent me and to accomplish his work.'[603] As human beings, food is not an optional extra, but something that sustains the very fabric of our lives. Jesus ate and drank, just as we do, but his entire life was consciously committed to one thing—doing his Father's will. Everything he did was aimed at fulfilling God's purpose for his earthly life, and he did this so perfectly that he had no hesitation in saying, 'I always do the things that are pleasing to him.'[604]

He came on a rescue mission. He made this clear by saying that he came into the world 'to seek and to save the lost.'[605] We often decide on what we would like to do with our lives when we see the kinds of things that interest us, or find skills we would like to develop. This can give us a sense of purpose in life, and some might even say they have found their life's mission. Yet the Bible says that in our endless search for life's real meaning 'we grope like those who have no eyes.'[606] By contrast, Jesus' mission in life was known 'before the foundation of the world.'[607] In the Bible, Jesus says that the person who 'walks in darkness does not know where he is going',[608] and claims, 'Whoever follows me will not walk in darkness, but will have the light of life.'[609]

One of the clearest statements about why Jesus came says, 'The Father has sent his Son to be the Saviour of the world.'[610] But how?—and why?—and to save us from what?

Why are you here?

The answer

A few years before he died in Tahiti in 1903, the French artist Paul Gauguin (1848–1903) painted a vast canvas that has been called his last testament, a statement of what he saw life to be. The picture is divided into three parts, which Gauguin said should be 'read' from right to left. On the right we see a baby and three young women; in the centre are several people, some animals and an idol; and on the left are two figures, one of them an old lady preparing to die. In the top left hand corner Gauguin wrote three French phrases—*D'où Venons Nous?; Que Sommes Nous?; Où Allons Nous*? In English they read as follows: 'Where do we come from? What are we? Where are we going?' There is no evidence that Gauguin found answers to any of his questions. Soon after he had finished the painting he tried to commit suicide, but lived for another five years, then died in agony, his body weakened by alcohol and syphilis.

The only answers that atheism can offer to Gauguin's questions are 'Nowhere', 'Nothing' and 'Nowhere', but these leave no possibility of finding any meaning to life. That being the case, John Lennox is right to ask another question: 'Might it not be wise then to ask exactly where the atheist bus is headed before jumping on board?'[611] Throughout this book we have seen that ruling God out without examining the evidence is not only dishonest but destructive. As we continue to look for the real answer to the question about the meaning of life it will help to recall what we have discovered so far.

Recap

After reviewing Stephen Hawking's approach to the issue, we began by seeing that the universe in which we live provides us with a cosmic clue that life on planet Earth is not accidental or haphazard. The Scottish biologist Donald Bruce says that as a teenager it made no sense to him to think that he had any significance in a universe that either had no purpose or a cause that was purely impersonal. He goes on, 'I reasoned that everything about me that I am, all that I had ever done or might do in life, everything I felt, enjoyed, feared, hoped, every relationship I ever had, anything to which I attach meaning—all these were utterly insignificant in the cosmos … Nothing would even register that I had existed.'[612]

Ravi Zacharias easily dismisses the idea that the laws of nature are responsible for all that we see: 'Suppose I took a trip to a distant planet and saw a crumpled piece of paper on which were written the words, "Hello, Ravi, did you bring some curry and rice with you?" I would not in a million years conclude that this note was produced by the laws of physics.'[613] The laws of physics can neither create anything, nor can they cause anything to happen; they simply describe what normally happens given certain conditions. We showed that the universe is neither eternal nor self-created, and that the more we discover about it the more it seems fine-tuned for the existence of intelligent life on our planet, with a precision that defies human understanding or imagination. Its amazing features demand an explanation; its creation by an eternal, all-powerful, intelligent designer is the only theory that fits the facts. We saw earlier that as Copernicus pursued his studies in astronomy, he became convinced of this, and wrote that the universe 'has been built for us by the best and most orderly workman of all'.[614]

We all owe a massive and growing debt to science for revolutionizing our lives, yet we saw that it could take us only so far. It is unable to tell us why the universe came into being, why the laws of nature exist, why it is so amazingly fine-tuned to support intelligent life on our planet, why we exist, and why we are persons and not merely physical objects. It can say nothing about our origin or destiny. It can make no comment about love, justice, freedom, beauty, joy or peace, nor can it make a distinction between right and wrong. It can say nothing about the existence or non-existence of God, and is unable to answer the one question this book asks: does life have any meaning? As Charles Moore wrote in *The Daily Telegraph* in 2014, 'It can have nothing to say about something that lies outside its realm.'[615]

For about 150 years one theory as to how we came to be here has outplayed all the others—the idea that over millions of years we evolved by a process of unguided, unplanned evolution, beginning when the first spark of life mysteriously appeared in non-living chemicals floating around in some kind of primordial 'soup'. Yet the American computer scientist Scott Huse is right to point out that the theory falls at the first hurdle, as the imagined leap from dead matter to life is 'a transition of truly fanciful dimension'.[616] Richard Dawkins desperately tries to bridge the gap between inanimate matter and living things, but as Kathleen Jones says, 'he cannot do more than to imagine that crystals have feelings'.[617] It is impossible to jump from molecules to meaning. Evolutionism has no explanation for humanity, nor can it say anything about truth, goodness, or the many aspects that mark us out from other species. After all, we are more than monkeys with clothes.

Relying on evolution to give a sense of meaning is pointless and illogical, as it says that our senses have no intelligent origin, so that any thoughts we have or conclusions we reach are controlled by forces that have no purpose and are not tied in to truth. Carried to its logical conclusion, the theory of evolution also robs us of any value or dignity and provides no explanation for the compassion, care and concern shown by human beings the world over for those in need. As the English preacher and author John Stott (1921–2011) asked, 'If the unimpeded progress of evolution were our chief concern, why should we care for the senile, the imbecile, the hardened criminal, the psychopath, the chronically sick, or the starving? Would it not be more prudent to put them to sleep like a well-loved dog, lest they hinder the evolutionary process?'[618]

We took some time to show that neither health, wealth, possessions, power, prestige nor pleasure contributed anything to the meaning of life, which is a far deeper issue than any of these. We heard testimonies from those who had reached heights of achievement that left the rest of humanity trailing far behind, yet who found their inner lives empty and meaningless. In a letter to a friend, the Swiss psychiatrist and psychotherapist Carl Gustav Jung (1875–1961) pinpointed the reason for this: 'Men cut themselves from the root of their being, from God, and then life turns empty, inane, meaningless, without purpose, so when God goes, goal goes, when goal goes, meaning goes, when meaning goes, value goes, and life turns empty in our hands.'[619] Ravi Zacharias writes of 'a slide into emptiness' and adds, 'I think particularly of our present generation, which enjoys more sophisticated toys than ever before, yet each toy has a shorter thrill-span than the previous one.'[620] Elsewhere, he says, 'It is not surprising that *boredom* is a very modern word, with no counterpart in the ancient or medieval languages.'[621]

We took two chapters to pinpoint seven things that mark us out from every other species and that give us reasons for believing that our lives must have meaning. Our physical make-up alone is a powerful pointer. The American statistician George Gallup (1901–1984), who pioneered survey sampling, went so far as to say, 'I could prove God statistically. Take the human body alone; the chance that all the functions of the individual would just happen is a statistical monstrosity.'[622] We are not only conscious, but self-conscious; we have a sense of our unique dignity. Francis Schaeffer claimed, 'If anything is a gift from God, this is—knowing who you are.'[623] We are *homo sapiens*, rational beings with vastly superior intelligence to any other. Our aesthetic instincts are so deep and fundamental that the Dutch scholar H. R. Rookmaaker (1922–1977) claimed, 'Our being cannot be satisfied unless the thirst for beauty is quenched.'[624] These five factors alone do more than hint that our lives have meaning; two others point even more strongly in the same direction.

The first is that we have a moral dimension. Even though we often try to ignore the fact, our consciences repeatedly remind us that we are subject to a moral law which we ought to obey. Kathleen Jones wrote, 'The whole of human life is concerned with morality, with the battle between our selfish instincts and our consciences.'[625] As the English philosopher, author and art critic William Hazlitt (1778–1830) neatly put it, 'Man is the only animal that laughs and weeps, for he is the only animal that knows the difference between what things are and what they ought to be.'[626]

The second is that we are unique in having a spiritual dimension. The English historian Richard Cavendish says, 'Religion is one of the things which distinguish man from other animals. Apes and dolphins, as far as we know, have no religions, but no group of human beings has ever been discovered which did not have religious beliefs.'[627] Some people assume that religion is past its sell-by date and that we are now moving into an era in which it will finally breathe its last. It may even surprise them to hear credible testimonies of life-changing faith. As the English scholar Jonathan Sacks says in *The Persistence of Faith*, 'For some reason, religious conviction in the modern world produces in us a mixture of surprise, fascination and fright, as if a dinosaur had lumbered into life and stumbled uninvited into a cocktail party.'[628] Yet the 'dinosaur' has never gone away. As Melanie Phillips writes, 'The secular society is a modern myth. The authorized version [she means the majority view in certain circles] holds that religion is doomed by the rise and spread of modernity. We are all now enlightened, rational beings who have no truck with the supernatural. *In fact, the evidence is to the contrary* ... the receding tide is washing away not spirituality, but organized religion. There's a difference.'(Emphasis added).[629] In the twentieth century alone millions of people were tortured, imprisoned or killed because of their Christian faith, but in his 2013 book *Atheists: The Origin of the Species*, the English author Nick Spencer reports one Soviet persecutor of Christianity as confessing, 'Religion is like a nail, the harder you hit, the deeper it goes in.'[630]

We then demonstrated that our plans and ambitions for life, and our thoughts and theories about whether life had any meaning, were framed by the fact that death will put an end to them all. The whole world is a hospital, and every person in it is a terminal patient; as soon as a baby begins to live it begins to die. Finally, we saw that in his birth, life and resurrection from the dead, one man—Jesus of Nazareth—pointed the way to discovering the true meaning of life. In this chapter we will see that he went further than that—he provided it.

Worldviews

A person's hope of finding whether life has any meaning depends entirely on their worldview—and everybody has one. Philosophers like to use the German word for it—*weltanschauung*—but in plain English a worldview is how a person views the world. If you wear a pair of blue-tinted spectacles or sunglasses everything you see will be affected by that colour, and similarly any other tint will affect what you see in the same way. Your worldview is what you 'put on' (that is, assume to be true) *before you look at anything*, whether it be the universe or your place in it, the natural world or your relationship to it, life as a whole, death or anything else. Your worldview is the position you take before you take a position on anything else—and it specifically affects the question as to whether life has any meaning or purpose

In Chapter 5 we looked briefly at the Bible's teaching on the subject through the writings of Solomon, and we need to take a closer look at this before we go any further. We concentrated on what he had to say about one particular worldview, that which saw life as 'under the sun', a phrase he used twenty-nine times and which means one that is purely self-centred and without reference to God. Although he had used his mind-boggling wealth to soak himself in all the earthly pleasures he could lay his hands on, this left him dissatisfied and disillusioned and he came to the conclusion that life 'under the sun' was pointless and meaningless. Without God at the centre of his thinking, nothing made sense.

The American author Teresa Turner Vining gives us a vivid modern example of life 'under the sun'. She tells of the time when, as a university student, the relentlessly atheistic worldviews of her professors were adding to a troubling doubt about her faith in God: what if it was all a lie? She records what happened when she returned to her apartment one day: 'Lying in bed surrounded by darkness, I tried to grasp the significance of it all. There is no God, I told myself. This life is all there is. No one really knows why we are here or how we got here. There is nothing more than self-centred, imperfect humanity in which to hope. There is no real meaning, no basis for knowing what is right and wrong. It doesn't matter what we do or how we live. There is no foundation, no right and wrong, no hope. *No!* something deep inside of me screamed. It could not be true. I couldn't believe that life was just a sick joke with humans and their capacity for love, appreciation of beauty, and need for meaning as the pitiful punch line. That went against all my experience as a human being. There had to be something more! ... Something deep inside me seemed to testify that somehow "good" is better than "bad" and "love" is better than "hate," and that meant we must be something more than just a sum of atoms.'[631]

Searching for a meaning to life while living 'under the sun', in other words seeing things from a purely human standpoint and without God at the centre of one's thinking, is not even like looking for a needle in a haystack, as there is no haystack. If we were not created by God, and are just biological accidents cobbled together with bits of our ancestors, why should anything we do have any more meaning or significance than the activities of a mouse or a worm? If we were born without purpose and are on our way to annihilation we can abandon any idea of life having ultimate meaning, and nothing we accumulate or pour into it will leave it anything other than empty and pointless. Woody Allen says that in a search for meaning we create a fake world, yet this too is 'a world that, in fact, means nothing at all when you step back. It's meaningless.'[632]

Yet Solomon's purpose in writing about the futility of life 'under the sun' was not to depress his readers. He encouraged them to enjoy life. He specifically mentioned the pleasures of food and drink, work, learning, marriage and home life. They were to realize that everything good in life is something 'God has given';[633] it is 'from the hand of God'[634] and 'God's gift to man.'[635] He wanted them to understand that life without God was utterly pointless, but also to see the big picture, which is that life on earth is not only 'under the sun' but 'under heaven'.[636] His readers now include you and me, and we should look at life using a wide-angle lens, giving us a worldview that puts God at the centre of the picture. Solomon put things in the right order when he wrote, 'God is in heaven and you are on earth.'[637] The American author Jay Wegter is exactly right when he says, 'Who God is and what he has said infallibly determines what is real, what is true and what is wrong.'[638]

This brings us right to the heart of what this book is all about. *CBBC* (a shortened version of its original name *Children's BBC*) is a digital channel for 6–12-year-old children that broadcasts twelve hours a day in the United Kingdom and has a hugely popular interactive website. Its strapline, carefully chosen to keep its viewers engaged, is 'It's all about you.' This may be an effective way of making children feel they are what makes *CBBC* tick, but it is the wrong starting-place in trying to find the answer to the question this book is asking. The same could be said of businesses that claim to 'put customers first'. To put it as simply as possible, *the meaning of your life is not about you!* As Michael Green says, 'If you want to know who you are, you have to start at the beginning. That means starting with God, the living, personal source of all there is.'[639] Vaughan Roberts tells about attending a concert of modern classical music at The Royal Albert Hall, in London. The music was way over his head and at one point he fell asleep, then was suddenly awakened by loud applause. Roberts then goes on, 'As the cheering continued the conductor beckoned to the wings for the composer to come on and take a bow. The triangle player, who had a very minor role in the piece, was sitting between the conductor and the composer's seat and thought that he was being invited to take the applause. He looked a bit confused but none the less stood and bowed. At that very moment the composer appeared on stage behind him and began to walk to the centre. The poor triangle player realized what had happened and sat down again with a very red face.'[640] As Roberts goes on to explain, the unfortunate triangle player made an innocent mistake, but most people remove God from his rightful place by choice. We can assume that when the wife of the English journalist and media personality Sir David Frost (1939–2013) was asked by a reporter whether he was religious, she had her tongue firmly in her cheek when she replied, 'Yes, he thinks he is God!'[641] On the other hand, Jean-Paul Sartre was being deadly serious when he went so far as to say, 'Man is the being whose project it is to be God.'[642] The Turkish philosopher and theologian Gregory of Nazianzus (c. 329–c. 390) took a very different line and pointed in the right direction when he wrote that 'the very best order of … every speech and action is to begin from God and to end in God'.[643] We were created *by* God and *for* God, and we will never have life in its right perspective until we grasp this.

Many people living 'under the sun' today may never have heard of the Greek philosopher Protagoras (490–420 BC), but he coined the phrase 'Man is the measure of all things,' now a central plank in secular humanism, which excludes God from its thinking and interprets life solely in terms of time and space here and now. Humanism says that our thinking about life—including its origin, relevance and destiny—should centre on us, and that we have the right to make all the judgements that need to be made about it. Protagoras has a lot to answer for!

The Bible points us in the opposite direction. Its worldview has God not only as the creator and sustainer of the universe, but as the one who sets out the purposes for which it was made and who establishes its values and meaning. It tells us, 'Seek the things that are above';[644] 'Set your minds on things that are above, not on things that are on the earth.'[645] It also gives us the best possible reason for having this kind of mind-set: 'For the things that are seen are transient, but the things that are unseen are eternal.'[646] This is what C. S. Lewis had in mind when he wrote, 'All that is not eternal is eternally out of date' and went on to say that when our worldview is God-centred 'our priorities completely change. No longer is life about what is satisfying here and now'.[647] The only worldview that can point us to life having any purpose and meaning is one that has God at its centre, not one that cobbles together our own likes and dislikes, views and opinions, hopes and fears, pursuits and pleasures, possessions and positions, then assumes that they somehow give life meaning. Nothing we have or do can fill the God-shaped gap in our lives. Health, wealth, work, pleasure or success may take our minds off it for a while, but they are no more than low-dose painkillers, and in the depths of our hearts we know that they do nothing to meet our greatest need.

At this point, countless people ask 'Where is God when things go wrong?' If God is an all-powerful and all-loving Creator in complete control of the universe, why does he allow so much evil, pain and sorrow? I have written about this elsewhere, examining how it plays out 'under the sun' and otherwise,[648] and atheism's reply to the question could not be more bleak. To quote Richard Dawkins, 'In a universe of blind, physical forces and genetic replication, some people are going to get hurt, some other people are going to get lucky, and you won't find any rhyme or reason in it, nor any justice. The universe we observe has precisely the properties we should expect if there is, at bottom, no design, no evil and no good, nothing but blind, pitiless indifference.'[649] Elsewhere, he rams home his miserable mantra: 'There is no special reason to ask, "Why do bad things happen?" Or, for that matter, "Why do good things happen?" The real question underlying both is the more general question: "Why does *anything* happen?" ... The universe has no mind, no feelings and no personality; so it doesn't do things in order to either hurt or please you. Bad things happen because things happen ... Unfortunately, the universe doesn't care what people prefer.'[650] As we are about to see, God has done everything possible to rescue us from the disastrous consequences of having this worldview. Lord Hailsham (1907–2001), one-time Lord High Chancellor of Great Britain put it like this:

'You do not get out of your philosophical troubles arising out of the fact of evil by rejecting God. For, as I have tried to point out before, the real problem is not the problem of evil, but the problem of good, not the problem of cruelty and selfishness, but the problem of kindness and generosity, not the problem of ugliness, but the problem of beauty. If the world is really the hopeless and meaningless jumble which one has to believe it to be, if once we reject our value judgements as nothing more than emotional noises, with nothing more in the way of objective truth than a certain biological survival value for the species rather than the individual, evil then presents no difficulty because it does not exist. We must expect to be knocked about a bit in a world which consists only of atoms, molecules and strange particles. But how, then, does it come about that we go through life on assumptions which are perfectly contrary to the facts, that we love our wives and families, thrill with pleasure at the sight of a little bird discreetly dressed in green and black and white, that we rage at injustice inflicted on innocent victims, honour our martyrs, reward our heroes, and even occasionally, with difficulty, forgive our enemies and do good to those who persecute us and despitefully use us? No, it is light which is the problem, not darkness. It is seeing, not blindness ... It is love, not callousness. The thing we have to explain in the world is the positive, not the negative. *It is this which led me to God in the first place*.[651] (emphasis added).

God steps in

As we saw in an earlier chapter, God created man 'in his own image'.[652] Elsewhere, the Bible tells us that man was 'created after the likeness of God in true righteousness and holiness'.[653] Our first parents not only had the right worldview, with God at the centre of their thinking, they were also obedient to all that God required of them, and as a result enjoyed a perfect relationship with him, with each other, and with all of nature. Then at some point things went disastrously wrong: 'Sin came into the world through one man, and death through sin'.[654] From the moment of Adam's calamitous disobedience, man's innocence and free will were lost, his nature was corrupted, and his worldview was skewed, becoming self-centred instead of God-centred. He rejected God's authority and believed he could determine right and wrong for himself.

What is more, Adam's children, and those of every generation since, inherited this fallen nature. This is why the Bible speaks so clearly about what is sometimes called 'original sin', something it emphasizes by words from two of the most important people on its pages. King David of Israel openly admitted, 'I was brought forth in iniquity, and in sin did my mother conceive me'.[655] The apostle Paul went even further, and pointed out that man's sinfulness had appalling consequences. He linked himself with his readers and warned them that they were all 'under the wrath of God by nature'.[656] This applies to us today. To put it bluntly, sin is contempt for God. Not only does our rebellion against God expose us to his righteous anger here and now, but left to ourselves we will experience this in much fuller measure after we die, when we will 'suffer the punishment of eternal destruction'.[657] We will not be annihilated, but as Jesus made clear, we will be 'sentenced to hell',[658] which he called a 'place of torment'[659] and 'eternal punishment'.[660] This teaching about final judgement is rejected by atheists, but this is nothing more than wishful thinking on their part. The Lithuanian-born author and diplomat and Nobel Laureate Czesław Miłosz (1911–2004), who lived through Soviet Communism's outworking of Karl Marx's claim 'Religion is … the opium of the people' wrote this: 'A true opium of the people is a belief in nothingness after death—the huge solace of thinking that for our betrayals, greed, cowardice and murders, we are not going to be judged'.[661] Yet if there is no final judgement there is no such thing as ultimate justice, and campaigning for it in the blink of time we call life on earth is pointless. The Bible is crystal clear that 'we will all stand before the judgement seat of God'[662] and that 'each of us will give an account of himself to God'.[663] It is equally clear that as far as heaven is concerned 'nothing unclean will ever enter it'.[664] Hell is not fiction, but fact.

Now we can see the answer to the questions asked at the end of the previous chapter. God stepped in to rescue us from this appalling fate. In the person of his eternal Son, the Lord Jesus Christ, he came into our broken world and provided a way by which we can have a living relationship with him, have our worldview transformed, begin living a God-centred life, avoid the horrors of hell and one day enjoy the wonder of living in his presence for ever in 'a new heaven and a new earth'.[665] In the person of Jesus, God became a man, lived a perfect life, then took upon himself the full penalty for human sin. In his crucifixion Jesus became as accountable for human sins as if he had been responsible for them. As John Calvin put it, 'He bore in his soul the tortures of a condemned and ruined man.'[666] He met the demands of God's law not only by obeying it in every part, but by paying in full the penalty it imposes on those who break it. The Bible makes it clear why he did so; it tells us that Jesus died, 'the righteous for the unrighteous, that he might bring us to God',[667] which means restoring our broken relationship with him.

This staggering truth lies at the very heart of the Christian faith, which may be why atheists like Richard Dawkins attack it so vehemently. He calls the idea that the innocent Jesus died in place of guilty sinners 'vicious, sado-masochistic and repellent' and 'barking mad'.[668] Christopher Hitchens called the Bible's record of this an 'ancient superstition' in which God was 'trying to impress humans',[669] but both Dawkins and Hitchens are blind to the brilliant truth that God did not punish an innocent third party and somehow get satisfaction from accepting his death in the place of others. Instead, he did the most amazing thing we could ever imagine—he took the punishment upon himself.

Ernest Gordon (1916–2002) was a company commander with the 2nd Battalion, Argyll and Sutherland Highlanders, and served in several campaigns in the Second World War, including those in Burma and Singapore. In *Miracle on the River Kwai* he told a remarkable story. When the prisoners had finished a particular day's work a Japanese guard shouted that a shovel was missing, and demanded that whoever had stolen it must step forward to be punished. When nobody moved, he raised his rifle and screamed, 'All die! All die!' When he aimed it at the first prisoner in the line a young Argyll Highlander stepped forward, stood stiffly to attention and said calmly "I did it". The guard then beat him to death, finally crushing his head with the butt of his rifle. When the prisoners marched back to camp and the tools were counted it was found that none was missing.[670] This is a stunning story of courage and sacrifice, yet it is only a pale reflection of what Jesus did in bearing in his body and spirit the punishment that other people rightly deserve.

Why do such a thing? The Bible's only explanation can be summed up in one word—*love*—and it expands this in several amazing statements. 'God shows his love for us in that while we were still sinners, Christ died for us';[671] 'For God so loved the world, that he gave his only Son, that whoever believes in him should not perish but have eternal life';[672] 'In this the love of God was made manifest among us, that God sent his only Son into the world, so that we might live through him.'[673] God does not love us because he finds us attractive or because we deserve his love. Exactly the opposite is the case; Jesus loved us by dying in our place 'while we were enemies'.[674] Michael Green is exactly right: 'A love which sacrifices itself not for its friends but for its enemies has no parallel in our world … You will not find anything in the other religions that remotely compares with it. It is utterly and gloriously unique. There is nothing in the whole wide world like the love of God for sinners.'[675]

We can also know that Jesus paid sin's penalty in full because he rose from the dead on the third day, the clearest possible proof that even death had been defeated, and that 'it was not possible for him to be held by it.'[676] As the Bible says elsewhere, 'Christ, being raised from the dead, will never die again; death no longer has dominion over him.'[677] C. S. Lewis put it brilliantly: 'He has forced open a door that had been locked since the death of the first man. He has met, fought and beaten the King of Death. Everything is different because he has done so. This is the beginning of the new creation. A new chapter in cosmic history has opened.'[678]

This amazing mission was not 'Plan B' on God's part. As we also saw in Chapter 9, it was something planned 'before the foundation of the world'.[679] Hundreds of years before Jesus was born, one of God's prophets said that the Messiah would come and pour out his soul 'to death' by bearing the sins of others.[680] As his birth approached an angel announced that he would 'save his people from their sins'.[681] His own mission statement was clear: 'The Son of Man came to seek and to save the lost',[682] —but how was he to do this? When his followers suggested a change of programme, he replied, 'My time has not yet come',[683] but a week before his arrest and crucifixion he told them, 'The hour has come',[684] and soon afterwards said, 'For this purpose I have come to this hour'.[685] A few days later he began his longest recorded prayer in the Bible with the words, 'Father, the hour has come'.[686] On the point of being arrested, he told his followers, 'See, the hour is at hand'.[687] These statements illustrate that God's rescue plan centred on Jesus dying in the place of sinners, bearing in his own body and spirit the penalty they deserved to pay. The English author Dorothy L. Sayers (1893–1957) wrote a controversial radio drama on the life of Jesus called *The Man born to be King*, but the title was misleading. Jesus was not born to be king—he was already 'King of kings and Lord of lords'[688] before he was born. He was not born to be king, *he was a king born to die.* In 2006 a man in the United States broke the world record by having his 1000th body piercing. Asked why he had done this, he replied, 'I wanted to do something useful with my life'! This triviality is in stark contrast to the fact that Jesus came into the world to do something that was truly astonishing—he 'laid down his life for us'.[689] His body was also pierced, not by choice but by a member of his execution squad, who 'pierced his side with a spear'[690] to make sure that he was dead.

In all of this, Jesus was not acting on a sudden impulse, or carrying out an idea that grew on him during his thirty or so years on earth. Nor was he reacting to changing circumstances. He made this clear when a few hours before his death he anticipated it by telling God the Father, 'I glorified you on earth, having accomplished the work that you gave me to do.'[691]

In this chapter we have seen that in an amazing demonstration of divine love, Jesus came into the world to save sinners from their appalling fate. Our final chapter explains what our response should be and how to find life's true meaning and purpose.

The end—and the beginning?

In the middle of the seventeenth century, a group of outstanding English and Scottish theologians and laymen met in London over the course of two years to produce a number of documents aimed at helping people get a clearer picture of the Bible's teaching. One of these was the Westminster Shorter Catechism, which is based on a long series of questions and answers. The first of these are:

Q: 'What is the chief end of man?'

A: 'To glorify God, and to enjoy him for ever.'

The word 'end' in the question means purpose or intention. During our lives we have countless motives and reasons for doing things, but the question asks about man's 'chief end', the supreme reason why he exists. It is one thing to know what we are made *of*, but more important to know what we were made for—and God says that man was created 'for my glory'.[692]

If you are not a committed Christian, the last paragraph may make little or no sense to you, but it gets to the very heart of what this book is all about. It also helps me to cut to the chase in this final chapter. To fine-tune things I want to write as much as I can in the second person singular, as if we were alone, talking to each other. This may veer from the usual style of book-writing, but I am more concerned to press home to you this chapter's vital importance and urgency than to toe any literary lines. It may not all make comfortable reading, but getting to the truth is more important than feeling good.

When all of men's theories, ideas and arguments have been heard, the fact remains that the way to discover life's purpose and to find its true meaning is to put God first. In writing the book of Ecclesiastes, Solomon took the same line, which puts us in the shoes of a humanist, someone whose worldview is self-centred, with God off-stage. He showed us that trying to find any meaning in life while ruling God out of one's thinking leads to frustration and futility, and that doing so is like chasing after the wind. After looking at life from many different perspectives he said that the bottom line is this: 'Fear God and keep his commandments'.[693] This was his way of saying that we should glorify God. *This is the overriding purpose for which we exist and is the key to discovering meaning in our lives.*

In looking to find the purpose for your life, and to discover why it has meaning, the right place to begin is not by shaking together a cocktail of your own thoughts, ideas, preferences and circumstances, but by recognizing that *God's glory is the most important truth in the entire universe.* The word 'glory' is not one we use a great deal in everyday life. One of the stands at White Hart Lane, the home of London's Tottenham Hotspur Football Club, has a huge sign reading, 'The game is about glory', but do the fans agree on what it means? Before we go any further, it is vital that we grasp two things: What does the glory of God mean? And what does glorifying him mean?

These questions may seem strange to you, and even some people who genuinely believe in God may not be sure of the answers, but they are fairly straightforward. There are over 350 words related to 'glory' in the Old Testament. The root meaning behind these is heaviness or weightiness, though they are rarely used in this literal way. Instead, they refer to a person who is honourable, impressive and worthy of respect. The word 'glory' appears well over 100 times in the New Testament, where its root has to do with rating a person's qualities very highly. Pulling all of this together, it is not difficult to see why the Bible has so much to say about the glory of God.

The ultimate truth

Everything the Bible says about this is summed up in four words: he is called 'the God of glory'.[694] God's glory is nothing less than all that makes him what he is by nature. It is his awesome and infinite majesty, radiance, beauty and perfection. 'Absolutely' is one of the most misused words in the English language today. No experience is absolutely delightful, no meal is absolutely perfect, no holiday is absolutely great and no person is absolutely wonderful, but when we describe God, 'absolutely' is always the right word to use. He is absolutely sovereign; 'his kingdom rules over all.'[695] He is absolutely perfect: 'God is light, and in him is no darkness at all.'[696] He is absolutely powerful; 'Surpassing power belongs to God.'[697] He is absolutely loving; 'God is love.'[698] He is absolutely just; 'All his works are right and his ways are just.'[699] Here are some of the ways in which the Bible says God reveals his glory:

- 'The heavens declare the glory of God, and the sky above proclaims his handiwork.'[700] In Chapter 3 we saw this as a cosmic clue that we are not accidental by-products of nature living on a tiny speck of dust lost in a mindless universe.

- Elsewhere we are told, 'The whole earth is full of [God's] glory!'[701] In spite of being polluted by man's sin, our planet's countless living things teem with evidence pointing to an intelligent Creator. The amazing complexity and elegance of the genetic code alone is sufficient to give Francis Collins 'a compelling demonstration of God's role in creating life.'[702]

- Jesus revealed God's glory when he came to earth. One of the Bible's names for him is 'the Word', and we are told, 'The Word became flesh and dwelt among us, and we have seen his glory, glory as of the only Son from the Father, full of grace and truth.'[703] As the English preacher Jeremy Walker puts it, Jesus showed himself to be 'the perfect transcript of what God is like.'[704]

- The glory of God was shown in the day-to-day life of Jesus; we are able to see 'the light of the knowledge of the glory of God in the face of Jesus Christ.'[705] In his unique wisdom, his perfect holiness, his countless miracles, his faultless judgement, his amazing grace, and in every other quality of his life, he revealed God's glory.

- The glory of God was shown in the death of Jesus. He did not come into the world as a diplomat, a politician, an economist, a psychologist or a scientist, but as a Saviour. He came to solve people's greatest problem and to bring them into a living relationship with God that would transform their lives now and for ever. Anticipating his death, Jesus told the Father, 'I glorified you on earth, having accomplished the work that you gave me to do.'[706] By dying in the place of sinners he revealed the glory of God's plan to rescue people like you and me.

- When Jesus returns to the earth (something promised about 300 times in the New Testament alone) he will do so 'in the glory of his Father'.[707] On that indescribable day, 'every eye will see him'[708] and in ways far beyond anything we can grasp, 'the glory of the LORD shall be revealed'.[709]

- The final day of judgement will reveal the glory of God. The American theologian Fred Carl Kuehner was right to say, 'In a world created by a sovereign and holy God, there must be a judgement, or else the very fabric of the spiritual universe is torn to shreds.'[710] The day of judgement will be an awesome declaration of God's authority, a dazzling display of his holiness and a perfect demonstration of his justice. The one who is 'righteous in all his ways'[711] will 'bring every deed into judgement, with every secret thing, whether good or evil'[712] and 'will judge the world in righteousness'.[713] As J. I. Packer points out, 'As our Maker, he owns us, and as our Owner, he has a right to dispose of us.'[714]

- God's glory will be revealed in the world to come, the 'new heavens and a new earth in which righteousness dwells',[715] when 'the earth will be filled with the knowledge of the glory of the LORD as the waters cover the sea.'[716] This new creation will be what the English author Christopher Ash calls 'the theatre of God's glory'.[717] With believers in mind, the Dutch theologian Anthony Hoekema (1913–1988) wrote: 'The Bible assures us that God will create a new earth on which we shall live to God's praise in glorified, resurrected bodies. On the new earth, therefore, we hope to spend eternity, enjoying its beauties, exploring its resources, and using its treasures to the glory of God.'[718] This is what the Westminster Shorter Catechism meant when it said that man was created to glorify God *and enjoy him for ever.*

These are some of the ways in which God's glory is revealed, but what do we make of the Westminster Shorter Catechism's statement that our 'chief end' is to 'glorify God'? God's glory is not something we can give him. Earthly rulers gain their position by inheritance, election or a coup, but by nature these rulers are no greater than any of their subjects. On the other hand, God is intrinsically glorious. He is glorious by nature, and we can no more make him glorious than we can make water wet. Nor can we add to his glory in any way, as he is infinitely and absolutely glorious. Neither can we diminish his glory; as C. S. Lewis put it, 'A man can no more diminish God's glory by refusing to worship him than a lunatic can put out the sun by scribbling the word "darkness" on the walls of his cell.'[719]

Then how can you respond to the Bible's command, 'Ascribe to the LORD the glory due his name'?[720]

When we want to be fair to someone, we might say, 'I'll give him his due.' To give God the glory due to him is to acknowledge his glory by worshipping him, by recognizing that he has the prior claim on your life, and by seeking to live in a way that draws attention to him. I am always impressed by the way in which good floodlighting draws my attention to something, such as a beautiful building. The Bible says, 'Let your light shine before others, so that they may see your good works and give glory to your Father who is in heaven.'[721] Floodlights are not put in position to draw attention to themselves, and God has placed you on this planet so that the quality of your life might reflect his glory and draw others to worship him. What is more, God wants this to be done in every part of your life: 'So, whether you eat or drink, or whatever you do, do all to the glory of God.'[722]

Reality check

How do you measure up? Can you honestly claim that your life draws attention to the glory of God? The Bible gives a blunt verdict that includes the entire human race: 'All have sinned and fall short of the glory of God.'[723] This simple statement uses two tenses to tell us some seriously bad news, and it is so fundamental in trying to find meaning to life that we will need to dig into it before we put the final pieces of this book's jigsaw into place.

Firstly, it uses the past tense and says that 'all have sinned'. Whatever pressures you may be facing as you read this book, your greatest problem in life is not physical, mental, psychological or financial. It is not centred on your family, your other relationships, your job (or lack of one), your health or your bank balance. Irrespective of your age, culture or circumstances, your greatest problem is that by nature and from choice you are a self-centred rebel against God. However you may try to excuse it or cover it up, you have a moral and spiritual track record that does not measure up to God's perfect standards—and so do I. Writing in *The Spectator* in 2002, the Hungarian sociologist Frank Furedi said, 'To be honest, as a humanist I don't much like the idea of sin.'[724] No sensible person would claim to be perfect, but we are good at trying to mask not only our run-of-the-mill failures but even the worst of our sins. At the time of the Holocaust, the Nazis called

the agency that arranged the sending of Jews to the killing centres
'The Charitable Transport Company For the Sick'. Some years ago
an American talk show had a guest who had been divorced seven
times. When the host asked, 'So are you committing fornication
with anyone right now?' the guest had no idea what he was getting
at. When it was explained to her she replied, 'I don't like to call it
that.' In some people's thinking, sin is limited to major crimes such
as murder, rape, violent assault or child abuse. The Bible gives a
very different picture—and pinpoints its source.

Lecturing in 1948, Albert Einstein said, 'The true problem lies
in the hearts and thoughts of men. It is not a physical problem, but
an ethical one ... What terrifies us is not the explosive force of the
atomic bomb, but the power of the wickedness of the human heart,
its explosive power for evil.'[725] Bertrand Russell said much the same
thing: 'It is in our hearts that evil lies, and it is from our hearts that
it must be plucked out.'[726] Although not known for their religious
principles, these two men were confirming something Jesus said:
'From within, out of the heart of man, come evil thoughts, sexual
immorality, theft, murder, adultery, coveting, wickedness, deceit,
sensuality, envy, slander, pride, foolishness. All these evil things
come from within, and they defile a person.'[727] This was not meant
to be a comprehensive list of sins, but it was reinforcing the point
that the root cause of man's moral and spiritual plight is to be found
in his nature, not in his culture. It is also worth noting that the list
of 'evil things' Jesus mentioned covered thoughts as well as actions,
and ranged from murder to envy and from adultery to pride. There
is no such thing as a trivial sin—and every sin has roots in man's
fallen nature. In his song 'Gravity' the American singer John Mayer
more than hints at this when he sings, 'Gravity is working against
me; and gravity wants to bring me down', then comes towards the
end of song by telling gravity to 'stay the hell away from me'. Finally

in desperation he pleads six times, 'Just keep me where the light is.'[728]

Secondly, the statement at which we are looking uses the present tense and says not only that everyone *has* sinned, but that we constantly '*fall short* of the glory of God'. In his fallen state man is a moral and spiritual wreck of the glorious perfection in which he was created. What is more, his thoughts, words and actions constantly fall far short of reflecting the glory of his Creator. You know perfectly well that you fall short of your own standards, let alone God's, however high or low you have set the bar. The Bible could not be clearer: 'If we say we have no sin, we deceive ourselves, and the truth is not in us.'[729] Solomon was equally blunt: 'Surely there is not a righteous man on earth who does good and never sins.'[730] If you try to soften this by claiming to be living a fairly decent life, you run up against Jesus' statement that the most important of all his commandments is, 'You shall love the Lord your God with all your heart and with all your soul and with all your mind and with all your strength.'[731] Claiming that you have never fallen short of that benchmark is proof that you have, and the same is true for everybody. The knowledge that we are moral failures has been called, 'the truth that can't *not* be known.' As Charles Colson wrote, 'The knowledge of right and wrong is in us, and we know in our heart of hearts that we have not measured up.'[732]

The heart of the human problem is the problem of the human heart, and left to yourself you are guilty, lost and helpless, cut off from the only one who can give your life security, stability, dignity and sanctity. As Ravi Zacharias puts it, 'The human condition at birth places us on a slippery slope and nothing can stop our downward slide.'[733] Using another picture, the English author G. K.

Chesterton (1874–1936) said, 'Not only are we all in the same boat, but we are all seasick.'[734]

Turn! Turn! Turn!

In the late nineteen-fifties the American songwriter Peter ('Pete') Seeger (1919–2014) released *Turn! Turn! Turn!* a song of which he wrote only ten words and the title. All the rest of the lyrics were taken almost verbatim from the book of Ecclesiastes. It is not clear why Seeger gave it that particular title, but the song repeats Solomon's words that 'for everything there is a season.'[735] Seeger is thought by some to have had the need for world peace in mind, which would explain why he inserted the words, 'It's not too late'. Be that as it may, his title points to a biblical message you need to hear. God says, 'Turn to me and be saved, all the ends of the earth! For I am God, and there is no other',[736] while elsewhere the Bible urges, 'Fear the LORD, and turn away from evil.'[737] Jesus drove the same message home by warning us of the alternative: 'Unless you turn and become like children, you will never enter the kingdom of heaven.'[738]

This means that if you are to get right with God, discover the purpose for which you were born, and find the true meaning of life, things will have to change! The first recorded words Jesus spoke in his public ministry explained what this involved: 'The time is fulfilled, and the kingdom of God is at hand; *repent and believe in the gospel*'[739] (emphasis added). A few years later the same double-barrelled message was at the heart of the apostle Paul's ministry, which called people to 'repentance towards God and … faith in our Lord Jesus Christ.'[740] The remaining pages of this book will spell out what this means.

'Full speed astern'

For many people, 'repent' is a cartoon word, aimed at those they would label religious fanatics, such as someone walking along in a public place carrying a sandwich board with the words 'Repent—the end is nigh!' written in threateningly large letters; but to treat it like that is to make a massively serious mistake. Sent by Jesus to begin their mission, his first followers 'went out and proclaimed that people should repent.'[741] There is a note of urgency in this, because God 'has fixed a day on which he will judge the world.'[742] That being so, it is hugely important that you get a clear grasp of what repentance means.

Repentance towards God is much more than regret or self-pity. Firstly, *it means a change of mind about sin.* It means realizing that sin—all sin—is not something that can be shrugged off as an excusable weakness, an error of judgement, or masked in some other way. Visiting the famous Cunard liner *Queen Mary*, moored in Long Beach, California, I noticed that the mirrors in the staterooms were rose-tinted. I was told that when sailing in rough weather and feeling unwell, wealthy passengers looking in the mirrors would think they had a healthy glow! No such trickery is possible when we use the Bible as a mirror, and it shows sin in its true colours. It reveals that all sin is an offence against the majestic holiness of God. Sin is described as a stain, a rebellion, a poison, crookedness, a burden, a storm, wandering, a sickness, a disease, a field of weeds, darkness, blindness, bondage, a debt, robbery and a curse. Sin is not trivial, but terrible. It is not superficial, but something deep-rooted in the human heart. It is not a psychological idea, but a spiritual fact. It is not a toy, but a killer. Sin brought God's curse on man, scarred the ecology of the whole universe, killed Jesus, the only perfect man in human history, and separates me and you from God. If you truly repent you will change your mind about sin.

Secondly, repentance means *a change of heart about sin*. It means realizing that sin defiles the sinner and defies God. Tempted to betray his boss by sleeping with his wife, one Old Testament man asked, 'How ... can I do this great wickedness and sin against God?'[743] Heartbroken when he realized the significance of his adultery, another confessed to God, 'Against you, you only, have I sinned and done what is evil in your sight.'[744] In a famous parable Jesus told, a rebellious son returned home and confessed to his father, 'I have sinned against heaven and against you.'[745] Genuine repentance will leave you deeply ashamed because you have sinned against the one who died for you and you have broken God's holy law.

Thirdly, repentance means *a change of will about sin*. Israel's King David is a good example of this as he prayed, 'Create in me a clean heart, O God, and renew a right spirit within me.'[746] He genuinely wanted to lead a new, clean, honest, upright life, one that was pleasing to God. Is this what *you* want? It is not enough to feel sorry that you have sinned, or because you have been found out. That could be no more than self-pity, which will add to your sins rather than removing them. The *Quiet American* is a novel by the English author Graham Greene (1904–1991). In it, a journalist adds murder to a long list of his other sins, yet in the closing lines he confesses, 'I wish there existed someone to whom I could say that I was sorry.'[747] Yet self-centred sorrow is concerned only with what sin has done to you; God-centred sorrow grieves over the fact that it has broken God's law. The Bible spells out the different results: 'Godly grief produces a repentance that leads to salvation without regret, whereas worldly grief produces death.'[748] True sorrow for sin must be marked by a deliberate change of direction in your life.

Repentance without turning away from sin is a contradiction in terms. It is much more than asking God to sweep your sins under the carpet. It means an honest longing to live a God-centred life and not a self-centred one. God's directions are clear: 'Do not be conformed to this world, but be transformed by the renewal of your mind.'[749] Is this what you want? This is true repentance, and the call to make this about-turn comes with a life-changing promise: 'Let the wicked forsake his way, and the unrighteous man his thoughts; let him return to the LORD, that he may have compassion on him, and to our God, for he will abundantly pardon.'[750] The English writer and broadcaster Marghanita Laski (1915–1988) once said, 'What I envy most about you Christians is your forgiveness, I have nobody to forgive me.'[751] If you truly repent, you will no longer be in that position. Instead, you will be able to lay hold of this promise: 'If we confess our sins, he is faithful and just to forgive us our sins and to cleanse us from all unrighteousness.'[752] Elsewhere in the Bible we are assured that God will remove the sins of those who repent 'as far as the east is from the west',[753] and that he will 'remember their sin no more.'[754]

Pulling all of this together, we can see that true repentance means a change of mind, a change of heart and a change of will about sin, leading to a new life, in which a person's views and values, affections and ambitions, motives and actions are no longer self-centred but God-centred. A person repenting does not suddenly become perfect, yet the change is so radical that C. S. Lewis called it going 'full speed astern'.[755] For many people, the first move is the most difficult, because it means admitting that they need help from God. As the Bible puts it, 'No one seeks for God.'[756] The Scottish educationalist Sir Thomas Murray Taylor (1897–1962) one-time Principal and Vice-Chancellor of Aberdeen University, hit the nail on the head when he said, 'Where the God of the Bible is concerned, men search for him in precisely the way that the average mouse searches for the average cat.'[757]

Yet God has revealed something of himself in the created order and in the human conscience, and try as they might, nobody can completely suppress this. Even those who have no other indication of God's moral law have it 'written on their hearts'.[758] In Augustine's words, 'Deep within man there dwells the truth.' In a March 1966 edition of the BBC radio programme *Any Questions?* Marghanita Laski was asked what were the most important issues any person had to face. She replied, 'We are lonely, we are guilty and we are going to die.' Even as an outspoken humanist she acknowledged a deep inner need.

Unless you admit that this is the case, there is no possibility of you finding God's intended meaning for your life. During the two years before my wife died I spent many hours with her in a waiting room at The Royal Marsden Hospital in nearby Sutton, a world leader in the research and treatment of cancer. There were always many other patients there, ranging from children to the elderly. Their particular forms of cancer were no doubt very different, but they all had one thing in common—they admitted they had a serious problem they could not deal with, so had come for help. This is the point Jesus made when he said, 'Those who are well have no need of a physician, but those who are sick'.[759] He then added, 'I came not to call the righteous, but sinners'[760] but as 'None is righteous, no, not one'[761] he obviously meant those who were self-righteous. Many people today feel that their lives are good enough to satisfy God, but as Michael Green says, 'Such an attitude stinks in God's nostrils.'[762] He is hardly exaggerating, as the Bible tells us, 'All of us have become like one who is unclean, and all our righteous acts are like filthy rags'.[763]

The apostle Paul, who wrote a great deal of the New Testament, had been deeply religious before he became a Christian, and had an impressive track record of doing seemingly good things, yet had come to 'count them as rubbish'.[764] True repentance does the same thing. It means a confession of sin, a hatred of sin and a genuine longing to turn away from it and to 'serve the living and true God'.[765] This is not a soft option, nor is it easily done. As someone has said, 'Like a well-worn pair of jeans, our [sinful] nature is easy to slip on and live in. Sin is what we know best as fallen creatures, and it is simple for us to go with what we know.'[766] This makes genuine repentance difficult, but Jesus gave an urgent warning of the alternative: 'Unless you repent, you will all … perish.'[767] The American author Dave Hunt says that for an unrepentant sinner to go to heaven 'would be as impossible as it would be for a worm to teach calculus or a lion to appreciate great works of art.'[768]

Do you accept not only that you have committed sins, but that you are a sinner? Can you really be perfectly relaxed about the certainty that on the final day of judgement you will face a holy God who has zero tolerance of sin? When the England football team won the World Cup at London's Wembley Stadium, the Queen presented the team's captain, Bobby Moore with the Jules Rimet Trophy. Asked by a reporter how he felt when going up to receive it, he said, 'It was terrifying, because as I was going up the steps to the balcony I saw that the Queen was wearing some beautiful white gloves. I looked at my hands and realized that they were covered in Wembley mud and I thought, "How can I shake hands with her like this? —I'll make her gloves dirty." A film of the presentation shows him frantically wiping his hands on his shorts, trying his best to get rid of some of the mud and hoping that his hands would be clean enough. Facing an awesomely holy God on the day of judgement will be much more serious. Are you hoping that you can wipe off enough of your life's 'mud' to make you able to face him with confidence, or with a clear conscience? Other people may speak well of you and commend your present behaviour and lifestyle, but their backing will count for nothing when you face a God who is 'majestic in holiness'[769] If you claim that your own level of goodness will save you on what the Bible calls 'the day of wrath when God's righteous judgement will be revealed'[770] you are making a fatal mistake because, as John Benton says, 'His character is right and good, and *all that offends against the holy character of God is wrong, and wrong in the most absolute sense*'(emphasis added).[771] A few months after I had been interviewed on a BBC television programme, a friend embarrassed me by repeating several things I had said in the studio before and after the interview. Unknown to me, every word had been recorded elsewhere in the building and my friend had got hold of the tape. He had great fun replaying it at my expense, but it will be no laughing matter for you to stand before God and be reminded of *everything* you have thought, said and done during your life on earth.

3-D faith

If 'repentance towards God' is often misunderstood or ridiculed, so is the Bible's teaching about 'faith in our Lord Jesus Christ', especially by those who deny that God exists. Richard Dawkins is a perfect example of this kind of thinking. In a lecture at the Edinburgh International Science Festival in 1992 he said, 'Faith is the great cop-out, the great excuse to evade the need to think and evaluate evidence.' In *The Selfish Gene* he writes, 'But what, after all, is faith? It is a state of mind that leads people to believe something—it doesn't matter what—in the total absence of supporting evidence. If there were good supporting evidence, then faith would be superfluous, for the evidence would compel us to believe it anyway.'[772] On being named 'Humanist of the Year' in 1996 he went even further and claimed, 'I think a case can be made that faith is one of the world's great evils, comparable to the smallpox virus, but harder to eradicate. Faith, being belief that isn't based on evidence, is the principal vice of any religion.' This is stirring stuff, but it could hardly be further from the truth. Faith in

God is not belief *in spite* of the evidence, it is belief *in light* of the evidence, and Alister McGrath points out that 'Dawkins' views on the nature of faith are best regarded as an embarrassment to anyone concerned with scholarly accuracy.'[773]

Turning from atheistic guesswork to the truth, we discover that, as with repentance, faith is three-dimensional; it involves the mind, the heart and the will. Firstly, *it involves the mind*: 'Without faith it is impossible to please [God], for whoever would draw near to God must believe that he exists and that he rewards those who seek him.'[774] This is faith at its most basic. If he does not exist, there can be no God-given purpose, meaning or value in your life. Do you believe that God exists? If you do, you have taken the first step of faith in finding it. There can be none unless you exist for a purpose, and only a living, intelligent being can give you this; God alone fits the bill. When C. S. Lewis was an atheist he believed that Christianity was 'a myth conveying as much of the truth as simple minds could grasp.'[775] Atheism was so fundamental to his thinking that in 1921 he told his brother that to admit God's existence 'would have upset my whole applecart.'[776] But eight years later his applecart *was* upset. As he himself put it, 'In the Trinity Term of 1929 I gave in, and admitted that God was God, and knelt and prayed: perhaps, that night, the most dejected and reluctant convert in all England.'[777]

In addition to believing that God exists, basic faith includes believing the Bible's testimony about Jesus. When his enemies challenged his claim to be divine, he replied, 'Unless you believe that I am he, you will die in your sins.'[778] This is not a one-off statement taken out of context, but a consistent New Testament truth. It speaks of 'the glory of our great God and Saviour Jesus Christ';[779] it calls him 'the true God and eternal life'[780]and 'the image of the invisible God';[781] it says that in him 'all the fullness of

God was pleased to dwell.'[782] What do *you* think of him? Countless people go no further than accepting that he was a fine man, a great teacher or an influential example, but this gets nowhere near what is needed. As C. S Lewis famously put it, 'Either this man was, and is, the Son of God, or else a madman or something worse. You can shut him up for a fool, you can spit at him and kill him as a demon, or you can fall at his feet and call him Lord and God, but let us not come with any patronizing nonsense about his being a great human teacher. He has not left that open to us. He did not intend to.'[783]

Secondly, biblical faith means much more than knowing who Jesus is; *it also involves the heart.* In one of the Bible's best-known verses David wrote, 'The LORD is *my* shepherd'[784] (emphasis added), and the apostle Paul wrote of 'the Son of God, who loved *me* and gave himself for *me*'[785] (emphasis added). Can you speak of Jesus in such a personal way? In the early days of the Christian church a man called Simon, who practised magic arts, 'believed' what Jesus' followers were preaching and attached himself to them. But his behaviour soon showed that his faith went no further than agreeing to facts, and when he tried to buy the power that God had given leaders in the church he was told in no uncertain terms that despite the facts he believed about Jesus he was not right with God.[786]

Writing to early New Testament Christians about Jesus, the apostle Peter told them, 'Though you have not seen him, you love him.'[787] Peter had spent a lot of time with Jesus, and had met with him after his resurrection. On almost the last time they met, Jesus asked him 'Do you love me?'[788] and Peter replied, 'Lord, you know everything; you know that I love you.'[789] Peter had been one of his inner circle of friends. He had seen him in private and in public, and had ample opportunity to hear what he said and see what he did. As a result, he had not only come to believe Jesus was 'the

Christ, the Son of the living God',[790] he had come to know and love him as a personal friend. Can you say the same thing?

Thirdly, faith in Jesus goes even further; *it involves the will.* It means committing yourself to him as your own personal Saviour. If you were flying somewhere on business or on holiday, it would not be enough to have detailed and accurate information about the airline, or even to believe that the pilot was capable of flying you to your destination. You would need to commit yourself to him by boarding the aircraft. In the same way, turning to God in faith means no longer trusting in your own moral or spiritual efforts, but committing your life to Jesus Christ, trusting him and him alone to save you from the guilt and consequences of your sin and to give your life the meaning it was intended to have. The greatest need in your life is to get right with God and until that issue is settled you will never know life's true meaning. As Melvin Tinker says, 'From beginning to end the Bible tells us that we were made for a relationship with God, and it is in this that we were meant to find meaning and satisfaction'.[791]

The only way in which you can have that relationship with God, and so find true meaning in life, is to put your trust in Jesus Christ. He made that clear by saying, 'I am the way, and the truth, and the life. No one comes to the Father except through me'.[792] The way to get right with God is by commitment, not to a programme or to a principle, but to a person.

Have you repented towards God, confessing that you are a sinner and asking him to enable you to live in a way that is pleasing to him? Have you turned in faith to Jesus Christ, acknowledging him to be God and trusting him to save you from your sins and to transform your life? If not, let me press home the point that repentance and faith are not human suggestions but divine commandments. Speaking to the city fathers in Athens, the apostle Paul told them that God 'commands all men everywhere to repent',[793] and elsewhere in the New Testament we are told, 'This is [God's] commandment, that we believe in the name of his Son Jesus Christ'.[794] Yet they are commandments aimed at ending your search for life's true meaning. They are urging you to escape from the confusing mess of human ideas and man-made religions and to fulfil the purpose for which you were made. There is meant to be more to life than just living until you die. Bertrand Russell said, 'Real life is, to most men, a long second best, a perpetual compromise between the ideal and the possible'[795] but Jesus came so that you might not just have life but 'have it abundantly'.[796] He came to bring you the 'forgiveness of sins'.[797] He came so that you might have 'peace with God'.[798] He came so that when this life is over you might live in his presence for ever, enjoying an eternal life in which there will be no more 'mourning nor crying nor pain'[799] and in which there is 'fullness of joy' and 'pleasures for evermore'.[800] All of this means that God's orders to repent and believe are also offers to receive and enjoy. Why would you refuse to accept them? If you do, the Bible warns you that 'because of your hard and impenitent heart you are storing up wrath for yourself on the day of wrath when God's righteous judgement will be revealed'.[801] Why choose to do this, and carry on living with no possible assurance that your life has any purpose or meaning?

On 22 November, 2013, fifty years after he died, a memorial stone to C. S. Lewis was dedicated in the floor of Poets' Corner in London's Westminster Abbey. It is inscribed with these words from one of his lectures: 'I believe in Christianity as I believe the sun has risen. Not only because I can see it but because by it I can see everything else.' Repentance and faith had brought him to that point.

Seize the day!

Bernard Levin once asked questions that you may also have asked: 'To put it bluntly, have I time to discover why I was born before I die? I have not yet managed to answer that question, and however many years I have before me they are certainly not as many as there are behind. There is an obvious danger in leaving it too late. Why do I have to know why I was born? *Because I am unable to believe it was an accident, and if it wasn't one, it must have meaning*' (emphasis added).[802] Levin was a sharp thinker, and nobody should duck his questions. In the previous chapter we saw that in looking for a meaning to your life it is pointless beginning with yourself. As Melvin Tinker puts it, 'Left to ourselves, we can no more find out the purpose of life than a man can pull himself up by his own shoe laces. What we need is for the meaning to be revealed to us from the *outside*.'[803] God has done exactly that and in the person of Jesus Christ has given you the opportunity to find that purpose and to find a satisfying meaning to life.

But the offer is time-sensitive. The day before the 9/11 terrorist attack in the United States a passenger on an American Airlines domestic flight noticed a stewardess breaking up ice with a wine bottle. Concerned that she might hurt herself, he asked if there was some other way of doing this. The stewardess was impressed that he should be so concerned, and some time later she was glad to accept a Christian tract from him. Before the flight was over she told him it was the sixth tract of this kind she had been given recently, and asked him, 'What does God want from me?' The man replied 'Your life', and then explained her need to get right with God through trusting Jesus Christ as her Saviour. Less than twenty-fours later she was on the first plane to crash into New York's World Trade Centre.

Your life may not come to such a violent and unexpected end, but however old you are it remains true that your life is 'a mist that

appears for a little time and then vanishes.'[804] An Old Testament
writer warns, 'Do not boast about tomorrow, for you do not know
what a day may bring.'[805] Death is now closer to you than it was
last year, last month and last week—closer than when you began
reading this book or reached the top of this page. God calls you to
'obey the gospel'[806] by responding to him in repentance and faith—
and delayed obedience is disobedience. I urge you not to take this
risk!

When his nation was in a spiritual tailspin, one of the greatest of
God's Old Testament prophets gave the people this warning: 'Give
glory to the LORD your God before he brings darkness, before your
feet stumble on the twilight mountains, and while you look for light
he turns it into gloom and makes it deep darkness.'[807] He imagines
a traveller on a mountain road, confident that he can reach his
destination in daylight, only to find himself in darkness and in
danger. This vivid picture is a warning against the fatal pride of
rejecting Jesus Christ, 'the light of the world'[808] who came 'to give
light to those who sit in darkness and in the shadow of death, to
guide our feet into the way of peace.'[809]

One last thing—something you may never have heard before:
you will glorify God sooner or later. In a stupendous statement about
the life to come we are told that 'at the name of Jesus every knee
should bow, in heaven and on earth and under the earth, and every
tongue confess that Jesus Christ is Lord, to the glory of God the
Father.'[810] Every intelligent being will join in agreeing that Jesus is
who he said he is. Even those 'under the earth', that is, who rejected
the gospel while on earth and are to spend eternity in hell, will be
forced to acknowledge this as they endure for ever their horrific
fate. Hell has rightly been called 'truth seen too late'.

The Bible urges you, 'Seek the LORD while he may be found; call upon him while he is near'.[811] It says, 'The LORD is near to all who call on him, to all who call on him in truth'.[812] It promises, 'Draw near to God, and he will draw near to you'.[813] It assures you that 'the free gift of God is eternal life in Christ Jesus our Lord'.[814] Eternal life is not merely life that goes on for ever, but life in a living relationship with God that begins here and now and never ends. Why turn your back on all of this? Why would you deliberately choose to remain 'having no hope and without God in the world'?[815]

When Thomas, one of his followers, heard that Jesus had risen from the dead, he doubted whether this could possibly be true, but when Jesus appeared to him, he gave him all the proof he needed and told him, 'Do not disbelieve, but believe'. Thomas responded by saying, 'My Lord and my God!'[816] When you can say that to God with all your mind, heart and will, then you will have found the meaning of life.

Seize the day! Time is not on your side.

Why are you here?

Appendix

Why believe the Bible?

n edited extract taken from John Blanchard's *Why believe the Bible?* (EP Books). For a fuller treatment, see Brian Edwards, *Nothing but the Truth,* EP Books).

The facts

Strictly speaking, the Bible is not a book at all, but a collection of sixty-six documents brought together over the course of about 1,500 years, the most recent dating from about AD 95. The word 'Bible' is based on the Greek *biblos,* the inner bark of the papyrus plant. The Egyptians used papyrus (the root of our English word 'paper') as a form of writing material, largely because it was relatively cheap to produce and could be rolled up into large strips. *Biblos* eventually came to mean a written scroll, volume or book.

The Bible is divided into two parts, the Old and New Testaments. A 'testament' (or 'covenant') is a solemn and binding agreement. These two covenants show in two distinctive, but not contradictory, ways God's determination to bring men and women into a right relationship with himself. There is a gap of 400 years between them, but their theme is the same. Both covenants are in complete agreement about the attributes and character of God, the nature of man and the way by which we can experience the reality of God's presence and power in our lives. The Old and New Testaments are like the two halves of a sentence: both are necessary before we can grasp the whole meaning.

The Bible's sixty-six books are not all of the same kind. Some record historical events; others concentrate on civil or criminal law; there are sections laying down rules and regulations about issues as diverse as temple worship and sanitation; parts are written as religious or lyrical poetry; there are large chunks of straightforward teaching; sometimes the writers have incorporated biography or autobiography; there is personal correspondence to individuals or groups of like-minded friends; there are poems, stories, speeches, prayers, hymns and sermons and also, very importantly, there are long passages of prophecy (more of that later). In their original form the books had no chapter or verse divisions. These slowly evolved over a period of some 700 years and the first complete Bible to contain our present chapter-and-verse divisions was the Geneva Bible, published in 1560.

No book in history has ever been under such sustained attack. Time and again it has been written off as 'a load of rubbish', or as 'myths' or 'folklore', while other attacks are more specific. These need to be faced and we shall look at some of them, beginning with those that ask fundamental questions about the entire biblical text.

Corrupt copies?

'How do we know that the text of our present Bible is anything like the original?' This is a perfectly fair question. The original books were all handwritten on perishable material and until printing was invented in the fifteenth century all we had were manuscripts copied by hand again and again over hundreds of years. How do we know that these copies were anything like the originals? There are at least three important tests that can be run on any ancient document and we will see how the Bile matches up to these.

Firstly, *how many documents do we have to work with?* The famous Dead Sea Scrolls, discovered from 1947 onwards, added 100 scrolls to the existing Old Testament documents, while we have well over 5,000 manuscripts of New Testament material in the original Greek and a total of some 20,000 sources to help us piece it all together. Other ancient works compare very badly. We have only nine or ten copies of *Gallic War*, by Julius Caesar (100–44 BC), twenty copies of *Roman History* by Livy (59 BC–AD 17), seven copies of the histories of Pliny the Younger (*c.* AD 61–113) and just two copies of *Histories and Annals* by Tacitus (*c.* AD 55–120). The closest rival to the New Testament's 20,000 sources is Homer's famous *Iliad*, with just 643.

The Bible easily wins the numbers game, but this leads to a second test: *how close in time are the manuscripts we have to the original text?* In the Bible's case the oldest major manuscripts get to within 300 years or so, though two important papyri are 100 years closer, the famous *John Rylands Fragment* is thought to date from AD 117–138 and three tiny fragments of papyrus in Magdalen College, Oxford, have been dated to the third quarter of the first century. Critics are quick to seize on these gaps as a reason for rejecting the Bible, yet ignore much bigger time-gaps for other documents which are accepted without question. Only one copy of Livy's *Roman History* gets closer than 400 years; with the works of Pliny the Younger the gap is 750 years; from Tacitus we have nothing closer than 900 years; and the oldest extant manuscript of Caesar's *Gallic War* dates from nearly 1,000 years after the events it describes.

No other known piece of ancient literature, religious or otherwise, can hold a candle to the Bible's credentials in this area. One can still see parts of Hadrian's Wall, which runs seventy-three miles across open country between the Solway Firth and the mouth of the River Tyne near the northern boundary of England. Nobody questions the fact that in AD 122 the Roman emperor Hadrian ordered the building of the wall to mark what was then the farthest extent of the Roman Empire—and 'to separate Romans from Barbarians'. Nor does anybody question the fact that one of Hadrian's predecessors, Julius Caesar, first invaded Britain in 55 BC, yet we now have only nine or ten manuscripts to support this and the earliest dates from over 900 years after the event.

Again, the Bible is way ahead of its rivals. As Sir Frederic Kenyon (1863–1952), one-time Director and Principal Librarian of the British Museum, said, 'In no other case is the interval of time between the composition of the book and the date of the earliest extant manuscript so short … and the last foundation for any doubt that the Scriptures have come down to us as they were written has been removed. *Both the authenticity and general integrity of the New Testament may be regarded as finally established*'[817] (emphasis added).

The third test is in some ways the most important: *how can we be sure that the manuscripts were copied accurately?* Again, this is a perfectly fair question, but before answering it is worth pointing out that not even printing eliminates mistakes. One version, published in 1631, was known as 'The Wicked Bible' because the word 'not' was left out of the commandment, 'Thou shalt not commit adultery.' In 1717 another became known as 'The Vinegar Bible' because one passage was headed 'The Parable of the Vinegar' instead of 'The Parable of the Vineyard'.

The much more serious question is whether, in the course of centuries of copying by hand, so many mistakes were made that we can no longer trust the text we have. There is no space here to go into detail, but the meticulous care with which the Jewish people copied their sacred Scriptures and the elaborate safeguards they put in place in an attempt to eliminate error almost defy belief. As a result, manuscripts dated hundreds of years apart are amazingly similar. To give one example, the Dead Sea Scroll manuscript of a particularly important chapter of the Bible is more than 1,000 years older than the earliest copy we previously possessed, yet of its 166 words only one (of three letters) is even in question, and the word concerned makes no material difference to the meaning of the passage. No other ancient document approaches anywhere near this amazing degree of consistency. In the *Mahabharata*, the national epic of India, about 10% of the lines are corrupt,[818] while Homer's *Iliad* has twenty times more instances than the Bible in which the original words are in doubt.

This is hugely significant, as the English author Brian Edwards illustrates: 'Suppose five children were asked to copy a sentence from the school wallboard, and only two produced identical copies. If we did not know the original sentence we might not be sure whether the two were right, or whether they made the same mistakes by coincidence. But if 500 copied the sentence and 200 were identical, we should be fairly certain that they represented the original exactly.'[819] Yet in 100 scrolls representing all but one of the Old Testament's thirty-nine books and some 20,000 fragments of Scripture copied during a period of over 1,000 years we have only trivial differences. Sir Frederic Kenyon had no doubt what this meant: 'It cannot be too strongly asserted that in substance *the text of the Bible is certain: especially is this the case with the New Testament.* The number of manuscripts from it, and of quotations from it of the oldest writers in the church, is so large that it is practically certain that the true reading of every doubtful passage is preserved in one or other of these ancient manuscripts. *This can be said of no other ancient book in the world*'[820] (emphasis added).

It is also worth noting here that no scientific *fact* (as opposed to a scientific theory) has ever proved the Bible to be in error, while many such claims have had to be withdrawn. To give just one example, the Bible contains many references to the Hittites, who occupied the region extending from northern Palestine to the Euphrates and who flourished for many centuries. When years of archaeology failed to turn up any signs of them, sceptics claimed that the Bible's record was either fiction or folklore—but later exploration uncovered masses of evidence confirming the Bible's record in great detail, and an entire museum in Ankara, Turkey, is now devoted to Hittite relics.[821] The English academic Alan Millard, Rankin Professor Emeritus of Hebrew and Ancient Semitic Languages, and Honorary Senior Fellow, at the School of Archaeology, Classics and Egyptology in the University of Liverpool says, 'We affirm that nothing has been found which can be proved to contradict any statement of the Old Testament. Archaeological research is a welcome aid to a richer knowledge of the Bible's message.'[822]

Miracles

In the eighteenth century David Hume, the Scottish philosopher and sceptic, launched a fierce onslaught on miracles. In a nutshell, his argument was that the laws of nature were based on the highest degree of probability, whereas miracles had the lowest degree of probability; so the wisest thing was not to believe in miracles. He even went on to say that the only miracle was that *anyone* should believe in them! *The Chambers Dictionary* describes a miracle as 'an event or act which breaks a law of nature',[823] and for many people this clinches the case: *in the absence of God,* anything that seems to contradict the scientific laws governing our world of time and space cannot be genuine and must have some other explanation. Notice the words I have emphasized! Once God is ruled out of the picture, events classified as miracles can be shrugged off as 'mysteries' or 'misleading' and, as its opening words are 'In the beginning, God created the heavens and the earth',[824] this would get the Bible off to the worst possible start!

One writer has identified 232 biblical miracles,[825] but this gives nothing like the complete picture, as the Bible says that many others were not recorded. If miracles never happen the Bible would self-destruct, but the right approach is not to begin by assuming the answer in advance, but by asking, '*Do* miracles happen?', and then examining each case in the light of the evidence. If the evidence does point to a miracle it demands an explanation, and to rule God out before considering that he might provide this is neither wise nor honest.

Dismissing miracles as non-events because they are against the laws of nature may seem a very 'scientific' thing to do, but the truth is exactly the opposite. The laws of nature never *cause* anything to happen, they are merely our assessment of how things normally happen, and the person who believes in God claims that they describe *what God normally causes to happen.* The question of miracles is not a scientific question at all, but a theological one. If God exists, and determines the laws of nature, he himself is not subject to them and can override them whenever he chooses to do so, bringing about what are referred to as miracles.

In a letter to *The Times* in 1984 thirteen prominent scientists, most of them university professors, quietly eliminated one of the main arguments on the issue of miracles: 'It is not logically valid to use science as an argument against miracles. To believe that miracles cannot happen is as much an act of faith as to believe that they can happen … miracles are unprecedented events. Whatever the current fashions in philosophy or the revelations of opinion polls may suggest, *it is important to affirm that science … can have nothing to say on the subject*'[826](emphasis added). Rejecting the Bible because it records miracles is simply a non-starter.

Out of touch?
Countless people take this line, brushing the Bible aside as being irrelevant in our modern world, yet this ignores the fact that the Bible marries right in to today's media headlines.

For example, the Bible has a great deal to say, directly or indirectly, about marriage, divorce, remarriage, alcoholism, substance abuse, stress and depression. It speaks to man's most damaging emotions, such as anger, guilt, fear, doubt and anxiety, and condemns dishonesty, immorality, arrogance, greed, selfishness and obscenity. It addresses issues such as violence, murder, war and natural disasters. Are these irrelevant? It sets out clear principles that relate to issues such as abortion, euthanasia, homosexuality, human cloning and other forms of genetic engineering. Are these not contemporary issues?

The Bible teaches extensively on stable family life, the proper enjoyment of sex, employers' and employees' responsibilities, social justice, business integrity and personal finances. It shows how to cope with poverty, sickness, rejection, bereavement and other personal traumas. To quote directly, it also points the way to 'love, joy, peace, patience, kindness, goodness, faithfulness, gentleness, self-control'.[827] Are these of no importance to us?

It directly addresses animal welfare and the care of the environment. It speaks powerfully about the 'haves' and the 'have-nots' and emphasizes our duty to help the sick, the disabled, the bereaved, the poor, the homeless and the dispossessed, sometimes pinpointing widows and orphans. Can we sweep this aside?

In his fine book *Grace—Amazing Grace*, Brian Edwards gives a stunning example of how much guidance for life is packed into the Bible: 'Deuteronomy 22 is an Old Testament chapter that deals with lost property, neighbourliness, cross-dressing, ecology, health and safety, agriculture and horticulture, marriage relationships, adultery and rape.' He then asks, 'Are we seriously suggesting that there is nothing for the … modern world to learn in a passage like this?'[828]

Critics sometimes condemn the Bible as being 'negative' rather than constructive, but this is a false contrast. For instance, it is true that eight of the famous Ten Commandments[829] begin with the words 'You shall not'—but does that mean that they are not constructive? Suppose your doctor prescribed some very powerful pills to deal with a serious sickness, that the prescription called for one to be taken every day for thirty days and that the container was clearly labelled, 'It is dangerous to exceed the stated dose.' This is a negative instruction, but if you were impatient at such a slow cure and took all thirty pills at once, your absence from work might well prove to be permanent! The negative command was not intended to harm you, but to do exactly the opposite—and the same is true of the Ten Commandments. 'You shall not murder' is negative, but obeying it preserves human life; 'You shall not commit adultery' is negative, but obeying it preserves the sanctity of marriage; 'You shall not steal' is negative, but obeying it safeguards personal property; 'You shall not give false testimony' is negative, but obeying it maintains integrity in our dealings with others.

The Bible goes even further and gives clear and coherent answers to the greatest questions we ever face as human beings, those to do with our origin, purpose and destiny. No other book ever written comes close to the way in which the Bible speaks to life in the twenty-first century.

Other roads up the mountain?
Another common argument for rejecting the Bible is to say that it is only one among many 'sacred writings' and that they may all be equally valid. Yet even a passionate atheist like Bertrand Russell squashed this idea: 'I think all the great religions of the world— Buddhism, Hinduism, Christianity, Islam and Communism—both untrue and harmful. *It is evident as a matter of logic that, since they disagree, not more than one of them can be true*'[830] (emphasis added).

Russell's last sentence hit the nail on the head, as the world's major religions are defined, not by their similarities, but by their differences. They can obviously agree on how to deal with certain social and moral issues, but they are poles apart on the most important matters, and most of all on the nature of God himself. In Christian teaching the one true God exists in three equally divine persons and his essential nature is love, while Islam's God is singular and distant, and Sikhism's is remote and impersonal. Hinduism says there are millions of gods; Zoroastrianism says there are two, and in Buddhism there are none. How can all of these religions be 'different paths to the same summit', as many people claim, when they disagree on the nature of the summit? In 1996 Prince Charles announced that in the event of his succession to the British throne he would see himself as 'defender of faith' rather than as 'defender of *the* faith', but as the *Daily Telegraph*'s Janet Daley pointed out, 'You cannot defend all faiths—at least not at the same time—because each has beliefs that render those of the others false.'[831] By the same token, it is illogical to equate the Bible with other 'sacred writings'.

Mistakes?

Many sceptics say that the Bible is riddled with mistakes, but this is easier claimed than proved and one of the many remarkable things about the Bible is the way in which its statements are confirmed by external evidence. Although the Bible is not a history book it does contain a great deal of historical data and *whenever it has been possible to check this against contemporary evidence the Bible has been found to be accurate.* There is no space here to develop this point, but four distinguished experts will help us set the record straight.

The American scholar Robert Dick Wilson (1856–1930), one-time Professor of Semitic Philology (the language and literature of the Middle East) at America's Princeton Theological Seminary, set himself a staggering forty-five-year study schedule, concentrating especially on Old Testament material. After exhaustive research into the Bible's record of about forty kings who had lived over a period of some 1,600 years, he came to the conclusion that while there were errors in other records, the Bible's data was perfect and that 'mathematically, it is one chance in 750,000,000,000,000,000,000,000,000 that this accuracy is mere circumstance'. Weighing this up, he added, 'No stronger evidence for the substantial accuracy of the Old Testament record could possibly be imagined than this record of kings.'[832]

William F. Albright (1891–1971) the American archaeologist and scholar, recognized as the world's greatest expert in Oriental studies, was Director of the American School of Oriental Research in Jerusalem, the author of over 800 books and articles, and the man whose verdict confirmed the authenticity of the Dead Sea Scrolls. In 1958 he wrote, 'Thanks to modern research we now recognize its substantial historicity. The narratives of the patriarchs, of Moses and the exodus, of the conquest of Canaan, of the judges, the monarchy, exile and restoration, *have all been confirmed and illustrated to an extent that I should have thought impossible forty years ago*'[833] (emphasis added).

The Scottish scholar Sir William Ramsay (1851–1939) was universally acknowledged to be one of the world's greatest archaeologists. A founder member of the British Academy, he originally went along with the trendy idea that the New Testament was largely mythology, rather than an accurate, contemporary historical record. For example, he was convinced that the book of Acts, written by the author of the Gospel attributed to Luke, a first-century physician, was nothing more than folklore cobbled together by an anonymous storyteller centuries after the events it claimed to record. Yet after painstaking on-site research Ramsay became convinced that Luke's data was so precisely accurate that he should be recognized as 'a historian of the first rank' who 'should be placed along with the very greatest of historians.'[834]

The American academic Nelson Glueck (1900–1971), the world's foremost biblical archaeologist, excavated over 1,000 sites in the Middle East, including the copper mines of King Solomon and the ancient Red Sea port of Ezion Geber. After years of meticulous research, he wrote of 'the almost incredibly accurate historical memory of the Bible and particularly when it is fortified by archaeological fact', and went so far as to say, 'It may be stated categorically that *no archaeological discovery has ever controverted a biblical reference*'[835] (emphasis added).

These are world-class testimonies and even if they do not of themselves prove that every historical statement in the Bible is true, they make nonsense of the cavalier claim that the Bible is 'full of mistakes'.

Contradictions?

A variation of the previous attack is to claim that the Bible is full of contradictions. From dates to doctrine, geography to genealogy and names to numbers, critics have claimed that the Bible often contradicts itself and can therefore be rejected out of hand. It would certainly not be sensible to claim that over many centuries of copying the Scriptures by hand there had never been a slip of the pen. Yet years of careful study show that these are few and far between, almost entirely confined to six of the Old Testament's historical books, and are just tiny discrepancies in numbers or an occasional word. Even more importantly, *not even one of these 'slips of the pen' makes a material difference to the meaning or significance of the passage concerned.* When textual criticism was at its height about 150 years ago scores of alleged errors and discrepancies were being touted, but patient research has steadily whittled away at these, and the American theologian R. C. Sproul rightly claims, 'There is less reason today to believe that the Bible is full of contradictions than at any time in the history of the church.'[836] Three other things can be said at this point.

Firstly, *an unanswered question is not the same as proof of a mistake* and an unsolved problem is not necessarily an error.

Secondly, it has been accepted for over 2,500 years that, with certain qualifications, *the benefit of the doubt must be given to the document concerned.* Simon Greenleaf (1783–1853), Royal Professor of Law at Harvard University, was one of the world's greatest experts on legal evidence. At one stage in his life he set out to debunk the credibility of the New Testament, but eventually came to the conclusion that it was utterly reliable and that 'the attributes of truth are strikingly apparent throughout the Gospel histories'.[837] Greenleaf's first rule of documentary criticism was this: 'Every document apparently ancient, coming from the proper repository or custody, and bearing on its face no evident marks of forgery, *the law presumes to be genuine and devolves on the opposing party the burden of proving it to be otherwise*'[838] (emphasis added). This puts the ball firmly back in the critic's court.

Thirdly, 200 years of determined attacks *have left the Bible unscathed.* At the end of 1974, *TIME* magazine ran an article entitled, 'How true is the Bible?' and came to this conclusion: 'The breadth, sophistication and diversity of all this biblical investigation are impressive, but it begs a question: Has it made the Bible more credible or less? … After more than two centuries of facing the heaviest scientific guns that could be brought to bear, the Bible has survived—and is perhaps better for the siege. *Even on the critics' own terms—historical fact—the Scriptures seem more acceptable now than they did when the rationalists began the attack*'[839] (emphasis added).

There are many people who not only ask 'Why believe the Bible?' but directly challenge its integrity and authority. Anyone who takes this position should ask himself the following questions: 'Is my opposition to the Bible fuelled by prejudice or principle? Do I have expert knowledge of the three languages (Hebrew, Greek and Aramaic) in which the Bible was originally written?

Do I have a clear grasp of the context in which each book was compiled? Do I have a correct understanding of every passage and of the sense in which the writer used words or numbers? Can I in every case identify the author's use of language, so that I can determine whether he was employing metaphor or hyperbole, or using a simile or a localized idiom? Am I certain as to whether any given passage is an allegory, a parable or a factual narrative? Do I understand the significance of every one of the religious and civil laws and customs of all the times and places covered by the Bible's writers? Am I certain that no amount of textual or archaeological research will shed any further light on any of the issues concerned? Am I honestly open to being convinced that the Bible really *is* the Word of God and that it speaks to me?' The person who can truthfully answer 'Yes' to all of these questions, may feel qualified to press on with their attack. If not, surely it would be wiser—and humbler—to try a different approach?

All together

One of the Bible's most impressive features is its unity. As we saw earlier, the Bible is not so much a single book as a 'library' of sixty-six separate documents written by some forty authors at intervals stretching over more than 1,500 years. They included a king, a statesman, a governor, a civil servant, a doctor and at least two fishermen, as well as a tent-maker and several of whom we know nothing but their names. They lived in vastly different times and places and only a few ever met any of the others. We can assume that if asked about any controversial subject other than religion they would have had as many different opinions as we might expect to hear on a media chat show. Yet without any collaboration or spin-doctoring, they have given us a body of writing that is amazingly coherent.

Commenting on this, the British-born Canadian theologian J. I. Packer says, '[The Bible has] an organic coherence that is simply stunning. Books written centuries apart seemed to have been designed for the express purpose of supplementing and illuminating each other … Truly, the inner unity of the Bible is miraculous: a sign and wonder challenging the unbelief of our sceptical age.'[840] Elsewhere he writes that the Bible 'appears like a symphony orchestra', with God as its conductor, and with each writer 'brought willingly, spontaneously, creatively, to play his notes just as the great conductor desired, in full harmony with each other, though none of them could ever hear the music as a whole.'[841] This is hardly proof that the writers were all telling the truth, yet, as truth unites and error divides, how else could everything they wrote fuse so perfectly together? The unity of the Bible is so amazing that one could be forgiven for thinking that all its writers were speaking with one voice—*or is this the whole point?* …

Their Master's voice

As we read the Bible, one overwhelming message that comes across loud and clear is its claim that *it is nothing less than the Word of God*. In the Old Testament, seventeen of its thirty-nine books major on prophecy and seventeen on history, while the remaining five are poetry. The prophets had no hesitation in claiming that when speaking in prophetic mode they were acting as God's mouthpieces and that their message was to be treated as coming directly from him—and the same claim runs through all the other books. Phrases like 'God said', 'God spoke', and 'the word of the LORD came' occur some 700 times in the first five (historical) books alone and some forty times in one chapter. In the Old Testament as a whole there are nearly 4,000 direct claims to divine authorship. No other literature known to man makes such clear, consistent and dogmatic claims.

We see the same kind of thing in the New Testament. The apostle Paul, who wrote at least thirteen of its twenty-seven books, not only described the Old Testament as 'the oracles of God',[842] but made no bones about the authority of his own writings: 'If anyone thinks that he is a prophet, or spiritual, he should acknowledge that the things I am writing to you are a command of the Lord'[843] Elsewhere, he commended those who received his message 'not as the word of men but as what it really is, the word of God',[844] insisting that he was God's mouthpiece, responsible not for devising the message, but for delivering it.

Other New Testament contributors said the same thing. The apostle Peter had no hesitation in claiming that his own writing came 'from heaven'.[845] The apostle John, another New Testament heavyweight, began the last book in the Bible by saying that what he was about to write was 'the word of God',[846] and signed off by assuring his readers that his words were 'trustworthy and true', having come to him directly from 'the Lord, the God of the spirits of the prophets'.[847]

The Bible's most concise claim to its divine authorship is to say, 'All Scripture is breathed out by God.'[848] 'Breathed out by God' perfectly translates the original Greek adjective, *theopneustos*, from the noun *theos* (God) and the verb *pneo* (to breathe). This tells us, not that the writers were *inspired*, but that what they wrote had been *expired*—that God 'breathed out' the very words they wrote down. As Peter himself put it when referring to Old Testament writings, 'For no prophecy was ever produced by the will of man, but men spoke from God as they were carried along by the Holy Spirit.'[849]

Critics quickly jump in at this point: 'To say that the Bible is the Word of God because it says it is the Word of God is to argue in circles.' This may sound as if it clinches the argument, but at least four things can be said in reply.

Firstly, we are all familiar with the idea of *appealing to higher authority*. In England, serious crime is tried in the Crown Court and a person convicted there could appeal on a point of law to the Criminal Division of the Court of Appeal. If this appeal failed, it could then be taken to the House of Lords. This is the final court of appeal in England, but the case could be taken one step further, to the European Court of Human Rights. But that is the end of the road, as English law recognizes no higher authority. In philosophy and religion the same point is inevitably reached.

Secondly, *all claims for absolute authority have such authority built in, or they could not be sustained.* For example, those who believe that human reason is the ultimate authority must look to human reason as the basis for claiming this to be the case. This is circular reasoning—but how can it be avoided? The same is true of those who claim that logic or science has absolute authority; only by presupposing what they are claiming can their claim be made.

Thirdly, we have already seen that *the Bible is no ordinary book.* Tested in every way possible, its integrity remains intact, with witnesses such as history, geography and prophecy providing impressive supporting evidence. This evidence is so solid that it is at least reasonable to suppose that the Bible can also be trusted when it speaks thousands of times about its own origin. The Bible is the only book we know that claims from cover to cover that it is God's direct, verbal message to man, and the American philosopher and theologian John Frame is not exaggerating when he says, 'If God's speech has an obvious location that location must be in the Holy Scriptures. There is simply no other candidate.'[850] With its impeccable track record, it is unreasonable and illogical to charge it with making thousands of false and blasphemous statements about its own authorship—and to do so without any evidence to back up the charge. Trying to avoid the Bible's central claim is like trying to avoid an avalanche by dodging individual stones. The Bible gives us many impressive reasons for believing that it is exactly what it claims to be—'the living and abiding word of God'.[851]

Fourthly, if God created all reality outside of himself and has sovereign authority over all of creation, *how could he turn to a greater authority to authenticate his own existence, attributes or purposes?* The Bible makes this very point in recording how God affirmed a covenant with the Old Testament patriarch Abraham: 'Since he had no one greater by whom to swear, he swore by himself'.[852] As the French theologian Hilary of Poitiers (300–368) commented, 'Only God is a fit witness to himself'.[853] By the same token, if the Bible is the Word of God, how can it possibly point us to any higher authority in order to authenticate its claims?

Some people try to find a middle road by saying that although the Bible is not the Word of God it is a highly moral book, with much to teach us, but this idea never gets off the ground. If the Bible were not the Word of God, yet claimed that it was, it would be the most dangerous, blasphemous and contemptible book ever written, lying to us about our origin, giving us a false basis for human dignity, faking a framework for the meaning and purpose of life and cruelly hoodwinking us about what lies beyond the grave. Calling the Bible a good book but not 'God's book' is illogical.

The Master's verdict

The Bible's message ultimately centres on the person and work of Jesus of Nazareth. This is hardly surprising, as careful researchers have pointed out that 'Scripture applies to Jesus every major name, attribute and title of God'.[854] If Jesus spoke with divine authority, his assessment of the Bible would be the best possible endorsement of its claims—and we are not left guessing as to what his assessment was. The only 'Bible' Jesus had in his day was the Old Testament, but he is recorded as quoting verbatim from it nearly forty times (from what are now thirteen different books) in the course of his teaching, and as referring to it on many other occasions. How did he rate it?

Firstly, he accepted without question that its history was reliable. He used at least fifteen events recorded in the Old Testament to illustrate spiritual truth about issues such as marriage, family relationships, miracles, the final judgement, heaven and hell.

Secondly, it was the only body of teaching to which he ever gave his approval and he acknowledged its unchangeable authority on every subject it addressed, telling his listeners, 'Scripture cannot be broken.'[855]

Thirdly, he was so concerned it should be properly understood that he frequently corrected those who were misinterpreting or abusing it.

Fourthly, he claimed that the entire Old Testament was a prophetic prelude to his own coming into the world; to give just one example, he pinpointed the three major divisions of the Old Testament and said, 'Everything written about me in the Law of Moses and the Prophets and the Psalms must be fulfilled.'[856] Jesus saw himself as the key to understanding everything the Old Testament said.

Fifthly, he made it crystal clear that he accepted the entire Old Testament as being the Word of God. Challenging those who questioned life beyond the grave, he asked, 'Have you not read what was said to you by God…?' and then quoted words spoken by Moses.[857] As far as Jesus was concerned, what the Bible said, God said.

The future—now!

The next endorsement of the Bible's claim to be the Word of God raises a subject that fascinates millions of people—foretelling the future. The human appetite for knowing what lies ahead seems insatiable. Millions read horoscopes published in countless magazines and newspapers, while others look for clues in crystal balls, tea-leaves or tarot cards. Yet it is fairly safe to say that hardly any who do so realize two remarkable things about the Bible—firstly, that about thirty per cent of it consists of prophecy of one kind or another; and, secondly, that *not a single prophecy made according to its own criteria has ever been shown to be false.* Surely this ought to get our attention?

Although genuine Bible prophecy sometimes concerns individuals' health, daily needs and family affairs, it never descends to the trivial nonsense traded by today's cranks, charlatans and con artists, which is largely aimed at massaging people's feel-good factor. Most prophecies in Scripture involve issues of national or international importance and make dogmatic forecasts of future events, sometimes being quite specific about their timing, so that their accuracy could be checked. This would hardly be surprising if the prophets were God's spokesmen and were passing on information he had given them, but this raised an obvious problem: how were people to know whether those claiming to be prophets were genuine and that their words could therefore be trusted? This was the test: 'when a prophet speaks in the name of the Lord, if the word does not come to pass or come true, that is a word that the Lord has not spoken; the prophet has spoken it presumptuously. You need not be afraid of him.'[858]

This is very different from saying that if any given prophecy turned out to be right the person making it was a genuine prophet. Anybody might make a correct forecast from time to time (as football pundits and horse-racing tipsters do today) yet this was no proof of his credentials. Instead, *if even one prophecy turned out to be false the prophet's claim to be genuine was in shreds.* It was no good his pleading that he was 'only human' and so 'bound to get things wrong from time to time'. A true prophet *always* got it right, even when his prophecy seemed to be ridiculous. Sceptics sometimes suggest that the 'prophecies' were made after the events they predicted, but there are so many cases in which the dating rules this out that the attack is pointless.

The argument that the Bible's prophecies could have been guesswork is not worth examining. Peter Stoner (1888–1980), co-founder of the American Scientific Affiliation, dealt with the issue by concentrating on just eleven prophecies taken from the writings of four prophets, Isaiah, Jeremiah, Ezekiel and Micah. These prophecies related to the land as a whole, the destruction of Jerusalem, the rebuilding of its temple and the later enlargement of the city—and they were all fulfilled to the letter. Calculating the probability of this happening by chance to be one in 8×10^{63}, Stoner illustrates what this means. He says that if we were to scoop together a pile of coins equal in size to 100 billion stars in each of two trillion galaxies in just one second, add to the pile at the same rate every second, day and night, for twenty-one years, then ask a blindfolded friend to pick out one previously marked coin from this incomprehensibly massive pile, his chances of doing so would be the same as the likelihood that these four prophets could have got their forecasts right by guesswork.[859] This is impressive enough, yet these are just eleven prophecies out of several hundred recorded in the Old Testament alone. What must the odds be against *all of them* being correct by guesswork?

Writing about the evidence for what he calls 'God's fingerprints on the Bible', the English author John Benton says that its prophetic teaching is 'probably the most direct evidence for the special involvement of God with this book'.[860]

Revolutions

Another reason for trusting the Bible is its unique record in changing individual lives and entire societies for the better. In New Testament times the Christian church in Corinth included in its membership those who had been sexually immoral, idolaters, adulterers, male prostitutes, practising homosexuals, thieves, greedy, drunkards, slanderers and swindlers, yet all had been transformed by biblical truth. Since then, millions have added their testimony that the Bible's influence has revolutionized the moral qualities of their lives for the better.

No identifiable group of people has had a more positive impact on their contemporary culture than those who have been motivated and directed by the Bible. Nobody is suggesting that only Bible believers have been involved in such work, but their record is second to none. It has been calculated that 75% of the social revolution that swept Western society in the eighteenth and nineteenth centuries was driven by biblical teaching, with names like William Wilberforce (the abolition of slavery), Elizabeth Fry (prison reform), the Seventh Earl of Shaftesbury (improving the status and conditions of the mentally ill) and Thomas Barnardo (housing destitute children) among those who took leading parts. Today, countries where freedom, justice and tolerance are the norm are almost all influenced by the Bible's teaching, in stark contrast to those that have deliberately rejected it. Of course there have been cases (the notorious and terrible Crusades and Inquisitions in the Dark Ages and Middle Ages are outstanding examples) in which religious leaders have grossly misapplied the Bible's teaching to justify appalling violence, but these are the exceptions that prove the rule, and the Bible remains an unparalleled influence for good.

R. C. Sproul says, 'If the Bible is trustworthy, then we must take seriously the claim that it is more than trustworthy.'[861] If we do, we will have sufficient reason for accepting its claim to be 'the living and abiding word of God'.[862]

Notes

1. Monty Python's *The Meaning of Life*, EMI Music Publishing.
2. As above.
3. As above.
4. Epicurus, Letter to Menoeceus.
5. Leo Tolstoy, *Memoirs of a Madman*, cited in Colin Wilson, *The Outsider*, Pan, p. 164.
6. Cited by B.A.G. Fuller, *A History of Philosophy*, Henry Holt and Company.
7. Jean-Paul Sartre, *Being and Nothingness*, trans. Hazel E. Barnes, Methuen, p. 566.
8. Cited by Gustav Janouch, Conversations with Kafka.
9. Albert Camus, *Lyrical and Critical Essays*, Vintage, p. 185.
10. Bertrand Russell, *Why I am not a Christian*, Simon & Schuster, p. 107.
11. Cited by Russell Stannard, *Doing away with God,* Marshall Pickering, p. 80.
12. See R. C. Sproul, *In Search of Dignity*, Regal Books, p. 92.
13. Rheinallt Nantlais Williams, *Faith Facing Facts*, Coverdale House Publishers, p. 35.
14. Cited by Bernard Palmer, *Cure for Life,* Summit Publishing Limited, p. 10.
15. See Ravi Zacharias, *Can Man Live Without God?,* Thomas Nelson, pp. 184–185.
16. Dave Tomlinson, *The Post-Evangelical*, Triangle.
17. Allan Bloom, *The Closing of the American Mind*, Simon & Schuster, p. 25.

18. See Michael P. Andrus, 'Conversion Beyond Mere Religious Preference' in, *Telling The Truth*, ed. D. A. Carson, Zondervan.

19. See Peter Kreeft, *C. S. Lewis for the Third Millenium*, Ignatius, p. 110.

20. John Benton, *Is Christianity True?* Evangelical Press, pp. 34–35.

Chapter 1

21. Kitty Ferguson, *Stephen Hawking: His Life and Work*, Transworld, p. 37.

22. *A Brief History of Mine,* BBC 4, 7 December 2013.

23. Ferguson, *Stephen Hawking: His Life and Work,* p. 31.

24. Usually referred to simply as 'Caius'.

25. See Michael White and John Gribbin, *Stephen Hawking: A Life in Science*, Dutton, p. viii.

26. *A Brief History of Mine.*

27. As above.

28. As above.

29. See White and Gribbin, *Stephen Hawking: A Life in Science,* p. 124.

30. Stephen Hawking, *A Brief History of Time,* Bantam Books, p. 192.

31. As above, pp. 156–157.

32. Stephen Hawking, *A Brief History of Time,* 2nd edition, Bantam Books, pp. 232–233.

33. Hawking, *A Brief History of Time,* p. 189.

34. As above, p.189.

35. Richard Lewontin, in *The New York Review*, 9 January, 1997, p. 31.

36. Hawking, *The Grand Design*, Bantam Books, p. 5.

37. As above, p. 30.

Chapter 2

38. Hawking, *The Grand Design,* p .5

39. *Oxford Dictionary of English*, Oxford University Press, p. 1323.

40. *The Atlantic*, 19 January 2012.

41. www.reasonablefaith.org/the-grand-design-truth-or-fiction

42. Hawking, *The Grand Design,* p. 5.

43. See John Houghton, *The Search for God: Can Science Help?*, Lion Publishing, pp. 13–14.

44. I have changed the order in which Houghton lists these.

45. *The Daily Telegraph Science Extra*, 11 September 1999.

46. Russell, *Religion and Science*, Oxford University Press, p. 20.

47. Allan Bullock and Stephen Trombley (eds.) *The New Fontana Dictionary of Modern Thought*, HarperCollins, p.75.

48. Donald M. MacKay, *The Clockwork Image: A Christian Perspective on Science*, Inter-Varsity Press, p. 43.

49. *Oxford Dictionary of English*, p. 1580.

50. *What Do You Care What Other People Think? Further Adventures of a Curious Character* by Richard Feynman as told to Ralph Leighton, in *Richard Feynman, the pleasure of finding things out*, Perseus Books, p. 146.

51. *The Daily Telegraph*, 19 August 2009.

52. BBC Radio Five Live, 22 September 2009.

53. Carl Sagan, *Broca's Brain: Reflections on the Romance of Science*, Ballantine Books, p. 96.

54. Karl Popper, *The Logic of Scientific Discovery*, Routledge Classics, p. 280.

55. Peter Medawar, *Advice to a Young Scientist*, Harper and Row, p. 31.

56. Francis Collins, *The Language of God*, p. 229.

57. John Blanchard, *Does God Believe in Atheists?*, EP Books and *Has science got rid of God?*, EP Books.

58. Michael Poole, *A Guide to Science and Belief*, Lion Publishing, p. 72.

59. Stephen Hawking, *Black Holes and Baby Universes*, Bantam Books, p. 90.

60. Edgar Andrews, *God, Science and Evolution*, Evangelical Press, p.36.

61. Cited by John Polkinghorne, *One World*, SPCK, p. 58.

62. *The Sunday Telegraph*, 18 February 2001.

63. *The Sunday Telegraph*, 17 April 1996.

64. Cited by Malcolm Jeeves and R. J. Berry, *Science, Life and Christian Belief*, Baker Book House, p.116.

65. Richard Dawkins, *The God Delusion*, Bantam Press, p.57.

66. Richard Feynman, *The Meaning of It All*, Penguin, p. 32.

67. As above, p. 43.

68. Paul Tournier, *The Whole Person in a Broken World*, Harper & Row, p. 149.

69. John Eccles, 'Science Can't Provide Ultimate Answers', *US News & World Report*, February 1985.

70. Cited by D. R. Alexander, 'Science: Friend or Foe?', *Cambridge Papers*, 4,3 (1995), p. 2.

71. Dawkins, *A Devil's Chaplain*, p. 149.

72. Andrew Miller, 'Biology and Belief' in *Real Science, Real Faith*, ed. R. J. Berry, Monarch Publications, p.95.

73. Erwin Schrödinger, *Nature and the Greeks*, Cambridge University Press.

74. *Soul of Britain*, BBC2, 11 June 1999.

75. Cited by Russell Stannard, *Science and Wonders*, Faber and Faber, p.168.

76. Collins, *The Language of God,* p.30.

77. *Radio Times,* 21 December 2013.

78. See *The Daily Telegraph,* 6 April 1998.

79. John Lennox, *God and Stephen Hawking*, Lion Hudson, p.73.

80. Isaac Newton, *Philosophiæ Naturalis Principia Mathematica*, cited by Rodney Holder, *Nothing but Atoms and Molecules?* The Faraday Institute, pp.60–61.

81. Dawkins, *A Devil's Chaplain*, p.151.

82. Cited by Denis Alexander, *Rebuilding the Matrix*, Lion Hudson, p.330.

83. *The Spectator*, 30 April, 2010.

84. *Evangelicals Now*, July, 2013.

85. As above.

Chapter 3

86. G. W. Leibniz, 'Nature and Grace', *Selections*, p. 527.

87. 1948 BBC radio debate with F. C. Copleston.

88. Cited by John Ankerberg and John Weldon, *Darwin's Leap Of Faith*, Harvest House Publishers, p. 59.

89. Stephen Hawking, *The Grand Design*, p. 180.

90. C. S. Lewis, *God in the Dock: Essays on Theology and Ethics*, ed. Walter Hooper, William B. Eerdmans, pp. 77–78.

91. Lewis, *Miracles*, p. 63.

92. Peter Atkins, *Creation Revisited*, Penguin, p.143.

93. John Lennox, *Gunning for God*, Lion Hudson, p.32.

94. Cited by Keith Ward, *God, Chance and Necessity*, Oneworld Publications, p.34

95. *The Daily Telegraph Review*, 14 December 2013.

96. David Hume, *Dialogues Concerning Natural Religion*, ed. Nelson Pike, Bobbs-Merrill, p.222.

97. As above, p.214.

98. Ward, *God, Chance and Necessity*, p. 109.

99. Cited by Peter S. Williams, *I wish I could believe in Meaning and Purpose*, Damaris, p.348.

100. *The Humanist*, January/February, 1996.

101. Cited by John Benton, *Is Christianity True?* Evangelical Press, p. 50.

102. Paul Davies, *God and New Physics*, Simon & Schuster, p. 189.

103. Melvin Tinker, *What Do You Expect?*, EP Books, p. 55.

104. Francis Collins, *The Language of God*, Free Press, p. 74.

105. Cited by Davies, *God and the New Physics*, p. 188.

106. See Jimmy H. Davies and Harry L. Poe, *Designer Universe*, Broadman & Holman, p.85.

107. Stephen Hawking, *A Brief History of Time*, pp. 135–136.

108. As above, p.138.

109. As above, p.134.

110. George Smoot and Keay Davidson, *Wrinkles in Time*, p. 110.

111. Cited by Fred Heeren, *Show Me God*, (Search Light Publishing) p. 179.

112. Hugh Ross, *The Creator and the Cosmos*, NavPress, p.198.

113. *The Daily Telegraph*, 18 March 2014.

114. As above.

115. Lewis, *The Personal Heresy: A Controversy*, Oxford University Press, pp. 29–30.

116. Hugh Ross, 'Astronomical Evidences for a Personal, Transcendent God', in *The Creation Hypothesis*, IVP, p. 141.

117. Hawking, *The Grand Design*, pp.8–9.

118. *The Spectator*, 30 April 2010.

119. Kathleen Jones, *Challenging Richard Dawkins,* Canterbury Press, p.41.

120. Cicero, *De Natura Deorum*.

121. N. Copernicus, *De revolutionibus orbium coelestium*, author's preface.

122. *New York Times*, 12 March 1991.

123. Cited by Carrie Boren, *Unconditional* (privately circulated), p11.

124. Cited by M. Browne, 'Clues to the Universe's Origin Expected,' *New York Times*, 12 March 1978.

125. Lewis, *Miracles*, p. 37.

126. Andrew Parker, *The Genesis Enigma*, Doubleday, pp. xii, 238.

127. Genesis 1:1.

128. Colossians 1:16.

129. Douglas Kelly, *Creation and Change*, Christian Focus Publications, p.45.

130. *Midweek*, 11 December 2013.

131. Richard Dawkins, 'A Survival Machine', in *The Third Culture*, ed. John Brockman, Simon & Schuster, p. 75.

132. Romans 1:20.

133. Stuart Olyott, *The Gospel As It Really Is*, Evangelical Press, p. 9.

134. Psalm 19:1.

135. Cited by Dan Graves, *Scientists of Faith*, Kregel Publications, p. 164.

136. John Houghton, in *Real Science, Real Faith*, ed. R. J. Berry, Monarch, p. 46.

137. Keith Ward, *Why There Almost Certainly Is a God*, Lion Hudson, p. 81.

138. See Richard Dawkins, *A Devil's Chaplain*, Weidenfeld & Nicolson, p. 13.

139. Robert Jastrow, *God and the Astronomers*, W. W. Norton, p. 14.

140. As above, p. 107.

Chapter 4

141. Stephen J. Gould, *Life magazine*, December 1988.

142. Dawkins, *A Devil's Chaplain*, p. 219.

143. Cited by John Currid, 'From the Renaissance to the age of Naturalism', in *Building a Christian World View*, ed. W. Andrew Hoffecker, Presbyterian & Reformed Publishing Company, vol. 1, pp. 154–155.

144. Ian Taylor, *In the Minds of Men*, TFE Publishing, p. 177.

145. *The Daily Telegraph*, 26 February 2014.

146. Charles Colson, *The Good Life*, Tyndale House Publishers, p. 213.

147. Cited by Phillip E. Johnson, *Darwin on Trial*, Monarch Publications, p. 101.

148. *NOVA: The Miracle of Life*, WGBH Educational Foundation.

149. Johnson, *Darwin on Trial*, p. 103.

150. Paul Davies, *New Scientist*, 12 July 2003.

151. See Mary Wakefield, 'The Mystery of the Missing Links' at www.arn.org/docs2/news/missinglinkmystery102803.htm

152. Francis Crick, *Life Itself: Its Origin and Nature*, Simon & Schuster, p. 88.

153. Antony Flew, *There is a God*, HarperCollins, p. 75.

154. Cited by Peter S. Williams, *I wish I could believe in Meaning and Purpose*, Damaris, p. 400.

155. Michael Denton, *Evolution: A Theory in Crisis*, Adler & Adler, p. 324.

156. Fred Hoyle, 'Hoyle on Evolution' in *Nature*, vol. 294, 12 November 1981, p. 148.

157. As above.

158. R. E. Dickerson, 'Chemical Evolution and the Origin of Life' in *Scientific American*, September 1978, p. 70.

159. Cited by J. White and N. Comninellis, *Darwin's Demise*, Master Books, p. 32.

160. Denton, *Evolution: A Theory in Crisis*, p. 261.

161. See C. M.Fraser, *et. al.*, 'The Minimal Gene Complement of *Mycoplasma genitalium*', in *Science* 270 (5235): 397–403.

162. See T. S. Kuhn, *The Structure of Scientific Revolutions*, 2nd edition, University of Chicago Press, p. 69.

163. Denton, *Evolution: A Theory in Crisis*, p. 250.

164. As above, p. 328.

165. As above, p. 264.

166. As above, p. 264.

167. Cited by Joe Boot, *Searching for Truth*, Crossway Books, p. 53.

168. Werner Gitt, *In the Beginning was Information*, Master Books, p. 107.

169. Dawkins, *A Devil's Chaplain*, p. 117.

170. George Wald, 'The Origin of Life', in *The Physics and Chemistry of Life*, Simon & Schuster, p. 12.

171. Dawkins, *Climbing Mount Improbable*, Viking, p. 259.

172. Dawkins, *The Selfish Gene*, Oxford University Press, p. 16.

173. Dawkins, *The Blind Watchmaker*, W. W. Norton & Co., p. 139.

174. Robert Shapiro, *Origins: A Skeptic's Guide to the Creation of Life on Earth*, Summit Books, p. 112.

175. *Ape Man: The Story of Human Evolution*, Arts and Entertainment Network, 4 September 1994.

176. Dawkins, *The Greatest Show on Earth*, Bantam Books, p. 8.

177. Christopher Hitchens, *God Is Not Great*, Atlantic Books, p. 82.

178. Charles Darwin, *The Origin of Species*, J. M. Dent & Sons Ltd, pp. 292–293.

179. Darwin, in a letter to Asa Gray, 5 September 1857, *Zoologist*, 16:6297–99, see p. 6299.

180. *The Guardian*, 21 November 1978.

181. Cited by Johnson, *Darwin on Trial*, p. 59.

182. Stephen J. Gould, *The Panda's Thumb*, W. W. Norton & Co, p. 184.

183. Steve Jones, *The Language of the Genes*, HarperCollins, p. 35.

184. Phillip Johnson, privately circulated article cited by Malcolm Bowden, *Science vs. Evolution*, Sovereign Publications, p. 227.

185. *The Sunday Telegraph*, 18 October 1998.

186. Richard Dawkins, *The Blind Watchmaker*, p. 112.

187. Lee Spetner, *Not by Chance!*, The Judaica Press, p. 160.

188. Malcolm A. Jeeves and R. J.Berry, *Science, Life and Christian Belief*, Baker Books, p. 206.

189. William B. Provine, *Origins Research* 16 (1/2): 9.

190. See *The New Yorker*, 6 September 1999.

191. Peter Singer, *Practical Ethics*, 2nd ed., Cambridge University Press, p. 331.

192. See Dawkins, *The Selfish Gene*, Oxford University Press, p. 2.

193. *World Magazine*, 22 March 1997.

194. Dawkins, *A Devil's Chaplain*, p. 81.

Chapter 5

195. Andrew Knowles, *Finding Faith*, Lion publishing, p. 9.

196. Written by Gerome Ragni, James Rado, Galt MacDermot; published by Channel H Productions; EMI U Catalog Inc.

197. O. Hallesby, *Why I am a Christian*, IVP, p. 43.

198. Rheinallt Nantlais Williams, *Faith Facing Facts*, Coverdale House Publishers, p. 35.

199. Rebecca West, *What I Believe*, Allen and Unwin, p. 176.

200. Cited by Johnson, *Darwin on Trial*, p. 114.

201. Jean-Paul Sartre, *Nausea*, trans. Lloyd Alexander, New Direction, p. 111.

202. See Ravi Zacharias, *Can Man Live Without God?*, Thomas Nelson.

203. William Provine, 'Scientists, Face It! Science and Religion are Incompatible' in *The Scientist*, 5 September 1988, p. 10.

204. *The Independent*, 27 December, 1995.

205. Thomas V. Morris, *Philosophy for Dummies*, IDG Books, pp. 286–287.

206. *The Observer*, 9 April 1995.

207. Dawkins, *River out of Eden*, Basic Books, p. 96.

208. Stephen Hawking, *Prospect*, August/September 1998, p. 6.

209. Cited in *This I Believe*, ed. J. Marsden, Random House, p. 48.

210. Charles Colson, *The Good Life*, Tyndale House Publishers, p. xiii.

211. Cited by Jonathan Gabay, *The Meaning of Life*, Virgin Books, p. 49.

212. John Benton, *Looking For The Answer*, Evangelical Press, pp. 38–39.

213. BBC Radio Five Live, 24 May 2014.

214. *The Times*, 21 November 2009.

215. Cited by Alister McGrath, *Bridge-Building*, IVP, p. 20.

216. Kriss Akabusi, *On Track with the Bible*, Bible Reading Fellowship. p. 9.

217. Cited by Zacharias, *Can Man Live Without God?*, p. 58.

218. Colson, *The Good Life*, p. 46.

219. Cited by Alister McGrath, *Intellectuals Don't Need God*, Zondervan, p. 15.

220. *The Daily Telegraph*, 11 November 2013.

221. Dennis Prager, 'The Key to Lasting Happiness', condensed from *Redbook*.

222. Cited by Michael Perrott, *The Christian Herald*, 20 August 1983.

223. Cited by David J. Randall, *Believe it or Not!*, Rutherford House, p. 99.

224. Cited by Vaughan Roberts, *Turning Points*, OM Publishing, p. 97.

225. *Melody Maker*, 1965.

226. Cited by Roberts, *Turning Points*, p. 100.

227. *The Sunday Telegraph*, 16 May 2012.

228. Ravi Zacharias, *Can Man Live Without God?*, p. 179.

229. Zacharias, *A Shattered Visage*, Wolgemuth & Hyatt, p. 86.

230. Augustine, *Confessions*, Oxford Paperbacks, pp. 22–23.

231. Cited by Randall, *Believe it or Not!*, pp. 74–75.

232. Colson, *The Good Life*, p. 79.

233. C.S. Lewis, *The Weight of Glory and Other Addresses*, Touchstone, pp. 1–2.

234. Roberts, *Turning Points*, pp. 4–5.

235. *The Sunday Times*, 16 May 1996.

236. *The Daily Telegraph*, 14 February 2014.

237. *The Observer*, 19 February 1995.

238. *The Times*, 16 January 1995.

239. *The Sunday Telegraph*, 8 December 2013.

240. Bruce Wilkinson and Kenneth Boa, *Walk Thru the Old Testament*, Thomas Nelson, p. 172.

241. Ecclesiastes 1:2.

242. Job 7:9.

243. Psalm 62:3.

244. Ecclesiastes 2:10.

245. Ecclesiastes 2:11.

246. Gareth Crossley, *The Old Testament Explained and Applied*, Evangelical Press, p. 488.

247. *The Daily Telegraph*, 2 August 2014.

248. Cited by R. Ferguson, *George MacLeod*, HarperCollins, p. 152.

Chapter 6

249. R. C. Sproul, *Lifeviews*, Fleming H. Revell, p. 167.

250. Benton, *Is Christianity True?*, p. 42.

251. Douglas Adams: *The Salmon of Doubt: Hitchhiking the Galaxy One Last Time*, Random House, p. 135.

252. John Polkinghorne, *Science and Creation: The Search for Understanding*, SPCK, pp. 20–21.

253. http://meaning of life.tv/video.php?speaker=Gingerich&topic=complete

254. Jonathan Skinner, *The Edge Of Known Reality And Beyond*, Evangelical Press, p. 57.

255. Cited by David Wilkinson, *Thinking Clearly About God and Science,* Monarch Publications, p 124.

256. Keith Ward, *God, Faith & the New Millennium,* OneWorld, p. 17.

257. John Blanchard, *Does God believe in Atheists?,* EP Books, 265–281.

258. Michael Denton, *Nature's Destiny: How the Laws of Biology Reveal Purpose in the Universe,* Free Press.

259. Alex MacDonald, *Why I Am Not An Atheist,* ed. David J. Randall, Christian Focus Publications, p. 83.

260. Paul Davies, *Superforce,* Simon & Schuster,p. 234.

261. John Polkinghorne, *One World,* SPCK, p. 57.

262. Owen Gingerich, *God's Universe,* The Belknap Press of Harvard University Press, p. 40.

263. http://www.leaderu.com/offices/schaefer/docs/bigbang.html

264. Cited by H. Margenau and R. A.Varghese, *Cosmos, Bios and Theos: Scientists Reflect on Science, God and the Origins of the Universe, Life and Homo Sapiens,* Open Court.

265. As above.

266. John Lennox, *Seven Days that Divide the World,* Zondervan, p. 99.

267. Christopher Darlington Morley, cited in *Draper's Book of Quotations for the Christian World,* Tyndale House Publishers, p. 109.

268. David C. K. Watson, *In Search of God,* Falcon Books, p. 42.

269. *The Book of Knowledge,* vol. 4., The Waverley Book Company, p. 140.

270. Cited by Keith Ward, *The Turn of the Tide,* BBC, pp. 28–29.

271. As above.

272. Richard Dawkins, *The Blind Watchmaker,* p. 21.

273. Dawkins, *The God Delusion,* p. 141.

274. Dawkins, *Climbing Mount Improbable,* p. 4.

275. Cited by Dave Hunt, *In Defense of the Faith,* Harvest House Publishers, p. 22.

276. *Start the Week,* BBC Radio 4, 9 December 2013.

277. Genesis 1:27.

278. C. Everett Koop in *Scientists Who Believe,* ed. C. Barrett and David Fisher, Moody Press, pp. 158–159.

279. Isaac Newton, *Opticks,* pp. 369–370.

280. Collins, *The Language of God*, p. 211.

281. Psalm 139:13–14.

282. Jerry Fodor, 'The Big Idea: Can There Be a Science of Mind?', *Times Literary Supplement*, 3 July 1992, p. 5.

283. A. C. Grayling, 'Body and Soul', in *Thinking of Answers*, Bloomsbury, p. 36.

284. Francis Crick in Susan Blackmore, *Conversations on Consciousness*, Oxford University Press, p. 68.

285. Sam Harris, *The Moral Landscape: How Science Can Determine Human Values*, Bantam, p. 158.

286. Dawkins, *The Selfish Gene*, p. 63.

287. Richard Dawkins, 'Is Science Killing the Soul?' at www.edge.org/documents/archive/knowledge53.html.

288. *The Meaning of Life.*

289. Jacob Bronowski, *The Identity of Man*, Penguin, p. 8.

290. Joe Boot, *Searching For Truth*, Crossway Books, p. 58.

291. C. Everett Koop, *Whatever Happened to the Human Race*, Crossway Books, p. 111.

292. C. S. Lewis, *God in the Dock: Essays on Theology and Ethics*, ed. Walter Hooper, William B. Eerdmans Publishing Company, p. 108.

293. Francis Schaeffer, *The God Who is There*, Crossway.

294. http://leicestercathedral.org/king-richard-iii-reinterred-march-2015-2/

295. *The Sunday Telegraph*, 20 July 2014.

296. *The Last Secrets of 9/11*, Channel 5 Television, 15 September 2014.

297. R. C. Sproul, *In Search of Dignity*, Regal Books, pp. 18–19.

298. *The Daily Telegraph*, 7 April 1996.

299. Knowles, *Finding Faith*, p. 9.

300. Leslie Paul, *The Annihilation of Man*, Harcourt Brace, p. 154.

301. Albert Camus, *Caligula*.

302. Genesis 1:27.

303. John 4:24.

304. Arthur Koestler, *The Ghost in the Machine*, Picador, p. 19.

305. Benton, *Is Christianity True?*, p. 90.

306. Francis Crick, *The Astonishing Hypothesis*, Simon & Schuster, p. 3.

307. J.B.S. Haldane, *Possible Worlds*, Transaction Publishers, p. 209.

308. Keith Yandell, *Philosophy of Religion—a contemporary introduction*, Baker, p. 49.

309. David Hume, *Of the Standard of Taste*, Essay 23.

310. Richard Dawkins, *A Devil's Chaplain*, Weidenfeld, p. 43.

311. Dawkins, *River Out Of Eden*, p. 120.

312. E. R. Emmet, *Learning to Philosophise*, Longmans, p. 119.

313. Richard Swinburne, *Providence and the Problem of Evil*, Clarendon Press, p. 52.

314. John Polkinghorne, *The Way The World Is*, Triangle, p. 17.

315. John Polkinghorne, 'Does God Exist?, in Harriet Swain (ed.) *Big Questions in Science*, Jonathan Cape, p. 6.

316. Francis Crick, *Nature* Magazine, 1974.

317. James P. Gills, 'The Magnificently Complex Cell', in *Darwinism Under the Microscope*, Charisma House, p. 42.

318. Denis Alexander, *Rebuilding the Matrix*, Lion Publishing, p. 253.

319. Anthony O'Hear, *Beyond Evolution*, Clarendon Press, Preface.

320. As above.

321. As above, p. 214.

322. www.philosophypathways.com/newsletter. Issue 47, 15 December 2002.

323. Douglas Groothuis, *Truth Decay*, IVP, p. 251.

324. Lennox, *God and Stephen Hawking*, p. 73.

325. Psalm 27:4.

326. Ecclesiastes 3:11.

327. Revelation 4:11

328. Keith Ward, *Religion and Creation*, Clarendon Press, pp. 267–268.

329. *Evangelicals Now*, April 1988.

330. Cited by Peter A. Angeles, *Critiques of God*, Prometheus Books, p. 296.

Chapter 7

331. C. S. Lewis, *Weight of Glory*, HarperOne, p. 46.

332. Psalm 139:13–15.

333. Psalm 32:9.

334. Genesis 1:27.

335. Isaiah 40:28.

336. C. S. Lewis, *Mere Christianity*, p. 21.

337. Darwin, *The Descent of Man*, p. 74.

338. See William Provine, 'Response to Phillip Johnson', *First Things*, No.6, 22 March 1997.

339. Provine, *The Scientist*, 5 September, 1998.

340. Rod Garner, *The Big Questions*, pp. 75–76.

341. Cited by Johann Hari, *TheIndependent*, 1 July 2004.

342. Julian Huxley, *The Stream of Life*, Watts & Co., p. 54.

343. Fyodor Dostoyevsky, *Selected letters of Fyodor Dostoyevsky*, ed. Frank and Goldstein, Rutgers University, 446.

344. Cited by Sproul, *Lifeviews*, p. 70.

345. R. C. Sproul, *Lifeviews*, pp. 118–119.

346. *The Observer*, 6 October, 1957.

347. Released as Track 2406 006 in the UK and as Decca DL79184 in the United States.

348. Written by Robert Fripp, Michael Rex Giles, Greg Lake, Ian McDonald and Peter John Sinfield. Published by Universal Music Publishing Group, Royalty Network.

349. C. S. Lewis, *Mere Christianity*, pp. 41–42.

350. Aldous Huxley, *Ends and Means*, Chatto & Windus, p. 273.

351. Scott Fitzgerald, *The Beautiful and the Damned*, Penguin, p. 249.

352. Aleksandr Solzhenitsyn, *The Gulag Archipelago*, Collins, p. 168.

353. Armand M. Nicholi Jr., *The Question of God*, p. 57.

354. As above.

355. *The Independent*, 12 April 1999.

356. Julian Baggini, *Atheism: A Very Short Introduction*, Oxford University Press, p. 62.

357. 'Nielsen's Opening Statement' at www.leaderu.com/offices/billcraig/docs/craig-nielsen2.html

358. Thomas Huxley, *Evolution and other Essays*, Romanes Lecture 1983, D. Appleton, p. 80.

359. *The Daily Telegraph*, 31 August 1992.

360. Dawkins, *The Selfish Gene*, p. 92.

361. Holder, *Nothing but Atoms and Molecules?*, p. 4.

362. *The Daily Telegraph*, 7 July, 1998.

363. *The Daily Mail*, 27 October 2000.

364. *The Daily Telegraph,* 31 August, 1992.

365. C. S. Lewis, *Mere Christianity,* p. 106.

366. Unpublished letter to R. A. Thornton, 17 December 1944.

367. Dawkins, *The God Delusion*, p. 80.

368. Dawkins, *A Devil's Chaplain*, p. 34.

369. Debate at the University of Alabama at Birmingham, 3 October, 2007.

370. John Lennox, *God's Undertaker: Has Science Buried God?*, Lion Hudson, pp. 39–40.

371. Paul Chamberlain, *Can we be good without God?*, IVP, p. 55.

372. Romans 2:15.

373. Collins, *The Language of God*, p. 218.

374. In a private letter to the author.

375. Joseph Gaer, *What the Great Religions Believe*, Dodd, Mead & Co., p. 16.

376. Houghton, *The Search for God*, p. 143.

377. Blanchard, *Does God believe in Atheists?*, pp. 211–240.

378. Samuel Zwemer, *The Origin of Religion*, Loiseaux Brothers, p. 26.

379. Martin Bell, *In Harm's Way*, Penguin, p. 72.

380. As above, p. 74.

381. Nikolai Lenin, *Selected Works,* vol. XL, Lawrence Wishart Ltd pp. 675–676.

382. See: J. M. Bochenski, 'Marxism-Leninism and Religion,' in B. R. Bociurkiw *et al*, eds., *Religion and Atheism in the USSR and Eastern Europe*, MacMillan, p. 11.

383. *TIME*, 7 April 1980.

384. Paul Johnson, *The Quest for God*, Weidenfeld and Nicolson, p. 6.

385. 'In God's Name: A Special Report on Religion and Public Life', *The Economist*, 3 November 2007.

386. Alister McGrath, *Why God Won't Go Away*, SPCK, p. viii.

387. Blaise Pascal, *Pensées and Other Writings,* Edition Pierre Cailler, p. 248.

388. Blaise Pascal, *Pensées and Other Writings,* trans. Honor Levi, Oxford University Press, p. 181.

389. Psalm 42:1.

390. Cited by Draper, *Quotations for the Christian World,* p. 412.

391. Cited by Charles T. Glicksberg, *Literature and Religion,* Southern Methodist University Press, pp. 221–222.

392. Ecclesiastes 3:11.

393. Lewis, *Mere Christianity,* p. 118.

394. Augustine, *Confessions,* 1:1.

395. Julian Barnes, *Nothing To Be Frightened Of,* Vintage Books, p. 1.

396. Douglas Coupland, *Life After God,* Touchstone, p. 359.

397. Genesis 1:27.

398. Genesis 1:28.

399. Kelly, *Creation and Change,* p. 224.

Chapter 8

400. Barnes, *Nothing To Be Frightened Of,* p. 126.

401. Bertrand Russell, 'A Free Man's Worship,' in *Mysticism and Logic and Other Essays,* Allen & Unwin, p. 41.

402. J. Ligon Duncan, *Fear Not!,* Christian Focus Publications, p. 10.

403. Zacharias, *Can Man Live Without God,* p. 113.

404. Epicurus, 'Letter to Menoeceus', in *Letters, Principal Doctrines and Vatican Sayings,* trans. Russell M. Geer.

405. Tom Stoppard, *Rosencrantz and Guildenstern are Dead.*

406. Recorded interview, shown on *Sky News,* 14 March 2014.

407. Sigmund Freud, 'Timely Thoughts on War and Death', cited by Walter Kaufmann, *The Faith of a Heretic,* Doubleday-Anchor, p. 357.

408. *The Daily Telegraph Review,* 29 March 2014.

409. *Q Magazine,* November 2006.

410. www.brainyquotes.com.

411. *The Daily Telegraph,* 7 February 1992.

412. *The Daily Telegraph,* 12 May 2014.

413. *The Daily Telegraph,* 23 June 2014.

414. Peter Atkins, *On Being*, Oxford University Press, p. 100.

415. Cited by John Ortberg, *When The Game Is Over, It All Goes Back In The Box*, Zondervan, p. 234.

416. Walt Whitman, 'Song of Myself' in *Leaves of Grass*, Pennsylvania State University, pp. 104–105.

417. Jean-Paul Sartre, *Being and Nothingness*, Part 4, Ch.2, III.

418. Ecclesiastes 3:19–20.

419. http://blogs.telegraph.co.uk/news/tomchiversscience/100122576/on-larry-king-and-an-atheists-fear-of-death/

420. *Tatler Magazine*, 10 January 2006.

421. Hebrews 2:15.

422. Job 18:14.

423. The Telegraph Ways with Words Festival, Dartington Hall, Devon, 2013.

424. Woody Allen, 'Death' (a play) in *Without Feathers*, Ballantine Books.

425. *The Daily Telegraph*, 24 May 2014.

426. *The Daily Telegraph*, 19 December 2013.

427. David Eccles, 'The Christian View of Time', in *Frontier*, August 1970, pp. 153–154.

428. Alister McGrath, *Bridge-Building*, Inter-Varsity Press, pp. 74–75.

429. Kenneth Williams, *Just Williams*, Fontana/Collins, p. 30.

430. *The Daily Telegraph*, 16 November 2013.

431. Julian Turner, 'Repulsion', in *Orphan Sites*, Anvil Press Poetry Ltd., pp. 42–43.

432. John Mortimer, *The Summer of a Dormouse*, Penguin Books, pp. 141–142.

433. *Billy Connolly's Big Send Off*, ITV, 7 May 2014.

434. 1 Chronicles 29:15.

435. Job 7:6.

436. Job 9:25.

437. Psalm 102:3.

438. Psalm 102:11.

439. James 4:14.

440. Luke 12:15.

441. 1 Timothy 6:7.

442. Genesis 3:19.

443. Emory Bancroft, *Elemental Theology,* Zondervan, p. 179.

444. Louis Berkhof, *Systematic Theology*, The Banner of Truth Trust, p. 691.

445. Christopher Hitchens, *God Is Not Great*, Atlantic Books, p. 282.

446. Ecclesiastes 12:7.

447. Genesis 1:27.

448. Cited by Ron Rhodes, *Heaven: The Undiscovered Country*, Harvest House Publishers, p. 65.

449. Cited by Sarah Kent, *Shark infested waters: the Saatchi Collection of British Art in the 90s,* Zwemer, p. 35.

450. Francis A. Schaeffer, *Death in the City*, Inter-Varsity Press, pp. 86–87.

451. C. S. Lewis, 'Dungeon Grates', in *Spirits in Bondage¸* William Heinemann, p. 41.

452. *The Sunday Telegraph*, 18 November 1990.

453. Cited in *The Daily Telegraph,* 14 August 2014.

454. Bertrand Russell, 'What I believe.'

455. Proverbs 15:3.

456. Genesis 18:25.

457. Hebrews 9:27.

458. Romans 14:12.

459. Luke 8:17.

460. Matthew 12:36.

461. Revelation 21:27.

462. 'The Campaign for Real God', Punch, 7 April 1989.

463. Psalm 145:17.

464. Lewis, *Mere Christianity*, p. 19.

465. J. I. Packer, *Knowing God,* Hodder & Stoughton, p. 172.

466. Romans 1:20.

467. Psalm 7:11.

468. Barnes, *Nothing To Be Frightened Of,* p. 70.

469. As above, p. 23.

Chapter 9

470. See John 1:46.

471. Luke 2:48.
472. Luke 9:58.
473. See John 2:18.
474. Luke 4:29.
475. See Mark 2:16.
476. Matthew 11:19.
477. See Mark 2:18,24.
478. See Luke 11:38.
479. John 7:12.
480. Mark 3:21.
481. Mark 3:30.
482. See Mark 3:22.
483. See John 8:59,10:31.
484. See Mark 8:17.
485. Mark 6:51.
486. See Matthew 13:10.
487. Mark 8:32.
488. Matthew 13:57.
489. E.g. Matthew 22:15.
490. See Mark 12:13–17.
491. John 11:53.
492. See Matthew 26:14–16.
493. See Matthew 26:47–49.
494. William Hendriksen, *The Gospel of Matthew*, The Banner of Truth Trust, p. 929.
495. See Matthew 26:60.
496. E.g. Luke 5:21; John 10:36.
497. Matthew 26:66.
498. Matthew 26:67.
499. John 18:38.
500. See Matthew 27:22–23.
501. See Matthew 27:24–26.
502. Matthew 27:24.

503. See Matthew 27:27–31.

504. Luke 23:35.

505. Mark 15:29.

506. See Matthew 27:57–61.

507. See Luke 20:24.

508. Kenneth Scott Latourette, *A History of the Expansion of Christianity,* vol.1, Harper and Row, p. 59.

509. See Matthew 27:62–66.

510. J.N.D. Anderson, 'The Resurrection of Jesus Christ', *Christianity Today,* 29 March 1968.

511. Géza Vermes, *Jesus the Jew: A Historian's reading of the Gospels,* Collins, p. 39.

512. John Blanchard, *Does God believe in Atheists?,* EP Books, *Meet The Real Jesus,* EP Books, *Jesus Dead or Alive,* EP Books.

513. J.N.D. Anderson, *Jesus Christ: The Witness of History,* Inter-Varsity Press, p129.

514. Mark 8:31.

515. Mark 15:43.

516. John 20:19.

517. Luke 23:55.

518. John 19:34.

519. John 20:6–7.

520. *The Times,* 15 September 1953.

521. A. Rendle Short, *Why Believe?,* Inter-Varsity Press, p. 51.

522. See Luke 24:13–27.

523. See John 20:27.

524. See Luke 24:28–32; John 21:1–14.

525. 1 Corinthians 15:6.

526. Peter Kreeft, 'Why I believe Jesus is the Messiah and Son of God', in *Why I am a Christian?,* ed. Norman L. Geisler and Paul K. Hoffman, Revised Edition, Baker, p. 250.

527. Ravi Zacharias, *Can Man Live Without God,* p. 163.

528. Anderson, 'The Resurrection of Jesus Christ', *Christianity Today,* 29 March 1968.

529. See Mark 14:66–72.

530. See Acts 12:1–3.

531. Acts 9:1.

532. Acts 26:11.

533. See Acts 8:1.

534. 1 Corinthians 15:8.

535. J.N.D. Anderson, *Jesus Christ: the witness of history*, Inter-Varsity Press.

536. Kenneth Scott Latourette, *A History of the Expansion of Christianity*, vol.1, p. 19.

537. John Blanchard, *Jesus Dead or Alive?*, EP Books, p. 164.

538. John Blanchard, *Jesus Dead or Alive?*, EP Books, p. 165.

539. www.hawaiichristiansonline.com

540. Roberts, *Turning Points*, pp. 133–134.

541. Romans 1:2–4.

542. Luke 4:21.

543. See Zechariah 13:7; Mark 14:50.

544. See Psalm 35:11; Matthew 26:60.

545. See Isaiah 50:6; Matthew 26:67–68.

546. See Isaiah 53:12; Matthew 27:38.

547. See Psalm 22:16; Luke 23:33.

548. See Isaiah 53:7; Matthew 27:14.

549. See Isaiah 53:12; Luke 23:34.

550. See Zechariah 12:10; John 19:34.

551. See Psalm 22:18; John 19:23–24.

552. Micah 5:2.

553. Matthew 2:1.

554. Luke 2:16.

555. Luke 2:40.

556. Luke 2:43.

557. See John 4:6.

558. Mark 11:12.

559. See John 4:7.

560. Luke 10:21.

561. Mark 14:34.

562. Hebrews 4:15.

563. See Hebrews 1:1–2.

564. John 3:13.

565. Cited in *Just Thinking,* RZIM, Winter 1998.

566. Matthew 1:23.

567. Luke 1:35.

568. See John 10:36.

569. John Lennox, *Seven Days That Divide The World,* Zondervan, p. 74.

570. Packer, *Knowing God,* p. 53.

571. Colossians 2:9.

572. John 14:8–9.

573. John Marsh, *Who does he think he is?,* Inter-Varsity Press, p. 25.

574. John 10:30.

575. John 10:31–33.

576. C. S. Lewis, *The Case for Christianity,* Touchstone Books, p. 40.

577. http://www.highflightfoundation.org/about

578. Hebrews 4:15.

579. 2 Corinthians 5:21.

580. 1 Peter 1:19.

581. Hebrews 7:26.

582. John 8:46.

583. Matthew 27:4.

584. Luke 23:47.

585. Michael Green, *Why bother with Jesus?,* Hodder and Stoughton, p. 21.

586. John 21:25.

587. See Matthew 8:26.

588. See Matthew 14:19–21.

589. Matthew 9:35.

590. Acts 10:38.

591. See Matthew 9:18–19; 23–26; Luke 7:11–17; John 11:1–44.

592. E.g. Luke 7:36–48.

593. C. S. Lewis, *Mere Christianity,* pp. 51–52.

594. Mark 2:7.

595. 1 John 1:5.

596. John 8:12.

597. John 4:24.

598. John 1:18.

599. 2 Corinthians 4:6.

600. See Psalm 33:12; Deuteronomy 26:11; Joshua 23:14; Psalm 103:8.

601. Peter C. Moore, *Disarming The Secular Gods*, Inter-Varsity Press, p. 158.

602. John 6:38.

603. John 4:34.

604. John 8:29.

605. Luke 19:10.

606. Isaiah 59:10.

607. 1 Peter 1:20.

608. John 12:35.

609. John 8:12.

610. 1 John 4:14.

Chapter 10

611. Lennox, *Gunning for God,* p. 12.

612. Donald Bruce, *Why I Am Not An Atheist*, pp. 25–26.

613. Ravi Zacharias, as above, p. 185

614. Copernicus, *De Revolutionibus orbium coelestium.*

615. *The Daily Telegraph*, 30 June, 2014.

616. Scott Huse, *The Collapse of Evolution*, Baker Books, p. 59.

617. Jones, *Challenging Richard Dawkins*, p. 189.

618. John R. W. Stott, *Issues Facing Christians Today,* Marshalls, p118.

619. Carl Gustav Jung, in a letter to E. Stanley Jones, cited in Paul Little, *The Answer to Life,* Crossway Books, p. 23.

620. Zacharias, *Can Man Live Without God?*, p. 88.

621. Zacharias, *A Shattered Visage,* p. 85.

622. Cited in Ray Comfort, *God Doesn't Believe In Atheists*, Bridge-Logos Publishers, p. 34.

623. Francis Schaeffer, *Genesis in Time and Space*, Hodder and Stoughton, p. 46.

624. H. R. Rookmaaker, *Art and the Public Today*, L'Abri Fellowship, p. 20.

625. Jones, *Challenging Richard Dawkins*, p. 165.

626. Cited by William Draper, *Quotations for the Christian World*, Tyndale House Publishers, p. 406.

627. Richard Cavendish, *The Great Religions*, Arco Publishing, p. 2.

628. Jonathan Sacks, *The Persistence of Faith*, Weidenfeld Paperbacks, p. 71.

629. *The Observer*, 16 April, 1995.

630. Cited in *The Daily Telegraph*, 30 June, 2014.

631. Teresa Turner Vining, *Making Your Faith Your Own*, IVP, p. 11.

632. Cited in Stig Björkman, *Woody Allen on Woody Allen*, Grove Press.

633. Ecclesiastes 5:18.

634. Ecclesiastes 2:24.

635. Ecclesiastes 3:13.

636. Ecclesiastes 2:3; 3:1.

637. Ecclesiastes 5:2.

638. Gary Gilley with Jay Wegter, *This Little Church Had None*, EP Books, p. 178.

639. Michael Green, *Critical Choices*, IVP, p. 23.

640. Roberts, *Turning Points*, p. 32.

641. *The Daily Telegraph*, 2 September 2013.

642. Jean-Paul Sartre, *Existentialism and Human Emotion*, Philosophical Library, p. 32.

643. Gregory of Nazianzus, *Oration 2*, para.1.

644. Colossians 3:1.

645. Colossians 3:2.

646. 2 Corinthians 4:18.

647. C. S. Lewis, *The Four Loves*, Geoffrey Bles, p. 188.

648. John Blanchard, *Where is God when things go wrong?*, EP Books and *Does God believe in Atheists?* (JB Classic Series), EP Books, pp. 585–651.

649. Dawkins, *River out of Eden*, p. 133.

650. Richard Dawkins, *The Magic of Reality: How We Know What's Really True*, Bantam, pp. 233,238.

651. Lord Hailsham, *The Door Wherein I Went*, Collins, pp. 41–42.

652. Genesis 1:27.

653. Ephesians 4:24.

654. Romans 5:12.

655. Psalm 51:5.

656. Ephesians 2:3, J. B. Phillips translation (*Letters to Young Churches*).

657. 2 Thessalonians 1:9.

658. Matthew 23:33.

659. Luke 16:28.

660. Matthew 25:46.

661. See *New York Review of Books, http://www.nybooks.com/articles/ archives/1998/Nov/19/discreet-charm-of-nihilism.*

662. Romans 14:10.

663. Romans 14:12.

664. Revelation 21:27.

665. Revelation 21:1.

666. John Calvin, *Institutes of the Christian Religion*, Christian Classics Ethereal Library, p. 444.

667. 1 Peter 3:18.

668. Dawkins, *The God Delusion*, p. 255.

669. Hitchens, *God Is Not Great*, p. 209.

670. See Ernest Gordon, *Miracle on the River Kwai*, Collins, pp. 88ff.

671. Romans 5:8.

672. John 3:16.

673. 1 John 4:9.

674. Romans 5:10.

675. Michael Green, *Why Bother With Jesus?*, Hodder & Stoughton, p. 42.

676. Acts 2:24.

677. Romans 6:9.

678. Lewis, *Miracles,* Fontana, p. 149.

679. 1 Peter 1:20.

680. See Isaiah 53:1–12.

681. Matthew 1:21.

682. Luke 19:10.

683. John 7:6.

684. John 12:23.

685. John 12:27.

686. John 17:1.

687. Matthew 26:45.

688. Revelation 19:16.

689. 1 John 3:16.

690. John 19:34.

691. John 17:4.

Chapter 11

692. Isaiah 43:7.

693. Ecclesiastes 12:13.

694. Acts 7:2.

695. Psalm 103:19.

696. 1 John 1:5.

697. 2 Corinthians 4:7.

698. 1 John 4:16.

699. Daniel 4:37.

700. Psalm 19:1.

701. Isaiah 6:3.

702. Collins, *The Language of God*, p. 106.

703. John 1:14.

704. Jeremy Walker, *The New Calvinism Considered*, EP Books, 2013, p. 79.

705. 2 Corinthians 4:6.

706. John 17:4.

707. Matthew 16:27.

708. Revelation 1:7.

709. Isaiah 40:5.

710. Fred Carl Kuehner, 'Heaven and Hell', in *Fundamentals of the Faith,* ed. Carl F. Henry. Christianity Today, p. 24.

711. Psalm 145:17.

712. Ecclesiastes 12:14.

713. Psalm 96:13.

714. Packer, *Knowing God,* p. 156.

715. 2 Peter 3:13.

716. Habakkuk 2:14.

717. Christopher Ash, *Remaking a Broken World,* Authentic Media Limited, p. 195.

718. Anthony Hoekema, *The Bible and the Future,* Eerdmans, p. 274.

719. C. S. Lewis, *The Problem of Pain,* HarperCollins, p. 46.

720. Psalm 29:2.

721. Matthew 5:16.

722. 1 Corinthians 10:31.

723. Romans 3:23.

724. Frank Furedi, 'Making a Virtue of Vice', *The Spectator,* 12 January, 1902.

725. Cited by Erich Sauer, *The King of the Earth,* Paternoster, p. 20.

726. Cited in 'Bertrand Arthur William Russell', http://www.giga-usa.com/quotes/ authors/ bertrand _arthur-russell-a1001.htm _russell_a001.htm

727. Mark 7:21–23.

728. John Mayor, 'Gravity', from the album *Continuum.*

729. 1 John 1:8.

730. Ecclesiastes 7:20.

731. Mark 12:30.

732. Colson, *The Good Life,* p. 253.

733. Zacharias, *Can Man Live Without God,* p. 173.

734. Cited in Dale Ahlquist, *G. K. Chesterton, The Apostle of Common Sense,* Ignatius Press, p. 43.

735. Ecclesiastes 3:1.

736. Isaiah 45:22.

737. Proverbs 3:7.

738. Matthew 18:3.

739. Mark 1:15.

740. Acts 20:21.

741. Mark 6:12.

742. Acts 17:31.

743. Genesis 39:9.

744. Psalm 51:4.

745. Luke 15:18, New International Version.

746. Psalm 51:10.

747. Graham Greene, *The Quiet American,* Viking, p. 249.

748. 2 Corinthians 7:10.

749. Romans 12:2.

750. Isaiah 55:7.

751. Cited in John R. W. Stott, *The Contemporary Christian,* IVP, p. 48.

752. 1 John 1:9.

753. Psalm 103:10.

754. Jeremiah 31:34.

755. Lewis, *Mere Christianity,* p. 56.

756. Romans 3:11.

757. T. Taylor, *Where One Man Stands,* The Saint Andrew Press, p. 84.

758. Romans 2:15.

759. Matthew 9:12.

760. Matthew 9:13.

761. Romans 3:10.

762. Michael Green, *Matthew for Today,* Hodder & Stoughton, p. 105.

763. Isaiah 64:6, New International Version.

764. Philippians 3:8.

765. 1 Thessalonians 1:9.

766. *Tabletalk*, May 2014, Ligonier Ministries, p. 51.

767. Luke 13:5.

768. Dave Hunt, *Whatever Happened to Heaven?* Harvest House Publishers, p. 28.

769. Exodus, 15:11.

770. Romans 2:5.

771. John Benton, *Is Christianity True?*, p. 97.

772. Dawkins, *The Selfish Gene*, p. 330.

773. Alister McGrath, *Dawkins' God*, Blackwell Publishing, p. 102.

774. Hebrews 11:6.

775. See Humphrey Carpenter, *The Inklings*, HarperCollins, p. 40.

776. C. S. Lewis, *Letters*, Fount, p. 138.

777. C. S. Lewis, *Surprised by Joy*, Fount, p. 178.

778. John 8:24.

779. Titus 2:13.

780. 1 John 5:20.

781. Colossians 1:15.

782. Colossians 1:19.

783. Lewis, *Mere Christianity*, pp. 40–41.

784. Psalm 23:1.

785. Galatians 2:20.

786. See Acts 8:9–23.

787. 1 Peter 1:8.

788. John 21:15,16,17.

789. John 21:17.

790. Matthew 16:16.

791. Tinker, *What Do You Expect?*, p. 150.

792. John 14:6.

793. Acts 17:30.

794. 1 John 3:23.

795. Cited in Jonathan Gabay, *The Meaning of Life*, Virgin Books, p. 112.

796. John 10:10.

797. Acts 13:38.

798. Romans 5:1.

799. Revelation 21:4.

800. Psalm 16:11.

801. Romans 2:5.

802. Cited by Green, *Critical Choices*, p. 18.

803. Tinker, *What Do You Expect?*, p. 66.

804. James 4:14.

805. Proverbs 27:1.

806. 2 Thessalonians 1:8.

807. Jeremiah 13:16.

808. John 8:12.

809. Luke 1:79.

810. Philippians 2:10–11.

811. Isaiah 55:6.

812. Psalm 145:18.

813. James 4:8.

814. Romans 6:23.

815. Ephesians 2:12.

816. John 20:27–28.

Appendix

817. Frederic G. Kenyon, *The Bible and Archaeology*, Harper & Row, p. 288.

818. See Norman L. Geisler and William E. Nix, *A General Introduction to the Bible*, Moody Press, p. 367.

819. Brian H. Edwards, *Nothing But the Truth*, EP Books (2nd edition, 1993), p. 179.

820. Frederic G. Kenyon, *Our Bible and the Ancient Manuscripts*, Harper & Brothers, p. 23.

821. See Dave Hunt, *In Defense of the Faith*, Harvest House Publishers, p. 69.

822. Cited by Edwards, *Nothing But the Truth*, p. 294.

823. *The Chambers Dictionary*, Chambers, p. 1069.

824. Genesis 1:1.

825. Henry M. Morris, *The Biblical Basis for Modern Science*, Baker Book House, p. 87.

826. *The Times*, 13 July 1984.

827. Galatians 5:22–23.

828. Edwards, *Grace—Amazing Grace*, Day One Publications, p. 69.

829. See Exodus 20:1–17.

830. Bertrand Russell, *Why I am not a Christian*, Watts & Co., p. 9.

831. *Daily Telegraph*, 28 May 1996.

832. Robert Dick Wilson, *A Scientific Investigation of the Old Testament*, Moody Press, pp. 70–71.

833. William F. Albright, *The Christian Century*, 19 November 1958, p. 1329.

834. William Ramsay, *The Bearing of Recent Discovery on the Trustworthiness of the New Testament*, Hodder & Stoughton, p. 222.

835. Nelson Glueck, *Rivers in the Desert: History of Neteg,* Jewish Publications Society of America, p. 131.

836. R. C. Sproul, *Reason to Believe*, Zondervan Publishing House, p. 26.

837. Cited by Hunt, *In Defense of the Faith*, p. 144.

838. Simon Greenleaf, *The Testimony of the Evangelists: Examined by the Rules of Evidence Administered in the Courts of Justice*, Baker Book House, p. 2.

839. *TIME*, 30 December 1974.

840. J. I. Packer, in foreword to Edmund P. Clowney, *The Unfolding Mystery*, Inter-Varsity Press, pp. 8–9.

841. Packer, *God Has Spoken,* Hodder and Stoughton, p. 106.

842. Romans 3:2.

843. 1 Corinthians 14:37.

844. 1 Thessalonians 2:13.

845. 1 Peter 1:12.

846. Revelation 1:2.

847. Revelation 22:6.

848. 2 Timothy 3:16.

849. 2 Peter 1:21.

850. John Frame, *Apologetics to the Glory of God*, P & R Publishing, p. 121.

851. 1 Peter 1:23.

852. Hebrews 6:13.

853. Cited by Edwards, *Nothing But the Truth*, p. 38.

854. Josh McDowell and Bart Larson, *Jesus, a Biblical Defense of His Deity*, Crossway Books.

855. John 10:35.

856. Luke 24:44.

857. See Matthew 22:31–32; Exodus 3:6.

858. Deuteronomy 18:22.

859. See Peter W. Stoner, *Science Speaks*, Moody Press, pp. 67–96.

860. John Benton, *Looking for the Answer*, EP Books, p. 14.

861. Sproul, *Reason to Believe*, pp. 31–2.

862. 1 Peter 1:23.